Christian Knöppler
The Monster Always Returns

D1670471

Film

Christian Knöppler (PhD) has taught American Studies at Johannes Gutenberg University Mainz and RWTH Aachen University. His research interests include American cinema, horror and cultural trauma, media and history, and comics and ideology.

CHRISTIAN KNÖPPLER

The Monster Always Returns

American Horror Films and Their Remakes

[transcript]

Financed by Research Center of Social and Cultural Studies Mainz (SoCuM).

Die vorliegende Arbeit wurde vom Fachbereich 05 - Philosophie und Philologie der Johannes Gutenberg-Universität Mainz im Jahr 2014 als Dissertation zur Erlangung des akademischen Grades eines Doktors der Philosophie (Dr. phil.) angenommen.

Bibliographic information published by the Deutsche Nationalbibliothek
The Deutsche Nationalbibliothek lists this publication in the Deutsche Natio-nalbibliografie; detailed bibliographic data are available in the Internet at http://dnb.d-nb.de

© 2017 transcript Verlag, Bielefeld

All rights reserved. No part of this book may be reprinted or reproduced or uti-lized in any form or by any electronic, mechanical, or other means, now known or hereafter invented, including photocopying and recording, or in any infor-mation storage or retrieval system, without permission in writing from the publisher.

Cover layout: Kordula Röckenhaus, Bielefeld
Cover illustration: Christian Knöppler, 2016
Printed in Germany
Print-ISBN 978-3-8376-3735-9
PDF-ISBN 978-3-8394-3735-3

Table of Contents

Table of Figures

(Note: all screenshots from DVD, taken by the author.)

Acknowledgements

This book marks the completion of a lengthy project, and it would not have been possible without the help of many. I would like to express my sincere gratitude to my advisor Oliver Scheiding for his enduring support, trust, and invaluable advice throughout this project and my career. I genuinely appreciated his productive criticism and his suggestions, even the ones I did not follow. I would also like to thank Mita Banerjee and my dissertation committee for their valuable comments.

Thanks are also due to the faculty and postgraduates of the American Studies department at JGU Mainz, who offered assistance and critical feedback at various stages of this project and were a tremendous help in getting it into shape. Likewise, my thanks to the many participants of conferences in Bonn, Hamburg, and Mainz, who gave encouraging responses to my early research and provided inspiration.

In addition, I owe a debt of gratitude to the Research Center of Social and Cultural Studies Mainz (SoCuM), which provided essential financial and intellectual support for the completion of this project. The SoCuM postgraduate group in particular facilitated a stimulating environment that helped to push my research in unexpected directions.

My thanks also to my volunteer proofreaders. Rest assured, any remaining mistakes are but my own.

Finally, I would like to thank my father Wulf Knöppler for his unwavering confidence and support.

Introduction

It is a Hollywood truism that no genre is more prone to repetition and reproduction than horror. Few successful horror films go without one or more sequels, and many yield long successions of ever more strained continuations and variations delivered on a regular schedule. Fewer classics of the genre still remain without a remake, a newly shot and updated version of that same film. While remakes regularly draw the ire of film critics and fans who view them as a sign of Hollywood's creative bankruptcy, they have also been an undeniable mainstay of the Hollywood film industry since its very beginnings. Remakes may be derided as easy cash-ins, and of course they are calculated to turn a relatively safe profit at the box office – no commercial film studio purposefully aims to take a loss, after all. That calculation, though, relies on the fact that remakes keep working, and they keep working because they fill a need in their audience and the broader cultural contexts. Likewise, the horror genre may be built on calculated successions of scare effects, but like any successful popular genre, it proliferates because it serves a cultural function. Consequently, I suggest that remakes of horror films are such a prevalent phenomenon because the two forms complement each other. This synergy of popular genre (horror) and production practice (remake) will be the subject of the following study.

I should emphasize that my approach is not at all concerned with notions of artistic value, and deliberately questions notions of originality. Even though horror films and remakes are not the most reputable types of films, I assume that they serve particular functions, and that these are accomplished independently from critical appreciation. The film studios' already stated commercial interests are likewise not detrimental to this purpose. The cycles of repetition on which popular genres and remaking are based may be antithetical to aesthetic concepts of originality, but I contend that they are in fact essential to their respective functionings, which I would summarize as follows:

Horror, with its clear focus on evoking fear and shock within the boundaries of its medium, negotiates fears and concerns that may not be confronted otherwise, or at least it offers a safe channel to experience and deal with various cultural fears.

Remakes adapt an earlier film for a new audience in a different historical or cultural context. The newly realized film either works because some of the material has remained relevant, or it makes an effort to stay relevant by making changes deemed appropriate to the current cultural climate.

In a nutshell, Horror deals with cultural fears, and remaking keeps them current, allowing us insight into their development processes by isolating variations of the same themes at particular points in time. With that in mind, I aim to analyze films and their remakes as one functional unit, a horror remake complex, which develops a particular discourse of monstrous difference. This approach helps to discern intertextual dynamics and synergies, and stresses the continuous refiguration of generic and cultural discourses.

In order to comprehend how horror film and remake complement each other, I need to consider them as separate phenomena first. My approach to horror and its function is partly derived from Robin Wood's model in "American Nightmare," which states the basic formula of horror as "normality is threatened by the Monster" (78) and suggests reading horror movies by analyzing the monster, normality (as constructed by the narrative), and the relationship between the two. The purpose of horror, then, boils down to enacting a return of anything that is repressed in society, embodied in the figure of the monster (75). While Wood's approach is steeped in his particular mesh of psychoanalytic and other theories, it is still simple and versatile enough to serve as a framework for the analysis of most horror films. For a more comprehensive understanding of how the horror genre and its monsters work, I also draw on a number of other texts, such as Carroll's *Philosophy of Horror,* and authors like Jancovich, Tudor, and Clover. For now, the short outline of the genre is this: horror film is designed to evoke a sense of pleasurable fear in its audience, using one or more monstrous figures as its objects of fear, which are positioned in complete opposition to normality.

Next, the concept of remake is perhaps more difficult to pin down. The term does not mark a genre of films defined by common themes or formal features, but more accurately describes a practice of reproduction. A remake, in short, is a new version of an existing film, a repeat production. Upon closer investigation, though, the boundaries of what constitutes a "new version" become blurred, and the remake may overlap with other reproductive forms like the adaptation or the sequel. Depending on one's concept of intertextuality, of course, all texts reproduce earlier texts, and the remake only stands out in its declared focus on a singular source. I will discuss these issues of definition, drawing on Verevis's multifaceted approach in *Film Remakes* and other key texts on remakes, and outline a working definition that supports a large field of films widely accepted as remakes. As overtly derivative works, remakes offer new perspectives on previous films and illuminate the reproductive character of popular genres.

With a basic understanding of both horror film and remake established, I move on to examine how the two concepts work together in specific examples. Simply put, my approach for the discussion of these sample films is a comparative analysis along two axes: first, reading monster against normality, and second, reading original against remake. The first step identifies the fears embodied by the monster and the ideological implications of the narrative, and the second traces their development over time, further highlighting their historical contingency. Given that the monster is the central feature of a horror narrative, and the most reliably recurrent element between multiple iterations of that narrative, it makes a convenient indicator of current cultural fears, and viewed in sequence, its permutations add up to a monster discourse.

In this context, I use the term "cultural fears" to clarify that these fears are not necessarily shared by every single member of the horror film audience, but that they are widespread enough to be identified as recurrent motifs in the cultural products of a particular time period. Horror is certainly not the only genre to channel cultural fears, but its singular focus on fear tends to put them front and center. This means that these motifs should be easily found in and compared between any number of horror films, and indeed, reading clusters of films as expressions of shared cultural fears is a fairly common approach in horror studies. For this purpose, however, there is still more untapped potential in horror remakes. Since remakes are readings and updates of existing material, they offer a much stronger basis for comparison than unrelated films from the same genre. They also have advantages over the most prevalent form of reproduction in the genre, the sequel. For the most part, sequels are produced too soon after the original film and too close to its production framework to feature interesting changes, whereas the remake, produced decades after its source, is free to reconceive previous ideas.

Despite lingering perceptions of being an outcast genre, horror film has been explored quite thoroughly by scholars over the past decades, and even though the field of film remakes has not drawn the same level of academic interest, it has nevertheless been the subject of several perceptive and compelling studies. Still, the intersection of the two forms has yet to be adequately considered. I seek to fill this blank, building on existing scholarship to develop a unified approach that closely integrates individual films, genre and remake. This should offer new perspectives on textual interactions as well as thematic breaks and continuities, and aid in tracing the historical trajectories of cultural fears through their monstrous embodiments. As horror remakes, all the sample films in this study have seemingly contradictory goals: to be the same, but different, and to be disturbing, but familiar. This tension holds substantial potential for research, and promises insight on either form as well as their combination.

APPROACH: TRACKING MONSTER DISCOURSE

Tracking a monster discourse across various iterations, or more specifically, versions of the same film, requires a methodical comparison of how the monster is depicted. In order to position a monster in discourses beyond the narrative itself, it needs to be located in relation to its cultural contexts. The dynamic between monster and normality, as introduced in the previous section, represents a convenient starting point for this examination. It yields two basic criteria for analysis and a number of subsequent questions: first, what is the monster, where does it come from, what does it do, and how is it defeated, if at all? Second, what is normality as constructed by the film, and which aspects of society are emphasized or left out, taking into account the historical and cultural contexts?

I should emphasize that the point of this analysis is not the development of a monster taxonomy, in the sense of compiling a catalogue of types and characteristics, along with a list of changes between iterations. Such an inventory would do little to further our understanding of these films.[1] Instead, I seek to understand how the monster is constructed and transformed, how it reacts to or shapes cultural fears, and which discourses of difference the monster draws on through the reuse of markers.

The tools for this approach will be derived from established theories of horror. While fixed criteria for comparison always risk falling short of capturing individual variations, they represent a starting point from which more accurate criteria can be developed where required. As a general example, Wood mentions a number of social Others that find their way into horror narratives as monstrous embodiments, such as "woman," "other cultures" and "alternative ideologies or political systems" (74). In a similar vein, Cohen claims that monsters are assembled from fragments (11), and that "monstrous difference tends to be cultural,

---

1   Besides monster catalogues of questionable value, there are of course more useful approaches that draw on categorization, such as Russell's system of generic classification based on monster types (cf. D. Russell).

political, racial, economic, sexual" (7). As a more specific example, Biskind deducts the ideology of 1950s monster movies from their depiction of authorities, that is, the interplay between government, military, and scientists, along with other groups and factors (cf. Biskind 121-22). These and similar approaches, while not without flaws, offer a range of possible factors in the analysis of individual films. As broad categories, normality, and all the systems that establish and support it on the diegetic level, and the monster, whether it comes from the inside or outside, work for all possible horror narratives.

Next, with these factors in mind, it is possible to contrast the various versions of a monster and the narratives in which it is embedded. The focus of the analysis will be on the transpositions that derive the hypertext of the remake from its hypotext, to use Genette's terms, such as transmotivations, amplifications and reductions. Alterations of the monster's motivations, from comprehensible to inhuman and evil, or a shifted balance with normality can radically alter the possible meanings of a narrative. Changes to both monster and normality may then be read in the context of social change in between iterations, while taking the circumstances of production into account where pertinent. Although extratextual details should not distract from reading or overshadow the text, production circumstances form part of the system and practice of cultural production and repetition that, ultimately, is the object of analysis here. With that in mind, larger trends can be identified in order to draw conclusions about the workings of the genre and the industry. Regarding the outcome, it is likely that some elements of a given monster discourse will endure, due to a lasting relevance to constants of American culture, while others are inextricably linked to their historical/cultural moment and therefore modified or removed entirely.

With the subjects of this study having been produced over a span of sixty years, the search for relevant historical contexts for interpretation brings certain challenges. It is easy to project a reductive, stereotypical view of a particular time period onto a particular film, or to mistake nuances of meaning which are difficult to grasp for modern day viewers. At the same time, contemporary films pose a different set of challenges, as the viewer may be too close to ongoing trends that have yet to be identified, or may find that an occupation with a narrow range of current concerns overshadows historical continuities. Admittedly, there is no easy way to resolve this dilemma, as neither historical omniscience, nor absolute objectivity are attainable. The readings in this study are obviously colored by culturally and historically contingent perspectives as well as theoretical backgrounds, most of all my own. Still, I aim to compensate for these limitations by balancing secondary sources and closely adhering to each text to avoid turning it into a blank projection space.

CHOICE OF FILMS

The goal of this study is not to offer an exhaustive listing of horror films and remakes. Instead, I chose six examples from different periods and subgenres for an
in-depth analysis. These films are not meant to cover all possible subtypes of
horror remakes, but they do offer some range in terms of themes and styles, and
serve to illuminate different approaches to remaking. Most of the initial films are
widely considered landmarks of one kind or another. They may be influential for
a cycle of films or the whole genre, lauded as particularly accomplished, or
charged with socio-political subtext. For example, three of these films, *The
Thing from Another World* (1951), *Invasion of the Body Snatchers* (1956), and
Halloween (1978), are part of the National Film Registry at the Library of Congress,[2] chosen for preservation as "works of enduring importance to American
culture" ("Frequently Asked Questions About the National Film Registry").
Even though the criteria of this and other canonizing authorities do not necessarily coincide with my areas of interest in this study, they nevertheless point to
a certain potential for interpretation.

As a consequence, however, my choice of films reinforces an already well-
worn genre canon. The potential problem with this should be obvious: an overre-
liance on a calcified inventory of supposedly classic texts runs the risk of ignoring recent and vital trends, as the conception of genre is filtered only through established past works. In the case of film remakes, though, treading on familiar
ground is hardly avoidable as the sources for remakes are almost by definition
canonical. Past success and recognition are pretty much prerequisites for a film
to be remade, and even less established films are elevated and canonized by the
act of remaking. Yet, while these initial films are usually part of a genre (or cult)
canon, their remakes are usually ignored, or confined to a lesser status due to
their derivative nature. By giving equal consideration to remakes, then, my study
amongst other things aims to broaden the respective genre canons.

Furthermore, my selection of films depends on a number of additional criteria, based on the goals set for this study. First, in order to explore the repetition
and transformation of filmic texts, I focus on films that do not have strong literary sources. This excludes most adaptations of classic Gothic narratives, such as
the genre-defining horror films following *Dracula* (1931) and *Frankenstein*

---

2   Along with horror genre milestones such as *Dracula* (1931), *Psycho* (1960), and *Night
    of the Living Dead* (1968) ("National Film Registry Titles 1989-2013").

(1931) in the 1930s and 40s, along with their extensive cinematic legacy.[3] Due to the well-established status of their literary sources, remakes of these films tend towards re-adaptation, meaning that they privilege literary over filmic source texts (cf. Leitch 45). Even though the processes involved in adaptation are similar to those of remaking, I intend to focus on the latter, and avoid the complications of inter- or transmediality.

Second, in order to trace historical trajectories of cultural fears, I concentrate on archival remakes, that is, American remakes of American films. This excludes international remakes, meaning American remakes of horror films originally produced in other countries, such as the wave of remade Japanese horror films in the 2000s (e.g. *The Ring* (2002)). Even though the adaptation of foreign works to an American context may yield intriguing material to illuminate specifically American fears, it is confined to a narrow historical moment, as international remakes are typically launched into production soon after the release of the original film. Archival remakes, by contrast, are the result of a self-reflexive process that takes place decades after the moment that brought forward the initial work. As indicators of discursive development, these films are far more promising.

With the pool of potential texts narrowed down to archival remakes without notable literary lineage, the selection of sample films needs to strike a balance between range and depth. Disentangling the complex intertextual relations between films and their remakes takes some space and effort, and the same goes for the analysis of cultural fears and the discourses of monstrosity in which they are embedded. At the same time, any speculation about broad cultural functions of horror, remakes, and the combination of the two would seem to require a larger body of texts to work with. With six horror remake complexes and a total of fifteen films, the thematic and historical range in this study will offer enough evidence to support some general conclusions, while still delivering a profound analysis of each individual text.

For a start, *The Thing from Another World* (1951) and *The Thing* (1982 and 2011) demonstrate the complex intertextual dynamics of film remakes as well as constantly shifting source text priorities. Where the 1951 film adapts its source text in a style that would be typical of 1950s science fiction/horror hybrids, the 1982 readaptation radically shifts to a contemporary body horror aesthetic. Along the way, the clear fronts of the budding Cold War give way to more introspective paranoia and an almost total dissolution of social and biological order.

---

3   A more recent example of a strong literary tradition in horror film might be adaptations of Stephen King's horror writings, some of which are getting old enough to be remade (e.g. *Carrie*, which was adapted or remade in 1976, 2002 and 2013).

To question textual categories further, I include 2011's *The Thing*, which is technically a prequel to the 1982 version, but also serves as a remake. Intertextual relations are slightly more straightforward for the second remake cluster, reaching from *Invasion of the Body Snatchers* (1956) to its three remakes *Invasion of the Body Snatchers* (1978), *Body Snatchers* (1993) and *The Invasion* (2007). The first film has been studied and analyzed exhaustively, whether as a prime example of 1950s hybrid monster movies, as an ambiguous filmic representation of Cold War paranoia, or as an unusually popular subject for remaking. The latter aspect in particular makes the four *Body Snatchers* films an essential inclusion in this study, and the repeated refiguration of the narrative's central themes, the fear of social conformity and the difficulty of distinguishing monstrous alien from human, is a promising subject for analysis.

The Crazies (1973) marks probably the most obscure case in this study. Generally considered a lesser entry in George A. Romero's filmography, it might have been passed over for remaking, were it not for Romero's brand name value. Still, the film's politicized horror makes it an interesting challenge for remaking, and the 2010 update struggles to substitute the pervasive Vietnam War allegory with a less ambitious narrative whose sense of insecurity is nevertheless attuned to the post-9/11 era. As Romero's more famous zombie films have proven to be popular subjects for remaking, his key work *Dawn of the Dead* (1978) and its 2004 remake are covered in this study as well. Again, the original film's social conscience and its transformation in the remaking process are in focus here, as its blatant critique of consumer culture and at times meandering narrative make room for a much slicker zombie horror experience.

The last two cases take a departure from the aliens and the undead towards the more mundane, but nonetheless monstrous psychopaths of the horror genre. Perhaps more than any other film covered in this study, *The Texas Chain Saw Massacre* (1974) enjoyed an almost mythical underground reputation of radical transgression and grotesque violence, which the more conventional, but still rather violent remake rode to box office success in 2003. Where the first film challenged basic sense and coherence, the remake adheres to fairly typical narrative structures and shifts the ideological implications of the backwoods cannibal scenario. Finally, *Halloween* (1978), with its simple story of a masked killer stalking suburban teenagers, stands out as highly reproducible, having served as a model for the wave of slasher movies that came to dominate the genre in the 1980s. That the film was remade in 2007 is as much a credit to its textual qualities as to film industry practices, and the new take exemplifies the conflicting goals of remaking. Furthermore, *Halloween's* (1978) preoccupation with young female victims has provided fertile ground for academic criticism, which should apply to the remake as well.

Given the constant production of horror films and remakes, there are of course many more films that could have been included in this study, even with the restriction to archival remakes. Along with *The Thing from Another World* (1951), several other monster movies of the 1950s were revisited in the 1980s, including *The Fly* (1958, 1986) and *The Blob* (1958, 1988). *Dawn of the Dead* (1978) may be the most famous entry in George A. Romero's zombie cycle to be remade, but both *Night of the Living Dead* (1968, 1990, 2006) and *Day of the Dead* (1985, 2008) saw new versions as well. As *Halloween* (1978) led the way for the slasher genre, its 2007 remake led a wave of slasher remakes, such as *Friday the 13th* (1980, 2009) and *Nightmare on Elm Street* (1984, 2010). And shortly after *The Texas Chain Saw Massacre* (1974) was remade, the redneck cannibals from *The Hills Have Eyes* (1977, 2006) also returned to cinemas. Beyond the subgenres treated in this study, a wide range of horror films has been remade, from revered classics like *Psycho* (1960, 1998) to highly disreputable rape-revenge exploitation fare like *The Last House on the Left* (1972, 2009) and *I Spit on Your Grave* (1978, 2010). Haunted houses were revisited in *The Haunting* (1963, 1999) and *The Amityville Horror* (1979, 2005), while demonic terrors of wildly different intensities were reconceived in *The Omen* (1976, 2006) and *The Evil Dead* (1981, 2013). Dozens more films could be listed here, but the point should be clear by now: horror appears to lend itself to remaking quite well.

A note on presentation and sources: The chapters on individual films will outline the relevant contexts for the subsequent interpretations, including production details, genre influences and legacy, as well as historical contexts. In many cases, I will also add information on the critical appreciation of these films at the time of release as well as box office numbers. While not entirely pointless trivia, this information is mostly offered to give a rough idea of a film's reception and remains of little consequence to my readings. Therefore, I have found it sufficient to quote non-academic websites such as review aggregators, which collect film reviews and calculate an average rating using various metrics, and databases collecting box office numbers. None of these sources fulfill academic standards, nor are they meant to. While one may be tempted to equate critical approval or commercial success with significance, I feel the need to emphasize that for the purpose of this study, these numbers are only a very limited, if any, indicator of the cultural relevance of these films. Moreover, as will become evident in the film chapters, the canonizing forces in academic, critical and fan cultures often work slowly and are prone to revising the initial reception of a given film.

This book is divided in two parts, the first of which explores the necessary key concepts in two chapters. Chapter 1 aims to give a brief introduction to the horror film genre, establish a working definition of horror, and explore how horror films function, with the figure of the monster as its key component. Therefore, the construction of monsters is examined in detail, and various theories on the ideological purpose of horror are discussed, as these lay the necessary groundwork for the identification of the genre's cultural function. In order to grasp the full scope of this function, the chapter also touches upon monstrous figures in discourses that go beyond the horror genre. As the monsters of horror are informed by and feed back into broader cultural discourses on monstrous difference, they also serve to illuminate these discourses. Chapter 2 focuses on remakes, and it is important to note that the term *remake* refers not to any form of reproduction, or indeed any derivative film, but more accurately to a particular type of derivative film, which is the result of a distinct practice in (re)production and reception. In a nutshell, a film remake is a newly produced version of a previously realized film, clearly declared and received as such. The chapter aims to give a brief history of the remake, survey the state of academic research, and address definitional issues. With these basics clarified, it will closely examine the intertextual mechanics of film remakes and go on to probe the margins of the concept by discussing related forms of reproduction and fan works. The second part of this book is devoted to the in-depth analysis of the sample horror remake complexes, grouped in roughly chronological order, in six more chapters.

Part I: Horror and its Remakes

1. Horror

HISTORY, DEFINITIONS AND STATUS

Histories of American horror film point towards the Gothic literary traditions of the eighteenth and nineteenth centuries, represented by British authors like Horace Walpole and Ann Radcliffe and American authors like Charles Brockden Brown and Edgar Allen Poe, as its primary source. In addition, theater, circus and freak show traditions also served as influences on the burgeoning genre (Neale, *Genre* 94-95), whereas the aesthetic of cinematic horror is frequently traced to the German expressionist cinema of the 1910s and 1920s, especially *Nosferatu, eine Symphonie des Grauens* (1922). The American horror film came into its own with the Universal films of the 1930s, such as *Dracula* (1931) and *Frankenstein* (1931), and prospered throughout the decade before eventually declining to minor status in the 1940s (Neale, *Genre* 95). The 1950s saw horror revitalized through an extensive hybridization with science fiction in monster movies such as *The Thing from Another World* (1951), *Them!* (1954), and *The Blob* (1958).

Many critics observe a clear shift in the genre during the 1960s, with either *Psycho* (1960) or *Night of the Living Dead* (1968) as the turning point towards a modern (Neale, *Genre* 96) or postmodern horror film (Pinedo 10). This new type of film marked a break with the established style and genre conventions of horror (cf. Neale, *Genre* 96), an end of security and a turn towards more paranoid horror (Tudor, *Monsters* 102-04).[1] In the aftermath of the end of the Hollywood

---

[1] Even though Tudor observes a fundamental and lasting shift in 1960s horror, he rejects the term "postmodern horror" ("From Paranoia" 105), since the loss of trust and ubiquity of fear in contemporary society are still rooted in modernity and capitalism (116). Furthermore, Jancovich disagrees with the widespread perception that *Psycho*

studio system, and with the ensuing boom in low budget independent filmmaking, horror film production increased significantly throughout the 1970s (Tudor, *Monsters* 25). The decade saw the rise of several celebrated horror filmmakers, including Wes Craven, Tobe Hooper, and John Carpenter, and brought forth numerous new cycles and subgenres, including the high points of occult and animal horror in *The Exorcist* (1973) and *Jaws* (1975), as well as the beginnings of the slasher and body horror, which would go on to flourish in the following decade.

Horror remained prolific throughout the 1980s, especially in the shape of teen slasher films and sequels, such as *Halloween* (1978) and *Friday the 13th* (1980), whose trails of successors lasted into the 2000s. The 1990s featured a wave of big-budget horror films aiming for respectability, including *The Silence of the Lambs* (1991) and new adaptations of Gothic novels (Jancovich, "Introduction" 6-7), along with a new, ironicized take on the slasher popularized by *Scream* (1996). Finally, the 2000s saw the emergence of subgenres such as found footage horror, following *The Blair Witch Project* (1999), and so-called torture porn, initiated by *Saw* (2004) and *Hostel* (2005).[2] In addition, remakes of earlier films and revivals of earlier traditions also appear regularly throughout all of these phases. For example, the Gothic saw a brief resurgence in the 1960s in Roger Corman's films (though much less pronounced than in the British horror film), and again in the 1990s, whereas the zombie resurgence of the 2000s easily eclipsed the genre's heyday in the late 1970s and early 80s.

This list of cycles and subgenres is by no means exhaustive, and attempts to further subdivide and classify the American horror film are complicated by overlapping subgenre designations variously created and employed by producers, critics and audiences.[3] Furthermore, even though horror film is widely recognized as a distinct genre, its exact boundaries tend to blur. Throughout its history, horror has successfully mixed with other popular film genres. Neale, for example, emphasizes the difficulty of distinguishing between horror and science fiction as well as the crime film and concludes that the tendency towards multi-

---

(1960) marked a break in the genre, and insists that it instead represents a continuation of trends existing in the 1950s (*Rational* 220-21).

2   So called because of the exploitative depiction of torture, not because of pornographic content.

3   Nonetheless, there exist numerous useful histories of horror film in general and American horror film specifically. Jancovich offers a concise overview both of horror film history and how its narratives are constructed ("Introduction"), as does Neale (*Genre* 93-99). More extensive coverage is offered by Skal (even though he strays beyond film), Tudor (*Monsters*), Wells, and for American horror, Rigby.

plicity and overlap makes "water-tight" definitions of these film genres hard to find (*Genre* 92; see also D. Russell 233).

Moreover, the troubles in delineating horror also highlight the problem of defining the concept of film genre as such. Jancovich identifies a number of possible approaches: horror as a formula, meaning that all examples share the same narrative pattern; structuralist approaches, which view the genre as a complex and meaningful system on which individual filmmakers can draw; and horror as consensus, meaning that an implicit agreement among the audience defines horror ("Introduction" 10-16). Representing the last approach, Tudor states that "genres are not fixed nor are they only bodies of textual material. They are composed as much of the beliefs, commitments and social practices of their audiences as by texts, better understood as particular 'sub-cultures of taste' than as autonomous assemblies of cultural artifacts" ("Why Horror" 49). Drawing on Naremore, Jancovich makes a similar argument, but focuses on discourse. Accordingly, genre is produced by discourses "through which films are understood" ("Genre" 151). As the audience of horror is internally fractured (153), not to mention other participants in the discourse of horror, genre distinctions are constantly contested: "Rather than horror having a single meaning, different social groups construct it in different, competing ways as they seek to identify with or distance themselves from the term, and associate different texts with these constructions of horror" (159).

These latter approaches probably come closest to appreciating the full extent of genres and the multitude of discourses that play part in their formation, yet at the same time, they run the risk of becoming hopelessly unwieldy. Whereas narrative formulas and textual structures can be located in the text, it is a significant methodological challenge to derive a solid consensus from a large and diverse audience. Tudor's subcultural expanse is largely beyond the scope of this study, not only due to practical considerations, but also because it would detract attention from the texts chosen as objects of study. His considerations nevertheless serve as valuable reminders that diverse audiences may arrive at divergent readings of the same texts, and that horror inevitably functions at an intersection of discourses.

It is also worth pointing out that despite the academic struggles with the boundaries of horror, the largest part of its potential corpus is fairly unproblematic. The canonical texts of the genre, whether drawn from scholarly or popular sources, will more than likely conform to any of the given definitions. From this perspective, the sample films treated in this study likewise elude the definitional dilemma, as they work with most prevalent conceptions of horror, whether according to textual characteristics and common narrative structures, or according to a significant section of critics and audiences. Still, in the interest of an in-depth textual analysis, this study will rely more on the former approaches rather than the latter.

The horror film is firmly established as part of the Hollywood film industry and has not only endured decades of changing audience tastes and media technologies, but prospered. Yet, it occupies a peculiar place in the perception of critics and the general public. Periodically, there are concerns about the genre or at least its extreme examples being immoral and harmful to its viewers or society, but these have done little to detract from the popularity of horror. The genre still carries the air of being objectionable, but at the same time, it is absolutely a mainstream phenomenon. The Hollywood horror film industry puts out a steady stream of product, as do independent filmmakers. In the US, horror films regularly top box office charts, especially around Halloween, which serves as the prime season for new releases. Despite this popularity, most horror films do not gain broader critical acclaim, at least not of the type measured in five-star reviews and awards.

The academic study of horror, by contrast, is well established since the 1980s, at least, and has been steadily gaining popularity in recent years. A large segment of research draws on psychoanalytic theory as a method of reading the monsters and scenarios of horror as signs and symptoms of society's repressed anxieties and urges; this includes key studies by Wood, Twitchell, Clover, and Creed, to name but a few (cf. Neale, *Genre* 98). At the same time, criticism of these psychoanalytic approaches has been voiced by a number of authors including Tudor, Carroll, and Jancovich. Judging by a survey of recent horror research, most of these authors are still relevant or even essential for the field, especially Carroll (for general purposes), Wood (for political/ideological readings), and Clover (for gender criticism).

A common thread among many of these studies is the claim that horror is marginal and disreputable, firmly located outside of commonly accepted cultural discourse. For example, Wood claims that "[t]he horror film has consistently been one of the most popular and, at the same time, the most disreputable of Hollywood genres" (77). Similarly, Brophy finds that horror is not accepted by mainstream film criticism (278), and Crane sees horror and its fans unfairly vilified (vii). The perceived marginal status of horror has often been invoked to validate the genre as a subversive cultural form and thereby legitimize its study (Jancovich, "Introduction" 1; Neale, *Genre* 93). For Jancovich, the increased academic interest suggests that the genre no longer has a marginal status, but then again, he admits that horror, like pornography, is subject to "considerable aesthetic criticism" as well as the "target of moral panic" (1).[4] The comparison to pornography may be flawed, since horror films run at multiplex cinemas and carry little or no stigma for their performers and directors. Furthermore, moral panics at the scale of the British "video nasties" debate of the 1980s have not recurred as new media such as video games have drawn the attention of concerned parties away from horror. The horror film may not be quite as beleaguered as it was in the 1980s and 90s, but the cited patterns of aesthetic and moral criticism still persist.

At this point, it is useful to distinguish between different discourses and canonizing authorities. Despite a certain overlap, academic film and culture studies have somewhat different interests than film critics writing for the review sections of mainstream newspapers or websites, or authorities concerned with the moral well-being of their communities. The acceptance of horror as an object of study in academia does not mean that its particular aesthetics are universally appreciated. Specifically, the genre's drive to challenge boundaries of taste in its depiction of violence inevitably leads to a constant struggle with ratings authorities and censorship, and to a sense of repression for more avid genre fans. In short, then, even if horror is not strictly a marginal genre in terms of production, profitability, and academic interest, it may nevertheless be marginalized by certain cultural authorities and institutions.

At times, even academic studies display a complicated relationship with the intertwined discourses of marginality and legitimacy. Gelder and Hantke, for example, want to preserve the marginal status of horror to preserve its effect (Gelder, "Introduction" 5; Hantke, "Shudder"). Since academic study already neglects the bodily effects of horror, argues Hantke, "[o]ne devastating effect academic criticism could have on horror would be to promote its canonization. This would place increasingly complex mechanisms of cultural mediation between the text and its reader, diminishing even further horror's ability to provoke a bodily response" ("Shudder" 7). From this perspective, the marginal status of horror would seem necessary for it to function at all, and a legitimization and fixation of horror would be harmful to its reception. Wells displays a related concern regarding academic criticism, arguing that the analysis of horror film "should not strain too far after meaning for fear it might undermine the sensation created" (1). Wells's argument is somewhat problematic, though; even if methodical analysis was to diminish the aesthetic effect of horror, it would hardly be appropriate to ask academics to hold back.

---

4   In addition, Jancovich's own examination of the disavowal of horror in the mediation of *Silence of the Lambs* (1991) shows that horror is far from universally accepted ("Genre" 156).

Another recurring notion in horror criticism is the perception of crisis. Several critics, especially among those who undertook influential studies of horror in the 1970s and 1980s, later expressed disappointment with the further development of the genre. Their criticism targets aesthetic shortcomings, a supposed loss of quality and innovation due to mass production, as well as perceived ideological shifts. Instead of subversive films that question social conventions, they claim, the film industry has turned to producing less intelligent, politically reactionary films. These complaints are by no means a recent development, as Wood already dismissed the genre in 1986, attesting its "decline – worse, the hideous perversion of its essential meaning – in the 80s" (70).[5] In his recent update to his 1977 book *Dark Dreams*, Derry likewise argues that American horror is in decline: "Horror films—like most Hollywood movies—are more than ever being reduced to the least common denominator; politically neutered, they are losing many of the subversive qualities so often associated with the genre" (7). He expresses dissatisfaction with the immature and ignorant contemporary audience of horror, a far cry from more sophisticated moviegoers of the 1970s (cf. 4; 110), and "feels great nostalgia for what the genre has lost" (11). Wood's and Derry's impressions are shared by many critics and fans, and the proliferation of remakes and sequels is seen as a key symptom of this decline, as film franchises "ad nauseam continue their unthinking onslaught" (Derry 111).

A counterpoint is offered by Steffen Hantke. While he agrees that when it comes to horror films, "not only does the present look bleak, the future looks dubious, too" ("'They don't'" xii), he also points out that remakes and sequels are nothing new and that "things have always been this way" (xvi). He admits there may or may not be a crisis, but concludes that the question seems impossible to answer (xvii). Instead, the talk about crisis points to an academic anxiety, which in turn stems from the "negotiation of legitimacy" and a "perpetual misalignment between film production and academic criticism" (xix). Academics solve that dilemma by holding on to a long-established genre canon. Fan frustration, then, may be a reaction of a subculture against the mainstream success of horror, an attempt to conserve the underground status of horror. Thus, the "rhetoric of crisis tells us more about the audiences than about the films they have been watching" (xxviii). The prevalent rhetoric of crisis only leads to a distorted perspective, as it serves as a self-fulfilling prophecy (xxiii-xxiv). Beyond Hantke's points, there are also generational divides at play, along with the simple problem that histories of horror are "narrative histories," which need to end either in fulfillment or tragedy (Jancovich, "General Introduction" 9).

---

5   The same point is echoed by Sharett, who laments a conservative turn in horror in "Horror in Neoconservative Culture."

All things considered, the perception of a crisis should have little relevance for my study. For one, the sense of decline is rather subjective, that is, dependent on particular aesthetic preferences and political views. As Hantke points out, the production and profitability of horror films are increasing ("They" vii), so clearly, a large audience is watching horror films and liking them enough to come back for more. That those viewers are content with supposedly thoughtless or reactionary sequels and remakes needs not be understood as a problem, but instead represents a revelation about the current cultural climate and indeed the function of the genre. As I stated in the introduction, the cultural functions of both horror films and remakes are performed independently of critical approval, and evidently, that includes the genre critics quoted above. In addition, the multiplicity of audiences cannot be neglected in the discussion. For these seasoned critics, the current crop of horror films may be dull and conservative, but how diverse audiences read them is a different question.

PARADOX PLEASURES: GENRE MECHANICS

As the name already implies, fear is what drives the horror genre. Carroll argues in his *Philosophy of Horror*, "The cross-art, cross-media genre of horror takes its title from the emotion it characteristically or rather ideally promotes; this emotion constitutes the identifying mark of horror" (14). Twitchell similarly puts the sensation of fear at the center of the genre: "Horror art is not, strictly speaking, a genre; it is rather a collection of motifs in a usually predictable sequence that gives us a specific physiological effect – the shivers" (8).

The audience of horror, in what seems like a paradox, wants to be scared, or at least to experience from a safe distance the thrill of danger. Horror narratives, whether fiction or films, are designed to evoke this affect of intense fear in their audience, using a variety of techniques, and direct it towards monsters, whether human or inhuman, natural or supernatural. These monsters are not simply dangerous, they are impure and unnatural, they disturb the order of things, and they go beyond categories of understanding, which distinguishes them from the threats in other suspense genres (Carroll 23; 34). This quality of disturbance is key, as the simple presence of monsters does not create horror on its own (Carroll 16; Tudor, "Why" 50). For Carroll, it is the criteria of "dangerousness and impurity" which "constitute the formal object of the emotion," that is, the focus of fear (28). Monsters must be threatening, whether to one's life or "psychologically, morally or socially," and also impure, involving "a conflict between two or more standing cultural categories (43). Monsters are thus (usually) morally and ontologically transgressive (200), with the latter frequently amounting to a form of hybridity, a fusion or fission of disparate categories or identities (43; 46).

In short, monstrous disturbance is the crucial feature of the generic horror narrative, which is neatly summarized in Wood's basic formula of horror: "normality is threatened by the Monster" (78). In this context, Wood points out, the term "normality" is nonevaluative and basically stands for "conformity to the dominant social norms" (78). According to Russell, Wood's formula comes closest to a general consensus among horror critics (D. Russell 238). As an alternative, Tudor offers a slightly more detailed basic plot: "a monstrous threat is introduced into a stable situation; the monster rampages in the face of attempts to combat it; the monster is (perhaps) destroyed and order (perhaps) restored" (*Monsters* 81). Tudor's criteria of stability and order roughly correspond to Wood's normality, but his plot outline already accommodates various outcomes. Numerous authors have likewise tried to condense a basic horror narrative, and usually arrive at similar terms, such as Pinedo, whose classic horror narrative starts with the "violent disruption of the normative order by a monster" and ends with the defeat of the monster (15). Nevertheless, a few still disagree with the defining role of the monster, such as Jancovich, who suggests that it is rather the victim that is common to all horror texts (Hills 15).[6] Since victims are indeed a necessary part of the normality under threat, and not all horror narratives feature easily identifiable monsters, it may be more constructive to adopt a more open conception of "monstrous threat," as implied by Tudor, to account for a maximum number of horror narratives (Neale, *Genre* 99). This way, the constitutive function of the monster may just as well be filled by unseen malignant forces.[7]

With monsters taking such a prominent role, it is necessary to point out another definitional dilemma: horror is defined by monsters, but not all narratives featuring monsters are necessarily horror. Many popular narratives, especially for child or young adult audiences, use established monster types not as threats, but in a manner akin to regular human characters, as protagonists and so forth. Any resulting generic confusion can, however, be resolved by keeping the central affect of horror in mind. After all, horror monsters are not just monsters because they fit an established subtype (vampire, zombie, etc.), but because they

---

6 Hills sees the view of emotions as object directed and occurrent as the major weaknesses of cognitivist approaches such as Carroll's and suggests that objectless fear and anxiety work as well (24-25); in fact, the interplay between the two may be key: "one of the pleasures of horror may in fact lie in the transformation of experienced affect into emotion and vice versa (28).

7 All things considered, the advantages of using the monster as the constitutive element of horror far outweigh the downsides (cf. Pabst).

perform a particular narrative function, as a dangerous, abnormal, terrifying contradiction to normality.

The disruptions of the horror monster, then, are presented in a manner intended to cause fear and discomfort in the audience. These effects are varied and depend on a complex interplay between narrative, cinematic technique, and audience expectations. A closer analysis of the audience's experience of fear is undertaken by Hanich, who distances himself from cognitivist approaches like Carroll's (cf. Hanich 13), and instead resorts to a phenomenological approach. Hanich describes and discusses a wide variety of fearsome viewing experiences and sets up a typology of cinematic fears, consisting of five categories: direct and indirect horror, shock, dread, and terror. Direct horror describes the discomfort of directly viewing morally repulsive acts, a "confrontation with vivid sound-supported moving-images of threatening acts of violence or a dangerous monster" (82). Indirect horror, then, encompasses the discomfort of seeing these same acts implied, creating "intimidating imaginations of violence and/or a monster" (109). Shock works differently, as a sheer unpleasant surprise, "a brief, highly compressed type of fear" reacting to "a threatening object or event that ruptures the situation suddenly and unexpectedly" (127). Dread, by contrast, is more subtle, describing the uneasy anticipation of an unspecified danger, such as "a vulnerable character slowly and quietly entering a dark, forsaken place harboring a threat" (156). Terror also builds on anticipation, but is more specific, being derived from "the quick and loud perceptible temporal approach of a horrifying threat" (203). Horror films typically draw on several or even all of these types of cinematic fear in succession.

The question why there is pleasure to be found in the normally deeply unpleasant experience of fear has been the subject of much discussion among scholars. Carroll suggests that the audience derives pleasure from gradually gaining knowledge about the ostensibly unknowable monster: "The disclosure of the existence of the horrific being and of its properties is the central source of pleasure in the genre" (184). Carroll's concept of cognitive pleasure is too purely rational for some (Jancovich, "Introduction" 22; Hills 17), and as a counterpoint, Shaw argues that the sheer power of the monster is already pleasurable and thrilling (Hills 20). Approaches that draw on psychoanalysis, such as Clover's, locate the appeal of horror in what is otherwise suppressed: "The 'ethnic' evidence suggests that the first and central aim of horror cinema is to play to masochistic fears and desires in its audiences . . . It may play on other fears and desires too, but dealing out pain is its defining characteristic" (Clover 229). Pinedo sees the draw in a "bounded experience," which she describes as "an exercise in recreational terror, a simulation of danger not unlike a roller coaster ride," which is controlled and therefore pleasurable (38). Pinedo also touches on psychoanalytic ideas by assuming that horror also "denaturalizes the repressed" and makes the "terrors of everyday life" accessible (39). Crane also invokes the roller coaster analogy, but stresses a collective experience of horror viewers and rejects prevalent approaches, as "New horror films refuse to entertain the unconscious as they, instead, offer meaningless death in response to the terrors of everyday life" (39).

This choice of quotes represents only a small fraction of theories regarding the appeal of horror. A few common threads emerge, and some link between the experience of horror narratives and real fears, with the former as a lesser version of the latter, is widely assumed. Nevertheless, there is hardly a general consensus, and most approaches are burdened with the same basic flaws. For example, Carroll denies that psychoanalytic approaches, figuring monsters as a return of the repressed, are generally applicable (Carroll 173-74). However, that criticism can of course be turned back on Carroll and his cognitive theory of pleasure, which may not be applicable to all audiences either (Hills 17).[8] Indeed, any universalizing account may be challenged for neglecting viewers who experience and enjoy horror in a different manner. Accordingly, Hills formulates the general critique that "[a]udience pleasures are constructed in line with specific theoretical presuppositions, and are then projected onto horror's 'ideal' readers and viewers" (13). In Hills's opinion, all theories impose limitations, "suppressing and marginalizing what become theoretically 'Othered' ways of thinking about horror's pleasure" (68). Similar concerns are voiced by Tudor, who views universalist explanations for the appeal of horror as problematic. Still, Tudor acknowledges that the alternative, resorting to particular accounts of horror reception, ends up with a multitude of reasons and has to resort to "disciplined speculation" when it comes to historical reception research ("Why" 53). Therefore, Tudor rejects questions regarding a general appeal of horror and instead recommends more specific inquiries, such as "why do *these* people like *this* horror in *this* place at *this* particular time?" (54)

At this point, it may be helpful to back up and realign with the goals of this study. The horror genre revolves around fear, in one way or another, and it focuses that fear in monstrous threats. That above all is its defining feature, and the enduring success of the genre proves the persistent appeal of the fearsome experiences it provides. How horror is received and how its audiences derive enjoyment from it (or indeed fail to) may be variable, but the core purpose of the genre is clearly stated and consciously pursued.

---

8   For his explanation, Carroll assumes "average consumers," but admits that there are others (193).

READING HORROR

Some authors suggest an ideological function behind horror's focus on fear and monsters. Stephen King, whose copious catalogue of horror fiction has frequently been adapted to film, claims that "the horror movie is innately conservative, even reactionary" (173). A similar assertion is made by Clover, who suggests that "[i]ts subject matter alone guarantees the cultural conservatism of horror" (15). The basic reasoning behind these (and similar) claims is that horror's focus on defeating abnormal intruders amounts to a defense of the sociopolitical status quo (cf. Carroll 196). This ideological function may be attributed to the themes or the basic narrative structures of horror.

As examples for the thematic approach, Carroll cites readings which consider the horror genre as xenophobic or as "scaring people into submissively accepting their social roles" (196). Support for either argument can be found, from Cold War invasion narratives to slasher movies, but the counterexamples of thematically progressive horror fictions disprove the claim that the genre is always "projecting ideologically repressive themes" (198). In his discussion of the structural approach, Carroll extensively quotes Stephen King and boils down the argument that "the horror story is always a contest between the normal and the abnormal such that the normal is reinstated and, therefore, affirmed," which posits horror as the "symbolic defense of a culture's standards of normality" (199). After a tentative analysis of the "deep structure" (200) of horror fiction and its carnivalesque elements (200-01), Carroll still finds the theory of horror's conservative structure less than compelling, since it fails to account for narratives in which the monster is not "expelled or eliminated" (201). Moreover, he takes issue with interpreting any violation of normality or moral code as a rebellion against a particular political status quo, since the two may not be intractably linked (203). The disruptions of the monster may thus occur at a level of abstraction that bears no relevance to the political or social order (203). Overall, Carroll firmly denies a consistent ideological stance for the horror genre as a whole and concludes on an ambivalent note: horror is neither always reactionary, nor is it always emancipatory (205).

Given the diversity of horror texts and audiences, it should come as no surprise that the idea of a single, ideologically narrow function for the entire genre is hard to sustain. Nevertheless, it may still apply to individual narratives or clusters of narratives. Numerous authors have undertaken investigations into the ideological foundations of horror, but Wood in particular remains highly influential (and useful) for such readings.

Wood's already quoted basic formula "normality is threatened by the Monster" (78) is versatile in its simplicity, and enables an ideological reading of any horror film through the examination of its fundamental dichotomy. In a nutshell, the monster is the polar opposite of normality and by its actions or its mere existence transgresses against it. In order to establish this dichotomy, a horror narrative constructs both sides of the story, the monster and the normality it targets. With these basics established, Wood draws on his readings of psychoanalysis as well as Marxist and feminist criticism to assemble his model of repression in the horror film. While basic repression is a necessary force, Wood argues, we are living in a culture based on "surplus repression," which shapes us into "monogamous heterosexual bourgeois capitalists" (71). Closely related to repression, he adds the concept of the Other, representing everything that bourgeois ideology cannot accept but must deal with, and onto which what is repressed in the Self is projected (73). Wood's list of Others includes other people in general, as well as women, the proletariat, other cultures, ethnic groups, or ideologies, deviations from sexual norms, and children (73-75).

Horror films, then, enact a return of the repressed: "One might say that the true subject of the horror genre is the struggle for recognition of all that our civilization represses or oppresses, its reemergence dramatized, as in our nightmares, as an object of horror, a matter for terror, and the happy ending (when it exists) typically signifying the restoration of repression" (75). Considering the approaches discussed earlier, this conclusion would seem to suggest a conservative function of horror, as it equates a "happy ending" with the persistence of the repressive status quo. Wood's model allows for more nuanced readings, though. The "restoration of repression" is not a universal feature of the genre, but one possible outcome. Alternatively, a victorious or at least surviving monster may represent the permanent disruption of repression and hence the social order.[9]

Wood's declared goal is finding "the means toward a political categorization of horror movies" (191), and he claims to have accomplished as much in his take on repression, but also admits that categorization can never be clear-cut (191). He finds a progressive potential realized in a number of horror films from the 1970s which defied the dominant ideology and offered the possibility of radical social change (84; 192). Following the radical horror film, Wood identifies a "reactionary wing," distinguished by the designation of the monster as simply evil, its presentation as totally nonhuman, the presence of Christianity and the confusion "of repressed sexuality with sexuality itself" (192-93). These characteristics, he argues, mark films that serve the dominant ideology by justifying and maintaining repression. For Wood, this ideological transformation indicates

---

9   E.g. *The Texas Chain Saw Massacre* (1974) (Wood 88-94, see chapter 7).

a "sinister and disturbing inversion of the significance of the traditional horror film," in which the monster was "not merely a product of repression, but a protest against it" (195). As examples, he names the "violence against women movie" and the "teenie-kill pic" (195), both of which would be folded under the slasher film as per Clover.

While influential for the field of horror film studies, Wood's approach has been met with substantial criticism, for its methodology as well as its goals. Hills, for instance, alleges that many psychoanalytic critics, especially Wood, were more interested in "defusing ambivalence" and "dividing horror texts into (bad) 'reactionary' and (good) 'progressive' instances" (46). The identification of a binary political stance assumes an ideal audience, onto whom "horror's pleasures are theoretically imagined or projected by Wood, in line with his project to validate and legitimate horror as deadly serious business" (51). Hills further takes issue with the "'return of the repressed' thesis" popularized by Wood (Hills 48), as the monster may just as often be repressive and not repressed (50; cf. Jancovich, *Horror* 16). Overall, Hills views Wood as performing "a vast semiotic fixing of horror's meanings" (52), which puts horror "in the service of a specific cultural politics" (53). Similar criticism is voiced by Russell, who argues that Wood's fixation on "ideological causality" and "libidinal determinism" is overly reductive and makes it "difficult to apply his system beyond its overt ideological purposes" (D. Russell 237).

While these critics have a point, Wood's approach is still more useful than they give it credit for. The simplicity and flexibility of his basic formula makes it a solid starting point for further analysis of horror films, as Russell admits (238). The criteria derived from this formula, the monster, normality and the relationship between the two, are likewise applicable to a wide range of narratives and function quite well with a lessened or adjusted focus on repression. Furthermore, a broader conception of normality expands its utility beyond ideological readings (D. Russell 239). Whether or not one finds Wood's take on repression convincing, simply analyzing how monstrosity and normality are constructed as opposites (or, in some narratives, revealed as related) offers plenty of material, and with more consideration for the ambiguities and contexts of individual films, the results are bound to go beyond a binary political categorization.

As another approach, Tudor's extensive survey of horror films ends up with an ideological divide, but locates it at a different historical breaking point. Tudor distinguishes two types of horror, secure and paranoid, each with different ideological underpinnings. Secure horror is basically conservative, supporting a hierarchical social order, the traditional family unit, the marginalization of women, sexual repression, anti-intellectualism and so forth (*Monsters* 220). Paranoid horror, by contrast, expresses doubt in the social order, and is ambivalent when it comes to the family unit, casting it both as a source of violence and the "only institutional defence" (222). The transition from secure to paranoid horror takes place in the 1960s, and Tudor carefully suggests a "post-sixties erosion of the foundations of social legitimacy in many western societies" as the reason (222). That would still (very roughly) align with Wood's notion of radical horror in the 1970s, but Tudor does not observe a conservative (or secure) turn afterwards. Instead, his update on horror between the mid-1980s and the turn of the millennium finds paranoid horror affirmed and continued, with a tendency towards internal threats and less legitimate authorities ("From Paranoia" 108-09). Most of the films chosen for this study fall outside of Tudor's secure horror, but the representations of authorities, institutions, and family remain valid criteria for analysis.

The portrayal of institutions is also the central factor in Biskind's survey of American 1950s cinema, which he sorts into centrist (pluralist and conservative) and radical (left and right) camps. The focus of Biskind's book makes it only marginally relevant for this study, but his coverage of science fiction/horror hybrids is at least pertinent. Even though he admits that Hollywood films "have no incentive to be politically clear" to avoid alienating audiences (5), Biskind has no trouble assigning an unambiguous political stance to each of the many films he covers, based on the relative role of government, science, military, and others. Thus, consensus marks a centrist scifi/horror film, with a coalition of scientists and soldiers in charge (102); a preference for scientists would mark a pluralist film and a preference for the military a conservative one. Opposition to established institutions and society, then, marks a radical film, with further subdivisions for left and right. Biskind's lack of flexibility in his readings, along with the rigidity of his radical-center model, limit the utility of his model, but the questions he asks on the (often monstrous) alien, whether it is "nature or culture," "Us or Them" (121-22), may still prove helpful in the discussion of monsters.[10]

It is evident that horror film and its confrontations of monsters and normality, of social order and transgression, invite questions of ideology. By necessity, its constructions of normality are informed by historical and cultural contexts, and may therefore reveal underlying ideologies, but that does not mean that horror film is tied to just one particular stance. Instead, its challenge of normality enables a negotiation that may reinforce or dissolve constructions of menacing Others, depending on the outcome of the narrative.

---

10 An extensive critique of Biskind is found in Jancovich's study of 1950s horror, *Rational Fears*.

Precursors and Permutations of Monsters

The concept of the monster predates the modern horror film and stretches to include a number of related concepts, from mythical beasts and apparitions to medical monstrosities and enemy images. Monsters, whether understood literally or metaphorically, are all around us, and have been for quite some time. The monsters of the horror genre are inextricably linked with the monsters of the real world, as both spring from the same discourses of normality, transgression, evil, and so forth.

The monster resists categorization, yet paradoxically, the monstrous itself is a category. Something can be marked as monstrous, excluded from normality as an offense against nature and/or morality. At the same time, the monster can never be completely understood and contained. Monsters negotiate the limits and failure of categories of knowledge, but they may also serve to reinforce conceptions of normality – by transgressing the boundaries, they remind us of their significance.[11]

The term *monster* encompasses a range of meanings, at various points in time referring to mythical creatures, humans or animals with congenital defects, or those guilty of extreme moral transgressions. Colloquial use of the term as a marker of extraordinary size or quality only retains a hint of its transgressive core. Academic studies of the monster frequently choose etymology as the starting point, deducting its function from the term's Latin roots. Cohen, for example, explains that "The monstrum is etymologically 'that which reveals,' 'that which warns,'" and notes that it "exists only to be read" (4).[12]

Attempts to trace the historical trajectory of monsters in European thought generally identify several distinct types and stages of development. The first type of monster originates in classical mythology and continues in medieval heroic epics, as extraordinary opposition for equally remarkable heroes. The next type consists of humans and animals with congenital defects or other variations deemed monstrous well into the early modern period. A multitude of reasons were invoked for these phenomena: "Monsters came from God and the Devil,

---

11 An earlier, more extensive version of this section and the next appeared in Knöppler, "The Mark(er) of Evil: Die Markierung von Monstrosität."

12 In addition, Hagner reports a distinction between "monstrositas" and "monstrum" well into the nineteenth century, the former referring to material beings with congenital defects and the latter fictional creatures. The two concepts are related, both liminal beings, the former a phenomenon requiring explanation, the latter a projection space for otherness and disgust (Hagner 9).

they were caused by stars and comets, they resulted from copulation with other species, and from flaws in their parents' anatomies" (Huet 1).

The Age of Enlightenment marks a clean break with this conception of monsters, as the perceived deviations were now understood as natural occurrences. While such monstrosities had been viewed as evil and incompatible with divine creation in the Middle Ages, the science of the second half of the eighteenth century now abolished monsters (Hagner 12-15). Explained away from the natural world, monsters instead took refuge in fiction (Röttgers 15) as the villains and creatures of the gothic novel and related cultural forms. At the same time, Foucault remarks, the figure of the "monstrous criminal," "the moral monster," appears and becomes ubiquitous in a range of discourses and practices, whereas the body monsters of the previous eras, all hybrid beings, are dissolved into a number of smaller abnormalities (75). Monstrosity thus moves from the exterior to the interior, and by leaving behind the body becomes flexible enough to attach to any kind of deviance (Gebhard, Geisler, and Schröter 19-20).

So far, the historical overview leaves us with at least two general types of monsters: body monsters, whose physical forms transgress categories otherwise considered inviolable, often through hybridity, and moral monsters, whose extreme transgressions against laws and morality mark them as inhuman. Scientific rationality may have eliminated the former from nature, but the latter thrive in tabloids and sensationalist news media; serial killers and pedophiles, genocidal dictators and terrorists are regularly labeled as the real monsters of the modern age. Both types of monsters, body and moral, can still be found in a variety of discourses, not least in the fictions of the horror genre. The longevity and flexibility of the monster are remarkable, and hint at an enduring cultural function.

The functions of monsters have been variously theorized. In seven theses, Cohen outlines "a method of reading cultures from the monsters they engender" (3). Monsters embody a certain cultural moment, Cohen argues, and as constructs and projections, they are made to be read (3-4). Monstrous figures are thus charged with meaning, and their analysis in turn allows conclusions about the context in which they originated. Not any cultural concept finds expression in the ever-changing monster; instead, it is "difference made flesh" and functions as a "dialectical Other" (7): "Any kind of alterity can be inscribed across (constructed through) the monstrous body, but for the most part monstrous difference tends to be cultural, political, racial, economic, sexual" (7). Explaining his point further, Cohen draws on René Girard: "Monsters are never created ex nihilo, but through a process of fragmentation and recombination in which elements are extracted 'from various forms' (including- indeed, especially- marginalized social groups) and then assembled as the monster, 'which can then claim an independent identity'" (11). In short, the monster is an amalgam of pre-existing markers of identity, and a careful reading should enable us to trace each part of the monster back to a particular group. Furthermore, the monster "polices the borders of the possible," prohibiting or permitting movements or behaviors as "vehicle of prohibition" (13-15). Cohen elaborates that notion with a reference to biblical monsters, concluding that "[t]he monsters are here, as elsewhere, expedient representations of other cultures, generalized and demonized to enforce a strict notion of group sameness" (15). As a foil, the monster reinforces difference and thereby group cohesion. Gebhard, Geisler and Schröter suggest a similar function of stabilizing the self and generating identity (23).

Given that the monsters of horror are part of the broader discourse on monstrosity, it should come as no surprise that Cohen's line of argument resembles approaches on the horror genre and its ideology quoted earlier. In a nutshell, Cohen assigns monsters a fundamentally conservative cultural function, in service of the social groups that create them. And as with similar claims about the horror genre, Carroll's critique of such claims may apply here as well: the construction of a deviant monster may of course enforce sameness, but depending on its framing narrative or discourse, it may also subvert it (cf. Carroll 197-99). Furthermore, on a more basic level, the monster also deals with the limits of knowledge. Designating something as a monster represents a first attempt at resolving a "category crisis" (Cohen 6), at taming the unknown or unknowable (cf. Gebhard, Geisler, and Schröter 22-23). At the same time, the classification as monstrous may already be understood as an admission of failure, as an acknowledgement that existing categories of knowledge are insufficient. The monster as such is an object of astonishment, and any successful transformation into an object of knowledge would dissolve its monstrosity (cf. Lehmann 199-200).

In summary, an approximate consensus about the cultural function of the monster can be formulated. It negotiates the experience (and fear) of difference, marks the boundaries of normality and reinforces notions of humanity or more specific group affiliations. The monstrous is a category that holds everything threatening that is to be expelled from the image of normality, yet at the same time it attests to the shortcomings of categorization per se. The monster is thus the site of a constant struggle over deviance, transgression and knowledge, and its cinematic embodiments deliver ample evidence of this struggle.

MARKING MONSTROSITY

As previously established, horror narratives pit monsters against normality, and for that opposition to work, the audience needs to be able to tell the two sides apart. Therefore, monsters have to be designated as different. For this purpose, any element of the film that signifies monstrous difference, from dialogue to audiovisual presentation of the monstrous body, functions as a marker of monstrosity. Even though the creation of suspense relies on uncertainties, a horror film monster is purposefully constructed as monstrous and needs to be clearly recognizable as such, even if the revelation is delayed until the climax of the narrative.

In particular, monstrosity is established and communicated through three sets of markers: the monster's body, its actions in the narrative, and the reactions of its opposites, the 'normal' characters or victims. While these three categories are by no means exhaustive, they cover a significant portion of the marking process. The audience of horror is already prepared to expect the monstrous by paratextual elements and supplementary materials, from posters and trailers to the opening credits, but these only serve a supporting function.

The most straightforward option for the designation of cinematic monsters is marking their bodies. A deformed body, not matching any familiar or 'normal' pattern, instantly exposes its deviance and as soon as it comes into view. In this regard, horror film monsters take some leads from mythical monsters, in that hybridity, "the mixture of what is normally distinct" (Carroll 33), is a key way of transgressing normality. The historical development of the body monster touched upon in the previous section finds its continuation in the wide range of cinematic monsters. A body that visibly merges human and animal, as in the case of werewolves, is instantly recognizable as unnatural. Likewise, a body that combines dichotomies like life and death, as in the case of the zombie, or one that completely defies conventional body images, like the shapeshifting Thing from the film of the same title, visibly violates categories by its mere existence. The same applies to monsters without physical bodies, as ghostly and other non-corporeal entities reject the body as such.

Markers get less obvious with human monsters, the psychopaths and serial killers, whose bodies rarely take radical departures from the norm. Yet, visual markers of their monstrosity are still widespread. For instance, the killers of slasher films frequently wear masks that obscure or remove their humanity. The killers of such prolific franchises as *Halloween* or *Friday the 13th* are almost never seen without their masks, and for an even more blatant example, the chainsaw-wielding maniac from *The Texas Chain Saw Massacre* (1974) wears a mask made of human skin to leave no doubts as to his monstrosity. Even a character like Hannibal Lecter is, in his most iconic appearance in *The Silence of the Lambs* (1991), covered in a restraining apparatus that masks his face in a monstrous visage. Unlike the previous examples, Lecter's mask is not his own choice, but the effect on the audience remains the same.

As a more subtle example, cinema's formative psychopath, Norman Bates of *Psycho* (1960), may appear unassuming, but nevertheless has his monstrosity visibly marked at the film's conclusion. Bates suffers from a split personality, as a projection of his long-dead mother takes over his actions and drives him to kill. Bates's monstrosity is thus based on an interior hybridity, which manifests during the fade into the film's final image: Bates's entirely 'normal' face is overlaid with the mummified skull of his dead mother. His body may appear unmarked at first, but the film's editing marks him on an extradiegetic level, that is, not in the reality of the film, but still visible for the audience. *Psycho* (1960) is frequently quoted as a turning point in the horror film genre, marking a shift towards a more psychological type of horror (e.g. Derry 27).[13] Arguably, the subsequent genres of serial killer and slasher films repeat the changes in the monster discourse at the end of the eighteenth century, by replacing the body monster with the moral monster. Nevertheless, these film genres still largely rely on visual markers of monstrosity.

Visual markers attached to the monster's body clearly play a crucial role in establishing its monstrosity, but that characteristic may also find expression in sound. Inhuman or merely unexpected noises or speech patterns can serve as markers of monstrous difference as well. Furthermore, the staging of the monster, the mise-en-scène, likewise effects or supports the marking of monstrosity. Horror films draw on a range of established techniques, such as lighting, camera angles, and editing to establish a sense of threat. The camera's view hides, implies and reveals the monstrous body bit by bit to raise tension, using what Hanich terms "suggested horror" (109). This strategy heightens the difference of the monstrous body, as its appearance alone is rendered mysterious and extraordinary. In addition, the soundtrack, as an extradiegetic element, gives the audience cues on how to read these scenes, as menacing crescendos or cacophonies also signal monstrosity.

So far, I have focused on what the monster looks and sounds like, as markers of a monstrosity conceived as physical. Few horror films remain at that stage alone, and the monster's actions in the narrative also function as key markers of monstrosity. In horror narratives, it is typically acts of violence that are impossible to reconcile with normality, whether due to the incomprehensible motive behind them, the cruelty or scale of execution, or the breaking of taboos like canni-

---

13 Again, the significance of *Psycho* (1960) is contested by Jancovich (*Rational* 220-34).

balism, as in *The Texas Chain Saw Massacre* (1974) and *The Silence of the Lambs* (1991). This is a crucial step for the moral monsters, as the body monster already establishes its deviance by appearances alone. If the decomposed dead rise and walk around, that alone marks a monstrous transgression of categories and a development irreconcilable with normality. Once these walking dead hunt the living, it merely raises the stakes. Intriguingly, though, it is possible to turn actions or characteristics that are solidly rooted in normality into markers of monstrosity, depending on the context. In *Invasion of the Body Snatchers* (1956), it is cool rationality that distinguishes the human-looking alien invaders and is thus, in context of the narrative, repurposed as a marker of monstrosity (cf. chapter 4). Calm, friendly behavior may thus take on as much menace as a monster's fangs.

Of course, these examples assume that the audience identifies these markers and finds them incompatible with their own morality, so much as to find them monstrous. That work is not left to the audience alone, though, as a monster is also identified by the other characters in the narrative. Their emotional reactions provide instructions and examples as to how the audience is supposed to respond to the monster on the screen. As Carroll explains, "Our responses are supposed to converge (but not exactly duplicate) those of the characters" (18). Clover agrees with Carroll, asserting that these responses serve "as a kind of instructive mirror to horror movie audiences, and that mirroring effect is one of the defining features of the genre" (167). Basically, the audience is horrified of something because they watch film characters being horrified and follow their lead.[14]

Since the earliest horror films, the most basic reactions to an encounter with the monstrous are bodily expressions of terror and revulsion on the part of the 'normal' characters, as they recoil and retreat from the monstrous body, their facial expressions filled with unambiguous horror, accompanied by the screams of female characters in particular. The intensity of this reaction serves as a measure of monstrosity. In addition to such moments of pure terror, monstrosity is also established in dialogue and exposition about the monster in question. For example, *The Silence of the Lambs* (1991) features an exchange in which a police officer asks whether Hannibal Lecter is a vampire, and the protagonist Agent Starling responds, "They don't have a name for what he is." The question associates the character of Lecter with a traditional horror monster, and the response reveals the failure of categories. Since Lecter cannot be understood by psychology

---

14 An even more intense expression of that effect is what Hanich calls "somatic empathy," which leads viewers to feel pain as bodily experience "a more or less automatic, but no more than partial parallelism between a character's and my own body's sensations, affects or motions" (103).

or law, he has to count as a monstrous deviant. The same pattern applies to a plethora of horror films: the characters that stand in for normality ask what they are dealing with, in an attempt to resolve the inexplicable by applying familiar categories. When that classification fails, characters may resort to calling it a monster, or, as an expression of helplessness, a thing, which is undetermined, but certainly not human. The zombies in *Night of the Living Dead* (1968), for instance, are mostly referred to as "those things," and *The Thing* (1982) already carries the capitulation of comprehension in its title.

In summary, the monster's audiovisual presentation (on screen and soundtrack), its actions (in the narrative), and its reception (by other fictional characters) need to express two key traits of monstrosity: first, a confusion of categories, or rather a crisis of understanding, and second, a sense of threat, whether to one's safety or one's worldview. Put even shorter, these traits are "dangerousness and impurity" (Carroll 28). As this section has shown, a wide range of markers may be employed to communicate these monstrous traits. The significance of these markers is by no means limited to horror narratives, as they overlap with other discourses (cf. Cohen 7-11). Since its markers carry multiple meanings, a monster may pick up and continue any of these discourses, and reinforce or undermine its ideological foundations, depending on how the story plays out (cf. Wood). Either way, the monsters of horror and the marking of their difference continue the discourse of monstrosity that historically developed through myth, religion and scientific (or pseudoscientific) approaches. Even if these conceptions of monstrosity have fallen out of use in their original contexts, they continue to exist side by side in various subgenres of horror.

2. Remakes and Remaking

THE SAME AGAIN, BUT DIFFERENT: FILM REMAKES

The film remake has been a fixture of the Hollywood film industry, and indeed filmmaking in general, since its very beginnings. Starting in the early 20th century, filmmakers would imitate their successful competitors' films after copyright law prohibited them from simply duplicating their prints (Verevis, *Film* 98-99). The transition to sound film in the 1930s led to a surge in remake production as silent films were remade with sound. At the same time, film studios began re-using previously realized scripts to cover the increasing demand generated by rapidly growing audiences. As the remake practice required no further payment to screenwriters at the time, it offered clear financial advantages, along with reduced development times (cf. Druxman 15).

While production fluctuated in the following decades, reaching a low point in the 1970s before increasing again, the remake has remained a standard among Hollywood's production practices. The appeal for commercially oriented studios remains the same: reworking a proven script facilitates production, and an already well-known title boosts promotion, turning a remake of a previously successful film into a relatively safe bet. Between the demand for a steady output of product and the need to curb financial risks, the advantages of film remaking are clear, whether the remakes are based on decades-old films from the studio archives or on the remaking rights purchased for foreign films.[1]

---

1   A note on terminology: since the 2000s, it has become commonplace to refer to remakes that are intended to serve as the new starting point of a franchise as "reboots," meaning that they reset narrative continuity after a series of sequels, spinoffs, and adaptations, and allow the entire system of production to start anew (or perhaps more accurately, continue with renewed vigor in a slightly different direction). Among the films discussed in this study, *Halloween* (2007) certainly qualifies as a reboot.

These perks do little to endear remakes to film critics, however. Even though remakes are well established as a type of film, they are commonly met with a distinct lack of appreciation. Film critics generally do not hold the practice in high regard, instead criticizing it as a result of Hollywood's commercial rather than artistic interest and as evidence of a terminal lack of ideas (cf. Forrest and Koos 2; Verevis, *Film* 4; Kühle 11). Similarly, dedicated fans regard most remakes as an affront to film classics, even reducing the value of the original films by merit of their very existence.[2] Of course, there are exceptions, especially when well-regarded directors are involved, or a relatively unknown or flawed film is remade. Martin Scorcese, for instance, received positive reviews for his 1991 remake of *Cape Fear* (1962), and several Oscar awards for *The Departed* (2006), a remake of the Hong Kong drama *Infernal Affairs* (2002). Despite these exceptions, remakes are still widely seen as lesser fare or "comfort food" for a less demanding audience (D. White).

The above criticism is based on an aesthetic standard that values perceived innovation over familiarity, and views art and industry as dichotomies. Academic studies based on different approaches, however, have recently discovered remakes as subjects for study. Accordingly, the remake's conscious and obvious acts of repetition sheds light on various cultural processes, whether by revealing the workings of commercial film production or documenting social changes between iterations (cf. Verevis, *Film* 3; Forrest and Koos 4-5; Horton and McDougal 6). Divorced from concerns of artistic value, the remake thus becomes intriguing as "a meditation on the continuing historical relevance" of particular narratives, concerned with "unfinished cultural business, unrefinable and perhaps finally unassimilable material that remains part of the cultural dialogue" (Braudy 331).

Judging by the number of publications since the turn of the millennium, the academic study of remakes has swiftly gained popularity, yet still seems insufficient considering the overwhelming number of remakes produced every year. English language studies often refer back to Druxman's *Make It Again, Sam* as a starting point for the study of remakes. While Druxman laid some groundwork for the discussion of remakes, his survey is, admittedly, more intended for film buffs rather than scholars (10). Published in 1975, at a low point in remake production, it is also outdated in some regards, as it predates the massive resurgence of remakes since the 1980s.

---

2   As an example for an irate fan perspective, see D. White. Similar articles or blog entries are abundant.

Further research is spread out over individual articles, such as Leitch's rhetoric of the remake in "Twice-told Tales" (1990),[3] and picks up with Horton and McDougal's anthology *Play It Again Sam: Retakes on Remakes* (1998). Among several articles exploring the range of remakes, Braudy's conclusion in particular attempts to locate the remake and stretch its unstable boundaries. *Dead Ringers* (2002), edited by Forrest and Koos, follows in a similar vein, but focuses more on the transnational remake and on American remakes of French films in particular. The first monograph and most extensive treatment of the subject is Verevis's *Film Remakes* (2006), which tracks the film remake as a concept in commercial, textual, critical, and other discourses. Verevis also recently co-edited an anthology with Loock, which investigates individual examples of remaking among other reproductive forms of popular culture. Across these works, a number of taxonomies and categories have been suggested in an effort to grasp all varieties of remakes, from Druxman's initial three types, or Leitch's four to Eberwein's taxonomy of fifteen types (Druxman 15; Leitch 45-49; Eberwein 30).

In addition, individual studies regarding specific remakes or series of remakes appear at a regular pace in film or cultural studies journals, yet considering the proliferation of remakes, research is still falling short. While complete coverage of all remakes is neither necessary nor achievable, there remain significant variations and recent developments in film remaking that are not yet accounted for.

Apart from the lacking scope of research, the theoretical approaches employed in the study of remakes have been criticized as well. Verevis warns against a tendency to reduce remakes to a canon of works and exclusive taxonomies, as these "risk essentialism" (*Film* 2), and Schaudig similarly alleges that indices of remakes only serve to disguise theoretical shortcomings (277). As another example, Quaresima levels similar complaints, and laments the often shallow, descriptive studies of remakes, without being able to offer an effective alternative (78). Claims that film remakes are a unique characteristic of the Hollywood film industry (Leitch 37) have been contested (Verevis, *Film* 13). More accurately, remaking is a fixture in film industries around the world and throughout the medium's history. While the Hollywood practice of remaking is distinct in its scale and methods, other film capitals, from India's "Bollywood" to Hong Kong have their own remake traditions (cf. Forrest & Koos 28), even though these go beyond the scope of this study.

---

3 A revised version of Leitch's article appeared in the anthology *Dead Ringers*, which is the version used for this study.

DEFINING THE FILM REMAKE

Although, or rather because the term remake enjoys widespread use in popular, academic and industrial contexts, there are serious disagreements about its boundaries. The initial definition of "a newly produced version of a previously realized film" still leaves the question what exactly makes a film a new version of another. The narrowest definition requires a completely new production, consciously drawing on an earlier film, which is officially confirmed and legally sanctioned by the use of the same title (cf. Leitch 38). The producers need to have obtained the rights to the previous film and announce that fact in the credits.

However, this requirement excludes a number of films that are commonly considered to be remakes due to their significant similarities to other films, but fail to acknowledge any sources. Allegations of plagiarism, or "rip-off" in more colloquial terms, are not uncommon in film criticism and fandom.[4] At the same time, the narrow definition still includes Druxman's category of "non-remakes," which covers films of the same title whose content has no relation to the previous film whatsoever (Druxman 15). This indicates a key problem in the discussion of remakes: If titles are insufficient as a marker, how do we measure the amount of elements that have to be repeated for a film to count as a remake?

Druxman understands remakes simply as recycled scripts, which means that a script from the studio archives is altered and rewritten for a new production (13). Therefore, a remake should be the same story (sequence of events) packaged in a new narrative discourse (presentation of events). Yet, determining whether or not the same sequence of events is present is highly subjective and cannot work as an absolute measure (Verevis, *Film* 29), especially considering Hollywood's use of standardized genre stories (Forrest & Koos 17). The distinc-

---

4   As a prominent example, Sergio Leone's western *A Fistful of Dollars* (1964) was accused of plagiarizing Akira Kurosawa's *Yojimbo* (1961), leading to a lawsuit and settlement. Today, DVD versions of *Yojimbo* point out the relation to Leone's more famous film on the box for advertising purposes (cf. Verevis, *Film* 89). A systematic strategy of plagiarism can also be found in the type of film derisively known as "mockbusters," cheaply made imitations of high-profile blockbusters, produced without legal sanction and designed purely to profit from the publicity surrounding the release of the originals. These straight-to-video releases typically employ titles and cover designs intended to appeal to, or rather mislead, audiences familiar with the original blockbuster.

tion between a story that repeats genre conventions and one that repeats a specific film is by no means clear.

Furthermore, several studies use broader definitions of "remaking." For instance, a remake could precisely reproduce the style and mood of the previous film, making it recognizable as a derivation without notable parallels in terms of story (Verevis, *Film* 28). Horton and McDougal go further by suggesting an extension of the term remake to cover other intertextual forms. Their definition calls the remake a "special pattern which re-represents and explains at a different time and through varying perceptions, previous narratives and experiences" (2). Given the vagueness of "narratives and experiences," the number of potential remakes would multiply under this definition.

Others view adaptations simply as remakes that occur in a different medium, as Lukas does in his discussion of films based on videogames (222). Likewise, Perkins concludes that sequels, too, can be a type of remake (15). While neither of these claims is without merit, and both will be discussed further in the next section, they also stretch the meaning of the term remake. Summing up too many phenomena under the label remake runs the risk of it becoming an unnecessary synonym for larger processes and concepts. Maes's (purposefully vague) definition – "In order to be called a remake, a movie must in some relevant way be comparable to a previous movie" (7) – demonstrates this dilemma by turning "remake" into an expression of general intertextuality. Therefore, in order for the term to serve a useful purpose in analysis, we need to differentiate the film remake from wider processes of filmic or transmedia repetition and reproduction.

Some of the issues with the term remake derive from its origin. As Braudy explains, "'Remake' is a term imported to academia from movie journalism and the movie business" (327). Therefore, any attempts to theorize the remake redefine a term from the discourse of industrial film production, which has also gained new meanings in popular discourses. This does not make the term ineligible for academic uses, but it requires an awareness of how the understanding of text differs between these discourses. In the end, the exact limits of the remake are drawn on the basis of particular preconceptions, which in turn depend on context, whether academic, industrial, or any other. As Verevis points out, "the identification of exactly which elements shall count as fundamental units of narrative . . . becomes . . . a theoretical construct" (*Film* 29). Accordingly, the construction of intertextual relations is already an act of interpretation, "limited and relative" to one's "interpretive grid" (Frow, quoted in Verevis, *Film* 29).

The outer limits of the remake may be blurry, but there is no disagreement about the center: the conscious, official, legally sanctioned remake that reproduces a previous film without any intimations of narrative continuity between the two. Therefore, this type of film promises to be a solid starting point for the discussion of remakes.

REMAKES AND INTERTEXTUALITY: REWRITING, REMAKING, READING

The remake defines itself by stressing one intertextual relation over all others. Verevis points out this fact in his definition of remakes as "intertextual structures which are stabilized, or *limited*, through the naming and (usually) legally sanctioned (or copyrighted) use of a particular literary and/or cinematic source which serves as a retrospectively designated point of origin and semantic fixity" (*Film* 21). Given the crucial importance of this concept, a further investigation of textual relations in the remake needs to discuss intertextuality first.

The concept of intertextuality, in the sense first coined by Julia Kristeva in reference to Bakhtin, refers to the many links between texts, and how "any text is constructed as a mosaic of quotations" (Kristeva 37). This describes a general property of all texts, but the term intertextuality has since been used to describe a more limited phenomenon, that of obvious and declared connections between particular texts. As the remake deals with more specific, explicit links between just a few texts, such a narrow perspective turns out to be rather useful, and some remake scholars draw on more structuralist models of intertextuality such as Gerard Genette's (cf. Horton & McDougal 3; Verevis, *Film* 20).

Genette's model replaces Kristeva's term intertextuality with transtextuality (cf. Allen 101), which has roughly the same meaning. However, Genette also uses intertextuality more narrowly as a subtype of transtextuality, referring to the presence of one text within another, usually in the form of direct quotations. He adds four more types of transtextuality, which are explicitly not meant as exclusive categories, but as open and overlapping (cf. Genette 7). These include paratext, defined as text on the margins of and threshold to the main text, such as titles. There are also metatext, which includes critical commentary, and architext, which determines genre links (1-4).

Most interesting for the discussion of remakes is the concept of hypertext, defined as "any relationship uniting a text B (which I shall call the *hypertext*) to an earlier text A (I shall, of course, call it the *hypotext*), upon which it is grafted in the manner that is not that of commentary" (5). The hypertext is derived from its hypotext by means of a transformation (5). Genette further details hypertextual types like parody and pastiche, but also offers more serious transformations or transpositions, which include the transposition into a different style or translations. Since all literary works draw on other works in one way or another, Genette admits that all works can be seen as hypertexts. In order to keep the subject manageable, he limits himself to those texts whose derivation is both "massive" and officially declared (9). Hypertextuality is thus declared through a paratextual sign, which works as a contract (8).

Working from these assumptions, we can view a film remake as a hypertext, which is derived from its hypotext, the previous film, through a series of transpositions. The declaration of hypertextuality through a paratextual note occurs through the usage of the same title and a reference in the credits. Transpositions such as reduction, amplification and transmotivation can all be found in film remakes. While Genette focuses on literary texts in *Palimpsests*, his discussion of Woody Allen's *Play It Again, Sam* (1972) as an example of "cinematographic hypertextuality" (156) confirms the applicability of the term in the context of film remakes. His mention of "hyperfilmicity" is more of an aside, though, which is why I will retain the term hypertextuality for further use.

The relationship between texts in a sequence of remakes is further theorized by Thomas Leitch. Instead of focusing on the dynamic between two filmic texts, Leitch adds a third element: that of the literary text, from which the initial film is adapted (39). This results in a triangular model between a film remake and its two source texts.[5] Depending on the remake's relationship to its sources, and whether it uses the literary of filmic text as its primary source, Leitch identifies four "stances." A remake that primarily draws on its literary source thus counts as a "readaptation" (45), while one that prefers its filmic source counts as "homage" (47). Both these stances aim to honor their sources, while the next two, the "update" (46) of a literary text and the "true remake" (49) are revisionist in intent.

Through these stances regarding their sources, Leitch assigns intent to the remake itself. In the case of the true remake in particular, this stance is aggressive, as the remake competes with its predecessor and aims to replace it (38). Of course, a remake cannot erase the previous texts from history, but it wants to establish itself as the definite version of the story in the minds of audiences and critics. Leitch expands this concept with a dynamic of acknowledgement and disavowal:

But disavowal – that is, the combination of acknowledgement and repudiation in a single ambivalent gesture – is apt in far more specific ways to the remake's model of intertextuality, since remakes by definition establish their value by invoking earlier texts

---

5   Leitch's triangular model may work for a large segment of remakes, but it is less fitting for films made from original scripts or films that have been remade several times.

whose potency they simultaneously valorize and deny through a series of rhetorical maneuvers designed at once to reflect their intimacy with these earlier texts and to distance themselves from their flaws. (Leitch 53)

The intertextual relationship of the remake is, according to Leitch, based on an ambiguous intention of the text itself. Yet the remake's goal of replacing another text does not seem very promising. While the previous film can certainly fall into obscurity once a new version appears, a remake is just as likely to achieve the opposite, as the mere existence of a remake confirms the value and canonicity of its predecessor. Therefore, Verevis considers remake and original to be in a symbiotic rather than a parasitic relationship, as they appeal to different audiences and a remake may well refresh interest in its predecessor (*Film* 17).[6]

Finally, Leitch also assigns the remake a stance towards its audience. Remakes, he claims, are not directed at viewers familiar with the previous version, but at an entirely new audience with only a marginal awareness of the original. For the more experienced viewer, only small details and in-jokes are offered as acknowledgement (42). But while Leitch assumes a heterogeneous audience, he also assigns it a single shared interest: "The audience for remakes . . . want the same story again, though not exactly the same" (44). This seems like a contradiction with his previous statement, which can be partly salvaged with his notion that the remake calls upon the "aura" of its predecessor instead of its memory. Awareness of an aura does not require the audience to actually have seen the film in question, especially in the case of more famous pop-cultural phenomena. Instead, the barest sense of familiarity should be enough to lure audiences into movie theaters, where they are then supposed to accept the remake as a standalone text, again uniting acknowledgement and disavowal.

Taking Leitch's argument one step further, the remake not only challenges the original, it challenges the concept of originality (cf. Horton and MacDougal 4). A remake is derived from an original, yet that original is never pure, as it also drew inspiration from other works, itself the mosaic of quotations Kristeva described (Kristeva 37; cf. Verevis, *Film* 27). In general, remakes stress a recurring story over individual narrative discourse, calling into question the very idea of an individual work (Quaresima 75). Even if the remake fails to replace its predecessor, its very existence undermines the uniqueness of the original by demonstrating how a story can be torn from its narrative discourse, thus proving that any work is replaceable. Yet, original and copy are "mutually constitutive concepts" (Grindstaff 275), as only the appearance of a copy can elevate a work to the sta-

---

6 A similar question arises for the literary adaptation, which may replace the book in the public imagination, or reinforce its status in the appropriate canon.

tus of *the* original. The paradoxical relationship of confirmation and challenge described by Grindstaff (277) closely matches the dynamic previously suggested by Leitch.

The question of originality ties into that of genre. Film remakes are mostly a genre phenomenon, and this study argues for the particular significance of horror remakes. By definition, all genre works repeat generic codes, and so do remakes of genre works. Yet, remakes possess a narrower focus, taking their cues more closely from one particular genre work. Verevis suggests that remakes constantly remake the intertext of the genre (*Film* 25). For Leitch, the remake is just an example of a genre work that wants its audience to expect genre conventions, but does not admit that it borrowed them from somewhere else (58). Braudy sees the link as grounds for reclassification and proposes that the remake might be "distinguished from adaptation and then treated as a subcategory of genre" (331). Indeed, it appears that we are dealing with the same process of cultural repetition on different levels of specificity here. The remake repeats one film, and the film genre repeats a set of conventions, in turn derived from multiple works.

So far, most approaches have tried to locate the remake in the text itself, and in the direct intertextual relations between original and remake. The remaining gaps may be filled by also considering the margins of the texts and extratextual factors, including reception by the moviegoing audience. Drawing on Altman's work on film genre, Verevis argues that film remakes are not only located in a corpus of works, but like genres, depend on audience activity. Like genres, he suggests, remakes "are located too in 'expectations and audience knowledge' and in 'the institutions that govern and support specific reading strategies'" (*Film* 23). Reading the opening credits may be sufficient to inform the audience that they are not watching the first version of a film, but in order to read that film as a remake, to recognize and make sense of intertextual connections, the audience needs a basic knowledge of texts and genre.[7]

In a wider sense, of course, audiences always read intertextually, actively making sense of any works based on their collected cultural experience. When it comes to specific genres and texts, however, particular strategies are required to read remakes, and the viewer constructs the remake by drawing on these strategies. The remake literacy of audiences has been steadily rising due to technological developments, from television and videotapes to DVD and internet streaming, which have created a higher familiarity with individual films and generic

---

7 It should come as no surprise that the arguments regarding the boundaries of the remake echo those on the definitions of the horror genre in the previous chapter. Even though remakes are emphatically not a film genre, the same questions of definitional authority between producers, consumers and critics apply here as well.

codes, thus enabling a more intertextual reading (Verevis, *Film* 17). In addition, these media technologies allow viewing remakes and their predecessors out of sequence (Verevis, *Film* 18). This upends the sequence of hypotext and hypertext, as the viewer may start at any point in a sequence of films, sequels and remakes and work their way back or forth, towards the original or away from it. Ultimately, production sequence may be replaced by viewing sequence, as the viewer repositions the various iterations.

The audience's production of meaning is directed and supported by factors that Verevis considers "extratextual" (*Film* 28). These include advertisements, film reviews and a wealth of other materials that are not part of the filmic text itself. In this context, Genette's model of transtextuality allows for a slightly more differentiated picture. Verevis's extratextual factors mostly fall under Genette's paratext and its subcategories, which includes elements on the threshold to and beyond the text. Among these are the epitext, which contains all materials outside the text (reviews, ads, interviews, online discussion boards etc.), and the peritext, which is on the threshold of the textual body (titles, credits etc.) (cf. Allen 101). The paratext creates an interpretive frame and determines the remake's intertextuality (Verevis, *Film* 130). It not only directs the reading towards a particular intertextual relation (towards the original), but, in the case of critical epitexts, also delivers hints on how to evaluate the remake, whether as worthless plagiarism or loving homage (Verevis, *Film* 176). This approach removes Leitch's stance of the text from the picture and instead puts focus on the paratextually directed reception, which structures intertextual reading.

Ultimately, though, even inter- or transtextual models may be insufficient to fully appreciate the scope of the film remake. Verevis, then, locates the remake at the intersection of a whole series of discourses:

Beyond textual approaches to film remaking . . . inquiries into the nature of remaking would locate it . . . not only in industrial fields and textual strategies, but in cinematic and general discursive fields, in such historically specific technologies as copyright law and authorship, canon formation and media literacy, film criticism and film reviewing. (Verevis, *Film* 29)

This approach yields the most thorough survey of the mechanics behind the remake, at the cost of spreading them out across so many levels of culture that they become hard to grasp.

MARGINS OF REMAKING: SEQUELS, ADAPTATIONS AND BEYOND

The previous sections already pointed out some of the difficulties in determining the boundaries of the remake. While a stable definition of the film remake is crucial for this study, it is also evident that beyond the grey areas already discussed, there are forms that serve similar functions of reproduction, but are typically distinguished from remakes.

The most obvious form of derivative film, the sequel, is a continuation of a previous film and enjoys a similarly bad reputation as the remake. While continuation and expansion seem different from starting all over in the remake, Perkins points out that the distinction is blurry, as "the process of continuation that the sequel undertakes is *also* a process of repetition" (15). The sequel, too, aims at repeating the experience of its predecessor(s), and narrative elements are simply repeated in a different form as they are continued. Perkins therefore suggests sequel types based on Druxman's remake taxonomy, such as the "nonsequel," as the "discourse of sequelization" lacks the terms to account for differences (15). With an open definition of the remake, she argues, one may "declare all filmmaking remaking, insofar as all filmmaking is (necessarily) intertextual" (16). Using such a definition, "there is no workable differentiation between a remake and a sequel," as the sequel "can be understood as a form of remaking" (16). However, even with a narrow understanding of remaking, the categories of remake and sequel can easily overlap, and a small hint towards continuity would be enough to turn the alternative narrative discourse of a remake into a sequel.

The relationship between original and sequel is also briefly covered by Leitch, who views the two in a more harmonious relationship than the parasitic competition he posits for the remake. Unlike the remake, a sequel can freely reference the original text, as the audience is deemed familiar with it, and it also serves as an advertisement for its predecessor (41). Thus, according to Leitch, the sequel is not vying for the same spot in the audience's mind, but gladly supports its predecessor. His argument is not quite conclusive, though. A sequel doing the same thing bigger and louder would seem to be in competition with the original, aiming to deliver an improved version of the same story in the same manner as the remake does.[8]

---

8   Most of these considerations apply to another type of derivative film, the prequel, which seeks to expand the narrative not by continuing it forward, but by adding previous events. The functions of prequel and sequel are mostly identical, as both types of film aim to deliver more of the same, albeit in a different chronological order.

Next to the sequel, Braudy considers the adaptation as the "close kin" of the remake (327), and Schaudig even terms the remake a type of adaptation (280). As the earlier discussion of Leitch has shown, there may be a significant overlap between remake and adaptation, depending on their priorities in source texts (cf. Leitch 45). If a new film draws on both the literary source and the previous film adaptation, it works as both adaptation and remake. If it exclusively draws on the literary source, it may not technically qualify as a remake, but as Verevis points out, even if the goal is a re-adaptation, the newest film in a chain of adaptations may be viewed as a remake (*Film* 82).

Despite these overlaps, the fact that adaptation involves a change in medium, whereas the remake remains within the same medium, serves as a hard distinction. Yet when it comes to sources from visual media such as comic books or computer games, Verevis argues, this distinction falls apart due to similar semiotic registers (*Film* 82). Lukas picks up on this argument to assert that "the move of video games to film and films to video game increasingly reflect [sic] remaking rather than adaptation," since the line between films and games is blurred (222).

Regardless of how this question of medium is resolved, the adaptation discourse proves relevant when it comes to "issues of fidelity and freedom" (Verevis, *Film* 82). The adaptation and the remake, along with the translation, are less interested in fidelity to their originals, but in the "potential of the original to generate further . . . cultural production" (84). Thus, in the context of larger, transmedia processes of reproduction, the distinction between adaptation and remake becomes less significant, as both repeat and reconfigure previous concepts and narratives.

Finally, as a less obvious example, alternate cuts of a film may in some cases border on remaking, depending on the severity of the changes and the insertion of newly shot scenes. The now common "director's cut," a home video release that deviates from a film's theatrical cut, does not qualify, as its additions were shot during the original production (cf. Arend 59). Even if the material were to be radically recombined at a much later point in time, it would still be more accurate to speak of a revision rather than a remake, even though the intent – to make a new version of the same story, in order to improve and replace the previously released one – may be similar.

The most compelling case for revisions as remakes would be significant additions of newly shot material. For instance, George Lucas drew fan criticism for repeatedly altering his first trilogy of *Star Wars* films (1977-1983), adding digital effects, entirely new scenes, and inserting characters to better tie together his film series. Likewise, in 2004, Lucas added digital effects to his debut film *THX*

1138 (1971), altering plot points and the film's overall mood and pacing. The reason usually given in press releases for these kinds of revision is that new technologies finally allow a director to realize their original vision. Perhaps more accurately, the director in question revises their work according to their current vision.

Adapting previous work to current sensibilities, those of the director in this case, is of course a key goal of the remake. However, the remake abandons the filmed material of the original completely, instead creating every bit of dialogue and image anew. The revision, except perhaps the most radical examples, is still bound by the original material; it changes the previous version of the film, but does not reenact it in the manner of the remake. Admittedly, alternate cuts subvert the idea of a fixed original and impose a reevaluation on the films in question. The basic distinction between revision and remaking remains, however, even though the former may include trace elements of the latter.

In conclusion, sequels and adaptations show clear parallels to the remake, in that they revisit, repeat and refigure a previous text. Like the film remake, they make their intertextual lineage explicit, but they rarely aim to displace their sources in the respective canon or public perception. Borderline cases aside, sequels and adaptations are more comfortable existing next to the texts they are derived from. Arguably, the contradictory stance of the remake (as per Leitch) complicates its production process and therefore makes for a more intriguing object of research. At the same time, all three of these reproductive forms likely serve similar cultural functions, by extending and renewing the reach of their texts through constant adaptation and repetition. This opens up perspectives for expanded research, and tracing the development of discourses through adaptations, sequels, and remakes may contribute to a better understanding of transmedia genres, their formation and transformations.

PARTICIPATORY CULTURE: AUDIENCE AND FANS

In this study, I view the chain of horror films and their remakes as instances in a continuously developing discourse, and suggest that the process of repetition and refiguration serves a cultural function. Yet these filmic iterations are embedded in a larger cultural frame, and in the years between the film releases, the relevant discourses keep shifting, taking on new meanings and forms as the filmic texts are reread and reworked by their audience. Each text emerges from a network of sources and relations, and again gives rise to a multitude of new texts as it takes its place in the intertextual web. The audience not only draws on this web of relations, it actively contributes to it by producing meaning, new texts fashioned from the material of previous ones. Therefore, the viewers of a horror remake are not passive recipients and consumers, but active participants in the reproductive process.

Since horror film as a genre is firmly located in popular culture, theorizations of popular culture shed light on the common underlying processes. John Fiske sees popular culture as a social process of making meaning and social identities, made by "subordinated peoples" from the resources available to them and always in process (*Reading* 1-3). The people, argues Fiske, choose from the offerings of the culture industries those texts they deem functional and relevant to their experience (*Understanding* 129-30).[9] Popular texts are not simply manufactured or imposed by an industry; they are elevated to that status by the choice of audiences who are, at the same time, consumers. To this end, a popular text needs to be "producerly," a term Fiske coins in reference to Barthes's categories of "readerly" and "writerly," to describe texts that are easily accessible, yet open to further production (*Understanding* 103-04). This requires gaps and contradictions in the text, to be filled by the audience. Drawing on Bourdieu, Fiske concludes that the resulting aesthetic and reading strategies are opposed to those of the bourgeoisie, which value a completed text and distance by the reader. In addition, Henry Jenkins identifies a popular aesthetic marked by novelty and an "affective intensity," meaning an intense emotional impact (*Wow Climax* 46). In the case of horror, this emotional impact is already in the name, as the previous chapter has demonstrated. Horror, to reiterate, is constructed specifically to provide the affect of fear (cf. Carroll 14).

Even though popular texts offer producerly qualities, their exploitation is not a requirement for consumption, and not all members of the audience draw on these resources to the same extent. For Jenkins, the fan experience is clearly different from the "bulk of the audience" (*Poachers* 287), whereas Fiske sees a difference only in degree, not in kind (*Understanding* 147). For Fiske, fans are "excessive readers," characterized by an "active, enthusiastic, partisan participatory engagement with the text" and whose main activities are "discrimination" (choosing texts and clearly delineating the object of their fandom) as well as "productivity" (146-47). The latter includes "fan gossip," which takes place both before and after readings or viewings and "reinterprets, re-presents, reproduces" texts (147), along with the creation of more elaborate pieces of prose fiction or

---

9   At first glance, the latter requirement would appear incongruous with the horror genre. After all, one should hope that the audience finds few parallels between the scenarios of horror and their everyday lives, but Crane argues the contrary, that horror films do indeed respond to the terrors of everyday life (39).

videos. To the fan, the original text is a cultural resource, from which numerous new texts are made (148).[10] The fan's producerly activity, then, "parallels that required to produce the original text," requiring cultural and social competence (148). In short, fans are themselves producers, constantly remaking and recombining texts.

Building on Fiske's theory and applying it to the horror film, I suggest at least two levels at which the audience in general and fans in particular may play a significant role in the production and reproduction of horror films, namely as consumers and as producers. First, the audience's consumption habits, from going to the movies to purchasing films on physical media or as digital content, directly influence the production of horror films. Almost without exception, horror film productions are deeply commercial ventures, and if the audience's appreciation results in financial success, more films in the same vein will be produced. A particular type of monster or horror subgenre may thereby rise in prominence, resulting in waves or clusters of films like the slasher films of the 1980s or the resurgence of zombie films in the 2000s, only to fall into obscurity as soon as audience interest drops. Since even relatively low budget horror films require significant financial investment, the development of a monster discourse in the medium of film may be facilitated or hindered by basic economic factors, as evidenced, for example, by George A. Romero's constant struggles to finance his films (cf. Gagne 21-23; 84-85).

Second, fans produce and discuss meaning in the form of new readings of horror films comparable to Fiske's category of fan gossip. This takes a wide range of forms, from a chat in person or an online discussion to elaborate amateur criticism and publications in non-commercial magazines, so-called fanzines. For decades, fanzines served as a mainstay of fan culture, offering an "alternative brand of film criticism" and functioning as critic, archivist or outlet for nihilistic urges (Sanjek 316). More recently, the internet has offered fans and amateur critics a much more open, easier means for communication and publication. Arguably, blogs and discussion groups have not only largely taken over the purpose of fanzines, but in fact expanded on it. Infrequent publication schedules and the difficulty of printing and obtaining a fan publication are negated by the internet, which allows a wider participation and the formation of larger, more effective interpretive communities. Blogs and news sites such as *Bloody Disgusting*

---

10 It is worth pointing out the distinction between Fiske's wide open concept of "text" influenced by cultural studies (all aspects of culture can be read as text), and the similar, yet more narrow sense in which Jenkins employs it. While Jenkins follows in Fiske's vein, text to him is more likely to mean "media text," i.e. fiction, television, film.

serve as information networks and link fan communities, as do a wealth of other fan websites dedicated to horror media. Due to the overlap of fan cultures, general media fan websites further add to the number of venues for discussion. The readings and responses generated in these communities may directly or indirectly feed back into commercial genre productions, including the production of remakes.

Since Fiske coined the term, the significance of fan gossip has not only increased manifold due to the spread of the internet and increased networking of fans, but it has also turned into a powerful commercial factor. Now, fan gossip is no longer private, but public, instantly accessible from around the globe. Amateur critics and the diffuse generation of "buzz" (rumors and speculation predating the release of a film) may influence the success of a film through word-of-mouth or cause alterations to a work in production. Information leaks from the production, be it gossip, complete scripts, or video material, spread quickly online and may help or hurt a film. One of the most publicized examples of this type of influence in the genre is 2006's *Snakes on a Plane*, which found a sizeable fan following based on its title and deliberately absurd premise alone. As internet users created parodies, fake advertisements and catchphrases, the studio staged reshoots to make the film conform to assumed audience expectations. These included the addition of graphic violence and lines of dialogue, resulting in a raised age rating and consequently a shift in target demographic. Ultimately, though, the producers' responsiveness to fan input did not pay off, as the completed film only drew moderate numbers of viewers (Waxman; *Snakes on a Blog*). This example suggests that internet buzz is as influential as it is unpredictable, and unsurprisingly, film studios frequently attempt to shape pre-release discussion through the controlled release of information, including purported leaks.

Finally, as a more elaborate form of production, fans may appropriate materials to create their own texts, reassembling and expanding on narrative elements from the subjects of their fandom. One of the most prevalent forms is prose fiction, known as fan fiction, which may range from short stories to multi-volume series of novels that supplement, continue, or reconfigure the narratives contained in their respective source texts. More relevant to the context of remakes, fan works also include videos, ranging from recut and recombined trailers and films to newly scripted and shot films cast with amateur actors. Both types of texts, along with many others put out by dedicated fans, find wide distribution on specialized internet platforms, general video streaming websites, and at fan conventions.

Evidently, the category of fan productivity covers a range of disparate phenomena. While fan gossip negotiates readings of the primary text in the sense of Genette's metatext, fan fiction or -films typically amount to hypertexts, in close intertextual relation to their hypotexts, but frequently self-contained narratives. The underlying attitude is quite different, as the latter type of fan text exhibits less of a respectful distance towards its subject, and instead nonchalantly appropriates or, for some, violates its source text. Significantly, fan gossip is not considered an infringement of intellectual property, unlike fan fiction in many cases (cf. Jenkins, *Convergence* 154).

Jenkins views this form of fan production in the context of a "convergence culture," in which the distinctions between various media as well as producers and consumers begin to fade, leaving only participants of different status (*Convergence* 132). This "grassroots culture" is enacting "the right of everyday people to actively contribute to their culture" (132). Jenkins further argues that where nineteenth century American folk culture built on borrowings from mother countries, "new convergence culture will be built from borrowings from various media conglomerates" (137). Regardless of its greater cultural significance, fan work is wide spread, and prolific amateur writers often exceed the output of their professional counterparts. Again, this is not a new phenomenon, but the internet allows for easy publication on any number of online platforms and archives. While horror does not draw as much fan activity as some other genres or particular media franchises, the largest internet archive for fan fiction, *fanfiction.net*, still offers a wealth of texts inspired by popular horror films. For example, a casual search for the films covered in this study yields 52 stories based on *The Thing*, 179 on *The Texas Chainsaw Massacre*, 604 on *Dawn of the Dead*, and 633 on *Halloween* as of this writing (*fanfiction.net*).

Furthermore, much to the concern of intellectual property holders, the internet has turned fan fiction into public texts in direct competition with their source texts. As Jenkins remarks on amateur films, they are no longer "home movies," but "public movies," intended for larger audiences, and "public in their dialogue with commercial cinema" (143). This suggests a significant elevation in status and recognition, and raises the question to what extent fan films may influence the development of commercial Hollywood films, including remakes.

Now, fan films have a similar relation to their source texts, and if they were to achieve the same significance as Hollywood studio products (reaching similar-sized audiences, responding to as well as shaping cultural attitudes), it stands to reason that they should be considered as relevant parts of the reproductive process outlined above. At the time of this writing, however, only very few examples of fan works travel beyond a limited audience and stand a chance to feed ideas back into the general genre discourse.

Furthermore, judging from my admittedly limited research, the number of fan films that aim for a full-fledged remake (earlier defined as a newly produced version of a previously realized film) appears to be negligible. It may be that the remake's goal of replacing the previous film runs counter to reverent fan attitudes, and even though fan works are frequently characterized by a nonchalant appropriation, they typically aim at expansion instead of substitution. And while parody is a complex form, fan-produced parodies likewise tend to function as a supplement and commentary on the source text, not as an attempted substitute. In addition, the amount of resources and organization required for the production of a full-length motion picture has to be daunting for all but the most dedicated and well-connected fan filmmakers. Despite the exuberant productivity of fan cultures, they have yet to claim the film remake, at least in the narrow sense used in this study.

In the discussion of the blurred lines between remakes, sequels, and other re-productive genre works, I decided to focus on the conscious, declared, legally sanctioned film remake. Almost by definition, fan films cannot fulfill the last criterion, as they are usually made without permission or approval by the owners of the respective intellectual properties. They can still fulfill the first two criteria, even though attempts to fully remake previous films may be exceedingly rare. A looser definition of remake, however, would find far more relevant material among fan productions. Clearly, fan works absorb and reproduce the material offered by films, including horror films, and contribute to the broader genre discourse despite their lack of authorization from the cultural industry. A study of larger, transmedia processes of cultural reproduction would arguably have to account for the manifold adaptations taking place outside of traditional and commercial venues. Even though these texts offer intriguing new perspectives for academic analysis, they are beyond the focus of this study.

Part II: Horror Remake Complexes

3. Alien Invaders and Shifting Bodies

The three versions of *The Thing* share a fear of invasion, with radically shifting vectors: in the 1950s, the alien monster comes from the skies and smashes its way into living spaces, but in the 1980s and 2010s, the monstrous Thing takes to invading the human body itself. The monster is restructured quite radically in the remake, and the balance of institutions representing normality changes as well. Under the Thing's attack, rifts between scientific and military authorities as well as experts and average people break open, and group dysfunctions quickly cost lives. Moreover, these three films already pose a challenge for the categories established in chapter 2, as their intertextual entanglements blur the boundaries of remake, (re)adaptation, and prequel.

THE THING FROM ANOTHER WORLD (1951)

The Thing from Another World is an early entry in the list of 1950s invasion narratives that combine horror and science fiction, frequently labeled "monster movies" (cf. Jancovich, *Rational* 11). Even though Christian Nyby is listed as the director, the film is frequently attributed to producer Howard Hawks, as the latter's style is noticeable in the pace of the film and the character dynamics, in particular their code of professionalism. For example, Morrison calls it Hawks's film, attributes all choices in the adaptation to him, and even speaks of "the craftsmanship of Hawks's direction" (184), ignoring Nyby's role in the production.

Since this study aims for a reassessment of film remakes, not literary adaptations, I have mostly focused on original scripts. *The Thing from Another World*, however, marks an exception, and it may be useful to take a brief look at its literary source, the 1938 pulp novella *Who Goes There?* by John W. Campbell, if only to place the changes of *The Thing* (1982) into context in the next section.

The Thing from Another World drags the novella into the present day, that is, the 1950s and the Cold War, and shifts the setting from Antarctica to the Arctic, now a more strategically relevant location due to its position between the USA and the Soviet Union. The shape-shifting monster of the novella becomes more straightforward, an "external evil, clearly demarcated outside the self" (Morrison 184), and its landing is no longer buried in the distant past – instead, it implies a clear and present danger. Furthermore, Morrison identifies the addition of two subtexts, political and sexual (184), which will be discussed in more detail.

The Thing from Another World follows a US Air Force rescue team, which is sent to the Arctic in order to investigate a possible plane crash near an American base. The mission is led by the protagonist Captain Hendry, who is joined by fellow Airmen and journalist Scotty. After a stop at the base, which allows Hendry to reconnect with his old flame Nikki, they fly out to the crash site with the lead scientist Dr. Carrington. The crashed plane turns out to be an alien flying saucer, which is destroyed during attempted salvage, but the team still manages to retrieve the saucer's passenger and return him to the base. The alien "Thing" is inanimate, frozen in ice, but soon returns to life as it thaws due to a guard's sloppiness. When it escapes and attacks human and animal inhabitants of the base, military and scientists disagree about the course of action to be taken. While Captain Hendry wants to stop the Thing, Dr. Carrington secretly conspires to protect and study it. Over several attempts to track and find the Thing, Hendry and Carrington clash repeatedly, until Carrington is knocked out by the Thing in a vain attempt to communicate. With a joint effort from the remaining scientists and military personnel, the Thing is lured into an electric grid and incinerated, and only then does Hendry give Scott permission to report the events to a wider public.

The beginnings of the Cold War are tangible throughout the film and imbue the Air Force mission with urgency. The Russians are mentioned as being "all over the Pole like flies," which at least suggests that their activities are unwanted and viewed as possible competition. Inseparable from the Cold War, the dawning Nuclear Age is also felt. Dr. Carrington is introduced as "the same one who was at Bikini." This reference invokes nuclear testing at the Bikini Atoll, which had served as a test site since 1946, and suggests that Carrington is among the leading scientists in the United States' nuclear weapons program. Carrington's purpose in the Arctic is not explained, however, and his exact area of expertise remains nebulous. Carrington is not the only connection to the Nuclear Age, as both the flying saucer and the monstrous Thing itself emit radiation. In fact, the base personnel are able to track the Thing using a Geiger counter. Between the Thing and Carrington, nuclear science and radiation are at least vaguely menacing, being only associated with the antagonists. Criticism of nuclear science also creeps into an exchange between Carrington and the military crew, when Carrington praises scientific discoveries with "We split the atom!" and earns the comeback "Yes, and that sure made the world happy, didn't it?" The airman's sarcasm points to the nuclear anxieties that were just beginning to grow when the film was released (the Soviet Union had gained nuclear weapons just two years prior, in 1949).

The casting of an untrustworthy nuclear scientist as an antagonist also echoes events shortly before the film's release in 1951.[1] High-profile cases of espionage laid the foundation for the McCarthy era and its fears of communist subversion, and the sale of nuclear secrets to the Soviet Union featured most prominently. In March of 1950, Klaus Fuchs, a member of the Manhattan project that developed the nuclear bomb, was convicted of providing crucial knowledge to the Soviets, and in August of the same year, Julius and Ethel Rosenberg were indicted under similar charges of espionage and treason. The character of Carrington reflects this moment of rising suspicion. He has no loyalties to a nation, and his insistence that "there are no enemies in science" makes him a liability in a conflict that is framed as war. The fact that scientists like Carrington are highly sought after only compounds his untrustworthiness, and Scotty is well aware of Carrington's value as a commodity: "If you were for sale, I could get a million bucks for you from any foreign government."

While these elements serve to date *The Thing from Another World,* the prime angle for analysis needs to be the group dynamics that develop over the course of the film. The Thing is certainly alien and menacing, but far from an unstoppable force. The challenge to the cast of characters is mostly the unification of their efforts, which is complicated by conflicting interests. Hendry wants to destroy the Thing, Carrington wants to study and communicate with it, the distant military command issues belated orders to the same effect, and Scotty wants to publicize events. The last issue may be counted as a sideshow, considering that Carrington's efforts actively endanger the lives of all human characters. Thus, the apparent divide between military and science stands out as the key conflict in the film, and its interpretation is crucial for any readings. It is worth pointing out that this conflict is not present in the literary source (Morrison 184). Not only is a group of military characters added, it takes over the protagonist role from the scientists. This may be read as a reassessment of importance or trustworthiness in the more war-like scenario of the film adaptation, which is after all informed

---

1   The internet movie database *IMDb* lists filming as October 1950-March 1951, and the premiere in April 1951 ("The Thing from Another World (1951)"), which puts it in the same timeframe as the trials of Fuchs and the Rosenbergs.

by World War 2 and the ongoing Korean War. In this context, the film can be easily interpreted as an allegory for US society at war. Even though the base is in a remote location, it is still a site of American normality, and as one of the Airmen remarks, it even "looks like Kentucky."

Science and Military, Authorities and Experts

According to Jancovich, the prevailing critical opinion views *The Thing from Another World* as an "authoritarian text" (*Rational* 31). As an example, he quotes Kawin, who bases his assessment on the familiar argument that horror as a genre defends the status quo, since it presents the unknown as threatening, whereas science fiction offers the possibility of liberation (31-32). The encounter with the Thing plays out in the horror mode, in that the Thing is an aggressive intruder that cannot be reasoned with. Therefore, in the conflict between violence and intelligence, the military, as personified by Hendry and his subordinates, is unquestionably right (32). Biskind is quoted with a similar conclusion: since all threats to the status quo are destroyed with violence, *The Thing from Another World* is a fundamentally conservative film that calls for a strengthening of the American state (32). In the same vein, Cumbow summarizes the conflict as "real-world conservative men of action . . . against ivory-tower liberal men of intellect" (Cumbow 112).

These readings are mostly developed from contrasting Carrington and Hendry as personifications of their respective institutions and related schools of thought. The film portrays Carrington in a tradition of mad scientist characters, obsessed with his research and unburdened with ethics or common sense. His appearance already marks him as different from the rest of the crew, as he wears a suit with an ascot inside the base, and a Russian-style fur hat outside (cf. Biskind 127, Warren 52-53). His sophisticated speech underlines the impression, with platitudes about the importance of science regularly reminding everyone (including the audience) of his calling. That dedication to what the film presents as pure scientific principles makes Carrington an active hindrance in any attempts to resolve the threat. First, his insistence that "there are no enemies in science, only phenomena to be studied" slows the response to the threat. More drastically, his conviction that "knowledge is more important than life" leads him to risk and sacrifice the lives of others. Despite Carrington's claims to pure reason, his conclusions are less than sound - that the Thing is "wiser" than humans is pure conjecture, and his expectation that the Thing would understand his pleas in English is absurd. Indeed, his admiration of the Thing and its supposedly superior biology, "its evolution not restrained by sexual or moral limits," renders him monstrous as well, as he holds up the blood-sucking alien monster as an ideal.

Captain Hendry, by contrast, is a rugged hero, good in a fight, clear-headed under pressure, and concerned about everyone's lives, while still finding the time to pursue his romance with Nikki. He sets himself up as an authority, ordering Scotty to keep events secret, and forbidding Carrington to pursue his research. Hendry also follows orders from his superiors, but only until those prove impractical and dangerous. Consequently, he values his own judgment over the structure he is part of, that is, the Air Force chain of command. As an emotional, practical and sexual character, Hendry is constructed as Carrington's polar opposite. Put this way, a clash between the two may seem inevitable, but it is questionable whether this personal conflict can be generalized to be read as the film's statement regarding the spheres of military and science.

First, Carrington and Hendry are the lead characters, but by no means the only representatives of their professions. The rest of the scientific staff at first goes along with Carrington's plans, but later aligns with Hendry to construct the trap that destroys the Thing. At the same time, Hendry's superior General Fogarty issues increasingly problematic orders that match Carrington in intent. Ultimately, the practical application of science is crucial to defeating the alien threat, whereas higher military leadership is counterproductive. In fact, the problem is not just the Air Force leadership, as the film frequently has Scotty point out the systemic flaws of the military as a whole. For example, when a message from Fogarty's headquarters suggests the use of Thermite, a procedure that has already proven disastrous at that point, Scotty sarcastically exclaims, "That's what I like about the Army: smart all the way to the top." Therefore, science as such is not the villain of this piece, and Morrison concludes that the film is not "antiscience," but "antidogma" (Morrison 184), promoting flexibility over stubborn adherence to any principle. Morrison here rephrases a slightly broader point by Warren, who defends the film against charges of anti-intellectualism (Warren 53).

Jancovich goes further in his reassessment of the film and shifts the axis of the ideological conflict. Carrington, he points out, is the one invested with the state's authority, not the soldiers. He is "clearly presented as one of the experts of the new Fordist order"[2] (*Rational* 34), whereas the "military heroes" are "far from experts" (35). Therefore, the conflict is not between science and military, but more accurately "between ordinary working people and the authority of ex-

---

2   For Jancovich, "Fordism" stands for the emergent economic, political and social order of the United States in the 1950s, "a system of centrally ordered administration which relied on an elite of experts," with a special emphasis on "scientific-technical rationality" (19).

perts" (35). It might be added that Hendry is certainly a leadership figure and an expert on flying planes, but clearly out of his depth during most of the film, and his rank of Captain still places him in the field, in contrast to Fogarty's staff. The military as a whole, then, is not depicted as positive, only the "soldiers on the ground"[3] are, as all orders from above are too late, or misguided (35), still asking for the Thing to be preserved when the situation has escalated to a life-or-death struggle. The same goes for standard operating procedures, themselves an expression of the structure (the Air Force) determining the actions of the individuals it contains (Hendry and his team). Standard procedures call for the use of Thermite to recover the alien craft from beneath the ice, which promptly results in its destruction. While the experts devising such procedures do not feature in the film, Carrington is very much in the foreground, constantly trying to enforce the authority of experts. Carrington in turn sees the alien Thing as the "'ideal' of the system of scientific-technical rationality" (36), unfeeling, dehumanized, with no impediments to efficiency (36). From this point of view, human sexuality is the root cause of irrationality, whereas the asexual reproduction of the Thing results in smoothly functioning duplicates, well-suited to a "centrally-ordered" Fordist system with strict social roles (36), instead of troublesome individuals. Interaction would then be removed in favor of functioning as interchangeable components.

This central "struggle between interaction and domination" (Jancovich, *Rational* 36) is noticeable in information and communication strategies throughout the film. Carrington withholds and manipulates information to his own ends, and frequently speaks in monologues. By contrast, Hendry, his crew and Nikki speak "in overlapping dialogue," developing ideas "out of communal interaction" (37). Even though Hendry acts as the group's leader, he does not dictate the course of action, but involves his subordinates, Scotty, Nikki, and the scientists. As an example, the plan to destroy the Thing grows as follows: Scotty asks what to do with a vegetable, Nikki suggests cooking it, Hendry picks up on the idea and passes it on to the scientists, who proceed to build an electric grid to incinerate the Thing. Carrington's lone interference only succeeds in getting himself injured.

Communication without hierarchical constraints, then, leads to success. The final communication of the story, though, is suppressed for the longest time. When finally given permission, Scotty puts the final spin on the story in a rous-

---

3   The film's endorsement of practically-minded men still has its limits; after all, it is the negligence of a soldier who cannot tell an electric heating blanket from a regular one that releases the Thing in the first place - Carrington's deviousness has nothing to do with the initial outbreak of the threat.

ing broadcast: "One of the world's greatest battles was fought and won today by the human race. Here at the top of the world a handful of American soldiers and civilians met the first invasion from another planet." In case the scenario was not clear enough, Scotty's monologue frames it as a war, evoking dramatic World War 2 broadcasts. After praise for the brave soldiers and a sad note for the fallen, Scotty inserts a Bible reference, thus covering nation and faith. He ends with a repeated warning that is often quoted in the context of 1950s paranoia: "Keep watching the skies."[4] The patriotic fervor stands in sharp contrast to Scotty's meek and sarcastic behavior so far, and it does much to support the initially quoted assessment of *The Thing from Another World* as authoritarian and conservative (cf. Jancovich, *Rational* 31; Biskind 126). Perhaps more terrifying than its lumbering vegetable monster, the film asserts in the most urgent tone that there is no safety, that there is an invasion yet to come - a fear that would persist throughout the following decades of the Cold War.

The Thing and Others

Compared to the discussion of group dynamics, the eponymous Thing itself tends to receive little attention from film critics and scholars. Glimpses at its frozen form make the soldiers uncomfortable, and its sudden reanimation sends a guard into panic. Its actual appearance on screen is somewhat less impressive, as its look and slow walk resemble Frankenstein's monster, by then already a horror film cliché. Its other characteristics read like movie monster pastiche: it drinks blood, regenerates damage, is impervious to bullets and possesses at least some intelligence, even though the audience never gets a glimpse of the superior intellect Carrington raves about. Despite its human body, it is a plant, inspiring Scotty's monikers "supercarrot" and "intellectual carrot," which only serve to diminish its menacing aura. On the other hand, the Thing's ability to multiply from seedpods adds to its menace, even though that potential is hardly explored in the film. In any case, the monster's vegetable origins emphasize its inhumanity, though not as successfully as the name made official in the title: *Thing*. As a pure embodiment of monstrosity, the alien cannot be contained by any category, and therefore the only adequate descriptor is that of a thing – no matter what it is, it is not human. Yet, even though the Thing is an unstoppable threat that treats humans as mere food sources (as we would treat cabbages, Carrington suggests), its most effectively monstrous trait is that it draws out the lingering inhumanity in Carrington and what Jancovich calls the scientific-rational order.

---

4   For example, Bill Warren's monograph on 1950s science fiction cinema uses that quote as a title.

In many regards, the Thing serves as a textbook example of an external monster that disturbs normality until its defeat. First, it intrudes from the sky, then from the cold outside into the living spaces of the base. Still, the narrative's central conflict suggests an expansion of the formula: we might as well consider the Thing *and* Carrington as the film's two monsters, both utterly alien to the average, that is, normal people occupying the Arctic base, and both completely careless when it comes to these lives. The association of mad scientist and monster is well established in the genre, and in the case of *The Thing from Another World*, the inhuman, asexual, bloodsucking Thing and scientific rationality - in its purest form, at least - are presented as uncomfortably close.[5]

So far, the discussion of difference in *The Thing from Another World* has focused on a monstrous alien and uncaring rationality. There is one more outsider to the group: Nikki Nicholson, one of only two female members of the base staff, and the only one with a speaking role. As an addition to the all-male cast of the literary source, she adds what Morrison calls a "sexual subtext" (184), her romance with Hendry serving to contrast human sexuality and the alien asexuality of the Thing (and arguably Carrington). She is portrayed as confident and self-sufficient, not as a screaming victim that has to be saved from the monster (indeed, fainting under stress is left to Scotty). Still, Nikki is relegated to a role in supporting staff. Her character alternately contradicts and conforms to female stereotypes: on the one hand, she is capable of drinking Hendry under the table; on the other hand, her key contribution to the Thing's defeat is her housekeeping skills (she suggests boiling vegetables).

Biskind puts Nikki in a tradition of women in "centrist sci-fi" with masculine names, who are "just one of the boys" (135). The relationship between Hendry and Nikki is given a Freudian spin by Biskind, who reads the Thing as a metaphor for Hendry's id, which needs to be subdued for a conventional relationship to form: "The extremes of head (Carrington) and heart (Hendry's id), culture and nature, both represented by the Thing, have given way, once again, to the golden mean" (135). Jancovich offers a different viewpoint, claiming that Nikki as a central character who outdoes males is evidence of the film's critique of the male/female distinction (*Rational* 39-40). The monster, he argues, is given traditionally male associations such as technology and rationality (39), while Hendry, as one of the "emotionally weak" (40) male characters, "must acquire traditionally feminine qualities" to defeat it (41). Jancovich likewise sees the film ad-

---

5   The parallels between the two also allow for an alternative reading in the context of the Cold War, as Warren admits that Thing and Carrington may both be "viewed as aspects of the Unfeeling Commie" (53).

vancing an ideal of balance, but not between the Freudian sections of the mind, but between genders.

In summary, *The Thing from Another World's* invasion scenario, heavily influenced by the Cold War, stresses the need for various groups to abandon impractical ideals and hierarchies to work together effectively. Despite individual and institutional shortcomings, the protagonists are capable of defeating a threat that comes unprovoked and cannot be reasoned with. The alien Thing and the detached scientist Carrington are both portrayed as inhuman and dangerous to average Americans. The conclusion leaves little doubt that America is under threat, and calls for vigilance.

THE THING (1982)

Director John Carpenter's admiration of both Howard Hawks and *The Thing from Another World* was evident in his filmography long before he began work on the remake. Carpenter's *Assault on Precinct 13* (1976) draws on Hawks's Western *Rio Bravo* (1959) to an extent that borders on unacknowledged remaking, and two years later, Carpenter quoted *The Thing from Another World* in *Halloween* (1978) (cf. chapter 8). Despite this attachment, the remake draws heavily from the earlier literary source by Campbell, restoring the Antarctic setting, the cast of characters, and the shape-changing monster (Morrison 183). These changes result in a film that differs significantly from its predecessor, yet the title still points to the 1951 film, now abbreviated to *The Thing* (1982). While Carpenter's take on the story was not well received at the time of release (Muir, *Carpenter* 27), it has since become a canonical text in the horror genre. It did not go on to spawn a film franchise, likely due to poor box office performance, but received belated honors with a prequel in 2011, which, as I will argue in the next section, also serves as a remake.[6]

While the story of the 1951 film is told in a quick and straightforward fashion, the 1982 version purposefully deals in uncertainties. It opens with a lone sled dog, pursued by a Norwegian helicopter, seeking refuge at an American Antarctic base. The Norwegian crew attempt to kill the dog and deliver a warning, but perish in a general confusion of gunfire and explosions, leaving the

---

6   The only realized sequels to the narrative of the 1982 film can be found in other media. Dark Horse Comics published a comic book series in the early 1990s, returning to the title *The Thing from Another World*, and a video game was released in 2002. Neither appears to have had a lasting influence.

Americans puzzled by what they just witnessed. The sled dog is locked up with the other dogs inside the base, while an expedition including pilot MacReady, the film's protagonist, investigate the Norwegian base from which the helicopter must have come. They find the base completely devastated, with all inhabitants dead, and bring back a burnt inhuman body. Before the crew can gain further insight, the adopted sled dog mutates into a grotesque monstrosity that attacks the other dogs until part of it is destroyed. Further examination reveals that the Norwegians had found a crashed UFO under the ice, from which they retrieved an alien being capable of assimilating other life forms and taking their shape. Now that the crew is aware of the threat the alien Thing poses, paranoia spreads, as anyone could already be assimilated. Blair, the scientist with the best understanding of the Thing, destroys the radio equipment to isolate the base from the outside world; a blood test is devised, but sabotaged by unknown parties, and the helicopter is likewise rendered unusable. After violent infighting, and deadly attacks by the Thing, MacReady takes charge and forces the survivors into a blood test of his own design. The test identifies one of the crew as a Thing, but results in further chaos and deaths. The remaining crew members proceed to find the Thing's subterranean lair, where MacReady blows up its last incarnation with dynamite. However, with the base in ruins and no way to escape, MacReady and the only other survivor are certain to freeze to death, with no guarantee that one of them is not also infected by the Thing.

Where the first film has the cast dig out the alien Thing shortly after its crash landing, a very direct, immediate interaction, there are multiple levels of distancing and framing in the 1982 remake. The main, that is, American characters are not the ones to find the Thing. Instead it was dug out by the Norwegian crew, whose remains serve as foreshadowing for the American characters and the terrors to come. The main action of the film has happened before, a hypotext contained in the traces of the Norwegian base and, most notably, the silent footage found therein. That footage restages quite closely images from the 1951 film, the measurement of the alien vessel and its unearthing using Thermite, all in black and white (Muir 110, see fig. 1). Thus, the characters of the remake are arguably watching parts of the first film on tape. The tapes are, on the one hand, a device for building suspense and foreshadowing – the same devastation is going to come to the Americans as well – and on the other, an acknowledgement that the narrative is not new and original, but a repetition.[7]

---

7   Another level of distancing comes with the Things's temporal dislocation, reintroduced from the novella. The alien craft has been frozen in ice for at least 100,000 years, which adds to the Thing's Otherness in that it comes from a distant place in

The complex relationship between *The Thing* (1982) and its sources serves to exemplify, and perhaps challenge, Leitch's model of film remakes (cf. chapter 2). At first glance, Carpenter's film is a readaptation, with the primary goal of fidelity to the literary source (Leitch 45). Muir stresses that its screenwriter was "extraordinarily faithful to the details of the Campbell story" in the recreation of particular scenes, characters and atmosphere (Muir 25), and Morrison likewise confirms that the 1982 film restored the essential premise and the central theme of *Who Goes There?*, along with the setting and major plot elements (Morrison 183). Given the 1982 film's focus on its literary source, Muir and Cumbow agree that it is not a remake (Muir 24, Cumbow 111), yet under Leitch's definition, even the most exact readaptation still counts as a remake (though not as a "true remake") and the 1982 film by no means disavows its filmic predecessor.

In fact, the 1982 film includes a clear homage to the 1951 film in the Norwegian videotapes, and adds more visual references in the image of a burning man running outside (Muir 110) and the "bed of ice" from which the Thing was extracted (Cumbow 112). The primary source is still the literary text, yet these quotations fulfill at least the first half of what Leitch states as the purpose of homage (as a type of remake), to "pay tribute to an earlier film rather than take its place of honor" (Leitch 47). One might be inclined to compromise by calling *The Thing* (1982) a readaptation with a trace of homage, but on closer inspection, even that proves inaccurate. The film does not limit itself to an accurate adaptation; it expands on and surpasses its source with deeper characters (Morrison 183) and a more terrifying and innovative monster. Carpenter's film shows that film remakes can easily blur Leitch's categories, and simultaneously pursue several competing purposes. The Thing (1982) aims to honor both its sources *and* to take their place as the definite version of the story. It succeeds on the second count, as the section on *The Thing* (2011) will show.

The historical context was quite tangible in the 1951 film, but the remake is less obviously attuned to its day. The political subtext is dropped entirely (Morrison 185), including all mention of Russians and nuclear weapons, as is the wartime rhetoric. These elements had been added to the story of the novella to make it relevant to the 1950s, yet the same approach is not followed to adapt the story to the 1980s. Instead, the transition to postmodernity expresses itself in a wide-ranging deconstruction of institutions, individuals and bodies. For Pinedo, *The Thing* (1982) is a prime example of postmodern horror (35-38), and specifically

---

both time and space. At the same time, the urgency of the 1951 film is removed, since there is no need to "keep watching the skies."

a "post-Vietnam film" (37) due to the inability to tell friend from foe.[8] Morrison reads the film's "single overriding fear of the future" (191) as a reflection of a profound pessimism in early 1980s America, resulting from the doubts and failures of the 1970s (191). For Muir, the fractured group of characters also mirrors a contemporary social development towards individualism and self-interest (*Carpenter* 107). Cumbow, in a similar vein, views the isolation of Antarctica as "metaphor for contemporary life" (117).

These statements refer to a general sense of social collapse in the film, but due to its vagueness, that sentiment is hard to attribute to a specific moment in history, especially since Carpenter's filmography shows a recurrence of similar themes from the early 1970s to the late 1990s. *Dark Star* (1974) features a similar degree of social dysfunction among a space ship crew, and *Escape from L.A.* (1996) still ends on the same pessimistic note as its precursor.[9] Without a doubt, however, the diffuse pessimism of the 1982 film remains striking when read against the 1951 film. It may not represent its era exclusively, but it insinuates how much conceptions have changed since the 1950s.

Individuality and Dysfunction

The social dynamics of *The Thing* (1982) stand in stark contrast to the 1951 film. Where the first film had clear institutions, order and a chain of command, with the Air Force officer Hendry effectively assuming authority over scientists and the press, there is only constant internal strife and suspicion among the crew of the Antarctic base. As Morrison remarks, the 1951 film has cooperation and camaraderie, while the 1982 version only has endless bickering and isolation (188-89). Morale is low even before the Thing arrives, and as the character Childs remarks, people are crazy already. There is no code of professionalism, and only little trust in the crewmembers' respective abilities, with the exceptions of physician Copper and scientist Blair. The rank structure is far from clear. It appears

---

8   Pinedo's link between *The Thing* (1982) and the Vietnam War is somewhat tenuous, though. The shapeshifting monster of the film goes back to the 1938 novella, and as the samples in this study show, examples of monsters assuming human shape or monstrous doppelgangers can be found in horror film long before the start of the war, as in *Invasion of the Body Snatchers* (1956). Likewise, the Vietnam experience is far more tangible in the films of George Romero, and *The Crazies* (1973) in particular.

9   Moreover, this study features a number of films that are quite bleak in outlook, yet appear at different times, and a broader survey of the genre will yield even more variation. For such an assessment to bear weight, then, it needs to be made with more specific textual (that is, filmic) evidence over the course of the following analysis.

that Garry is in command, as he occasionally gives orders, and his behavior and manner of speech point towards a military background. He also wears a uniform, albeit without insignia, and carries a gun at all times. Still, he gets little respect, is mockingly called "el capitan," likely a reference to his rank, and his orders are obeyed only grudgingly or openly challenged. After Garry's trustworthiness is cast in doubt, he freely gives up control of the station keys and his gun to a chosen successor, who refuses. Childs steps up, but is refused by Clark, until MacReady takes over. This chaotic passing around of authority demonstrates that no effective structures are in place. The lack of trust is amplified by the revelation that the shape-changing monster could be anyone. As a result, the crew's pursuit of the Thing is highly ineffective, and infighting is as dangerous as the monster. Shortly after his informal promotion to leader, MacReady comes under suspicion (despite being human) and is locked out of the base to freeze to death. He only survives by forcing his way inside, and in one of the ensuing confrontations, he kills Clark (later also proven to be human). With little direct action by the Thing, the crew's fear already has lethal consequences.

Since allegiances among the crew are fleeting, there are no persistent lines of conflict. There is no clear opposition between military and science, nor between average workers and experts. Thanks to its fractured state, the group is oddly egalitarian. While the military (as personified by Garry) is irrelevant, the scientist Blair still plays a key role, first as a scientific authority, then as an antagonist. After providing crucial knowledge about the Thing and its abilities, he turns on the group, trying to ensure their isolation and eventual death. Blair's motivations are markedly different from Carrington in the 1951 film, as he does not act out of an unhealthy fascination with the Thing, but out of concern for the rest of the world. Thanks to his expert training, he knows just how dangerous the Thing is, and perhaps driven insane by the realization, concludes that the sacrifice of the base crew is the only way to keep it from spreading. It would seem that scientific-rational thinking again has no concern for individual lives, whether in the 1951 or 1982 film, but at least Blair appears to be driven by altruism as opposed to pursuing knowledge for its own sake.

However, even that motivation is not beyond doubt, because Blair is later revealed as the final incarnation of the Thing, even its most dangerous one. As with most of the Thing's victims, it is never resolved when exactly Blair is infected, and therefore, it is impossible to determine whether his actions are guided by personal or scientific-rational principles or by the alien monster. This uncertainty also complicates what stance the film might take regarding experts. Blair's decision, if taken deliberately, would point towards a suspicion of experts, whose preoccupation with the larger picture leaves little concern for the suffering of average individuals. That reading would match the "disavowal of intellectualism" (Woods 22) found throughout Carpenter's films. Ultimately, though, the scientist in *The Thing* (1982) cannot be fully trusted either way: either he tries to get the crew killed in order to protect the rest of humanity, or he tries to get the crew killed because he is the Thing.

If the expert Blair is a somewhat ambiguous character, the film casts its protagonist MacReady in a more heroic role, as he constantly works to outwit and physically destroy the Thing. MacReady is emphatically not an expert; for example, his constant confusion of Swedes and Norwegians implies a combination of general ignorance and disinterest. When the crew speculate about the Thing's capabilities, MacReady gives his ideas ("'Cause it's different than us, see? 'Cause it's from outer space."), but refuses to assume authority and instead refers to Blair ("What do you want from me? Ask him!"). He is an outsider who reluctantly takes charge when he believes it necessary, the first time with the crew's approval, the second time by threatening to blow up everyone with dynamite. He is disrespectful of authority, suspicious of others, independent and resourceful. In a nutshell, MacReady is a rugged individualist, specifically in the filmic tradition of terse Western characters (visually emphasized by MacReady's frontier hat). This characterization notably departs from the literary source, which describes its McReady as an almost mythical heroic figure (Campbell 2), a multi-talented meteorologist with a working knowledge of medicine (36), a clear leader and the team's second-in-command (35). Given the remake's relative fidelity to the literary source, at least compared to the 1951 film, the recasting of the protagonist as more of a reluctant everyman stands out.

A comparison of 1982's MacReady and 1951's Hendry reveals some superficial similarities. Both are independent-minded leaders (and even pilots by profession), but upon closer examination, the parallels end. Hendry is certainly a man of action who values his own judgment, but he is also eminently social, from drinking and joking with his men to his romantic interest in Nikki. MacReady is far more individualistic, and prefers living in a small shack outside the base, with just a chess computer and a bottle of whiskey for company. He rises to the challenge when needed, but his leadership is a mixed success at best. Unlike Hendry, MacReady does not derive the strategy from group interaction, but rather enforces his own ideas. His blood test nicely demonstrates this approach: MacReady, only trusting himself, ties everyone else to a couch while he performs his test. The test works, but thanks to the restraints, the human crew are also defenseless when the Thing appears, and MacReady struggles to stop the monster on his own. Furthermore, MacReady has no romantic interests like Hendry does. The sexual subtext of the 1951 film is removed (Morrison 185), and with that another possible level of trust and attachment. The only remotely female presence on base is arguably the voice of a chess computer, dismissed by MacReady as a "cheating bitch." White takes the scene as a critique of the "phallicized hero's inability to tolerate the slightest challenge to his self-image as master of every situation" (E. White 400), but as an indicator of the film's gender relations, it has little to offer.

Overall, human relations are in a hopeless state in *The Thing* (1982). Cooperation might be more successful in containing the Thing, but it seems impossible to achieve due to general distrust and dysfunction. Institutions and authorities are either absent or ineffective. In the chaotic situation, the tough and resourceful everyman MacReady does better than designated experts and leaders, but whether he succeeds is still left unresolved. If nothing more, the film seems to express a fondness for the rugged individualist, but fails to endorse him as a success model.

A Thing without Shape

The Thing of the 1982 film is not a pastiche of familiar horror clichés like its 1951 counterpart, and it also transcends the shapeshifter of the novella. The special effects realizing its many transmutations were lauded as new and unique, even by the film's detractors, who frequently saw the transformation spectacle as the film's only commendable quality (cf. Muir 98). Perhaps more than any other horror film monster, the 1982 Thing embodies a transgressive monstrosity: it is impossible to grasp with any conventional category simply because it has no permanent shape.

The Thing operates in two modes: hidden and openly. First, it infects or inhabits a human being, remaining indistinguishable from the regular person. The potential for horror arises from the difficulty of identifying the monster and the resulting paranoia, and from the possibility of being infected and losing one's identity. The film's central dilemma is summarized in this exchange:

MACREADY. Somebody in this camp ain't what he appears to be. Right now that may be one or two of us. By spring, it could be all of us.
CHILDS. So, how do we know who's human? If I was an imitation, a perfect imitation, how would you know if it was really me?

The second mode has the Thing reveal itself, breaking out of its host body as a constantly mutating mass of flesh. It quickly grows new appendages, whirling tentacles, huge teeth, and splits up into new creatures in increasingly grotesque variations. In this mode, horror is generated very differently, not by a sense of dread, the fear of the unseen, but by the explicit display of impossible bodily distortions. *The Thing* (1982) keeps these mutations in full view, leaving little to the audience's imagination as flesh and skin stretch and tear and blood and less identifiable body fluids spurt. The film's characters react with astonished horror, clearly unable to process the monstrous display. In one scene, the human head of one of the Things detaches, drags itself forward using its tongue, then grows spider-like legs to scuttle away (see fig. 2, center), prompting one of the characters to pause and then exclaim, "You gotta be fucking kidding me." His statement serves as comic relief in a tense scene, but also transports genuine despair with the incomprehensible shapes of the Thing.[10] The failure of rational categories is a more profound source of discomfort next to the sheer disgust of witnessing the Thing's permutations. That the Thing possesses no true form makes it an affront to normal bodies and clearly defined concepts alike.

The depiction of mutation and the explicit destruction of human bodies also tie into a crucial subgenre of 1980s horror film, the body horror found in films by David Cronenberg and others. Body horror works with deconstructing the body, with flesh and bone becoming weak and unstable, whether by focusing on its destruction or on its radical change. Jancovich mentions that "body/horror," like a more general crossing of genres, is "associated with a supposedly postmodern collapse of distinction and boundaries" ("General Introduction" 5). More specifically, the monstrous threat in these films "is not simply external but erupts from within the human body, and so challenges the distinction between self and other, inside and outside" (Jancovich, *Reader* 6). *The Thing* (1982) integrates this contemporary horror trend into the framework of the novella and the earlier film, thereby first complicating and then dismantling the "oppositions of interior human security and exterior alien threat" (Morrison 186) that had remained distinct in the 1951 film. The Thing attacks both the antarctic base and individual human beings from the inside.

Telotte claims that the Thing's power of duplication renders "the self almost irrelevant" ("Human Artifice" 45), and that it reveals the "alien potential" for distrust and hostility, "a certain *thing-ness* within man, an absence or potential abdication from the human world" only visualized through doubles (47). At the end, assertions of the characters' humanity are hollow because the film has undercut "all certainty, all dependable knowledge, certainly all reliance on appear-

---

10 Taking a cue from Brophy, Neale analyzes Childs's exclamation as a sign with multiple meanings, an expression of the film's self-awareness, and uses it as a launching point for a discussion of narrative and knowledge in science fiction (Neale, "You've Got to Be Fucking Kidding").

ance" (47). Muir comes to a similar conclusion, namely that *The Thing* (1982) is about "the frailty of human flesh, and the dehumanization of man and his increasing paranoia in the modern age" (Muir 103). Cumbow likewise considers the film a "sustained metaphor of the collapse of identity, responsibility and trust in the modern world" that deals with the "growing indistinguishability of the monstrous from the human" (Cumbow 111). As noted earlier, critics link the film's uncertainties to a vaguely defined anxiety of modernity, yet there are also attempts towards more specific historic references.

The Thing is capable of absorbing and imitating other life forms at a cellular level. A crude animation of cellular hijacking, visible on Blair's computer screen, visualizes this subtle invasion, and emphasizes the conceptual shift the Thing makes from its 1951 (and literary) counterpart. In this scene, it is depicted not as a somewhat complete entity, but as a virus. This trait, and the fact that a blood test is used to find out who is infected, led some critics to view *The Thing* (1982) as a metaphor for not only disease in general, but HIV/AIDS in particular (cf. Muir, *Carpenter* 105). With awareness of the AIDS epidemic rising in the time after the film's release, the all-male group of the Antarctic base was also interpreted as "a metaphor for the homosexual lifestyle," which Muir rates as "pushing the matter a bit" (105). Glasberg, by contrast, asserts that "a fear of homosexual contact within homosocial groups permeates each iteration of the Thing meme" (Glasberg 202), while further discussing the Thing as viral. However, the HIV/AIDS discourse does not, and cannot, due to the historical sequence of events, inform the film to the same degree as the Cold War did for the 1951 film.[11] *The Thing's* (1982) later reception may be colored by that discourse, but its production most certainly was not.

White reads *The Thing* (1982) more specifically as an effort to "dramatize the import of evolutionary theory" (E. White 399). To him, "The Thing powerfully registers the anguish and horror occasioned by the recognition of human subjection to evolutionary process," as well as the "dread at the prospect of losing definition and essence" and the "potential of becoming other" (399). The horror of change is so strong, argues White, that the station's inhabitants prefer to destroy themselves "in other words, destroy civilization - rather than consent to a universe in flux" (400). To be fair, though, said "universe in flux" means the death of every human being on Earth, and the film's characters act with this consideration in mind. Like its 1951 counterpart, the 1982 Thing attacks and kills

---

11 Given *The Thing's* release date, it is rather difficult to link the film to public awareness of HIV/AIDS. According to *IMDb*, the film was released in June of 1982 ("The Thing (1982)"), which predates even the introduction of the term AIDS later the same year.

without provocation and cannot be reasoned with. In addition, the choice of MacReady and his few surviving allies to destroy the base rather than allow the Thing to survive is hardly voluntary. Due to the damage caused by sabotage or fighting the Thing, they are cut off from any help, with the only options being absorption by the Thing, or destruction of the Thing and themselves. The latter at least carries a benefit to the rest of the world, which appears to be a surprisingly altruistic act from the otherwise divided and self-absorbed crew.

While this reading attributes a certain degree of heroism to the final actions of MacReady and company, the outside world that may be saved by their sacrifice plays a remarkably small role throughout the film's dialogue. There are no dramatic speeches as in the 1951 film, and no mention of friends or families back home. Blair's calculation regarding the global spread of the Thing and MacReady's speculation about a rescue party are the only implications of a world beyond the base. Since the stated approach of this study includes reading the monster against the normality it opposes, this begs the question what exactly constitutes normality in *The Thing* (1982).

Simply put, normality should be the state of the film's world before the monster's arrival. In the case of the Antarctic base, this means a very specific situation, a confined, dysfunctional community, where individuals are without purpose and constantly at odds with one another. Cumbow claims that 1950s invasion movies are about disturbing order, but in Carpenter's films "things are already out of joint" (113), that is, the world is already wrong and distrust reigns (114). Put that way, the Thing merely accelerates the slow social collapse that already defines normality. In more abstract terms, however, the Thing would, by virtue of its fluid nature, automatically be opposed to any normality understood as a fixed status quo.

Allegations of right wing thought keep recurring in criticism of John Carpenter's work in general, fueled by Carpenter's penchant towards Us vs. Them scenarios (cf. Woods 22). Taking up Robin Wood's approach of tracing the politics or ideology of a horror film by its monster, Smith concludes that a number of Carpenter films, including *The Thing* (1982), would classify as reactionary (35), because a "small, enclosed community" is threatened by a "seemingly irresistible and relentless external force" for reasons hardly understood (36). Indeed, the Thing as a monster appears to be a clear-cut case for Wood's categories, as the violent expulsion of the Other, and thereby the restoration of repression, is the only way to resolve the problem. In his critique of what he considers a shift towards reactionary horror films, Wood names monsters that are "simply evil" and "totally inhuman" as criteria (Wood 192). Both apply to *The Thing* (1982), as well as to *The Thing from Another World.* [12]

The comparison between the two films shows the limitations of assigning a political stance based on a handful of key criteria. The basic claim is as follows: an ambiguous monster created or provoked by some aspect of regular human life would mean that normality is inherently problematic and needs to change, while an unambiguously evil, external monster would mean that normality is not flawed and can rightly go back to the way things were once it has repelled the threat. Since the latter case affirms the status quo, it is interpreted as conservative. In the case of *The Thing from Another World*, the final call for unity leaves no doubt that America is worth preserving in the face of alien aggression and must stand together. The crew's way of life in *The Thing* (1982), however, appears neither desirable nor sustainable, as there is little to save in the first place. In addition, the refusal of closure in the 1982 film also poses a problem for interpretation. If we presume that a conservative ending entails the defeat of the monster and the return to normality, then radical or progressive endings may deny the return to normality by letting the monster roam free (a tendency Wood sees realized in 1970s horror film (87)). In *The Thing* (1982), it is never conclusively proven whether or not the monster is destroyed, and with the destruction of the base and the certain deaths of the last two survivors, normality cannot be restored. The film's denial of a definite resolution makes it impossible to determine a definite stance beyond a general nihilism. In the 1951 film, professional cooperation defeats the monster, but in the 1982 film, the best case scenario is that everyone is dead. The progression from the first film to the remake resembles a broad deconstruction of institutions and individuals, in both their bodies and identities. Nothing, whether man or monster, is likely to survive the film's conclusion.

THE THING (2011)

The Thing (2011) is a borderline case for this study. Officially, it is a prequel, that is, a film whose narrative is set before that of the 1982 film. The two films

---

12 Another point is "the presence of Christianity" (Wood 192), which might only be extrapolated from one remark by MacReady: "Trust is a hard thing to come by these days. Tell you what: why don't you just trust in the Lord?" Given the delivery of this line and the absence of any other mention of faith in the film, it should most likely be read as sarcastic.

are supposed to be in continuity. Therefore, it is not explicitly a new version of either *The Thing* film, and thus should not count as a remake for this study. The relation is slightly more complicated, however. *Prequel* is the official designation for this film, and some effort is made to ensure that the narrative of the 2011 film leads into the 1982 one. *The Thing* (2011) tells the story of the Norwegian base found in the 1982 film, and various details are arranged to match, including an axe stuck in a door, a particularly recognizable monstrous body, and a suicide scene. The prequel concludes its main narrative arc, with its protagonist surviving and out of the picture, but leaves another character and iteration of the monster for an epilogue that exactly recreates the opening of the 1982 film, set to the same soundtrack. The transition is almost seamless, which suggests that tremendous work was put into recreating the set, costumes and props.

The continuity of the prequel is not perfect, however. While a few memorable details match the 1982 film, others do not. Most importantly, the Norwegians do not recover the alien body in the same manner as implied by the black and white footage found in the 1982 film, which also eliminates the homage to the 1951 film. Thereby, the 2011 film takes the place of the 1951 film in relation to 1982, now serving as a hypotext and as an alternate version at the same time. Furthermore, one vehicle should be left at the alien crash site that does not appear in the 1982 film, the overall design of the UFO is different, and a multitude of small set details likewise do not match. These are, of course, discrepancies that would only occur to the more discerning viewer, and even the most dedicated film crew would find it next to impossible to perfectly recreate the sets and props of a film made almost 30 years earlier. The intention of the film to serve as a faithful prequel is hardly diminished. Yet, there are a few elements that point to the 2011 film being a new version of the 1982 film, rather than a completely new narrative that merely shares continuity, and I will argue that it may be categorized as a *remake*.

The plot of *The Thing* (2011) is fairly similar to that of the 1982 version, perhaps unsurprising, given that it is supposed to tell that film's back story. As the devastated ruins of the Norwegian base foreshadow the horrors in wait for the American crew in the 1982 film, the reverse logic should apply for the prequel: the characters of the 2011 film will have to live through the same horrors as those of the 1982 film. The story, set in 1982, is as follows: After crew members of a Norwegian Antarctic research station find an alien space craft buried under ice, a research team is assembled by the Norwegian scientist Sander, including the protagonist Kate, an American paleontologist. The combined American and Norwegian team finds a frozen alien body, which soon breaks free and begins to kill the crew of the base, taking the shape of its victims to attack the rest. While the crew desperately tries to contain it using guns and flamethrowers, Sander's attempts to preserve a scientific discovery are at odds with Kate's efforts to stop the alien Thing. As a blood test to identify those infected by the Thing is sabotaged, Kate comes up with a much simpler way of determining who is human: the Thing cannot duplicate tooth fillings (or body piercings), therefore those with immaculate teeth must be alien duplicates. The discovery fails to resolve the situation, however, and the death toll from the Thing's attacks and the crew's infighting rises. Once the base is burned down, Kate and a fellow American track the now possessed Sander to the alien craft, where she destroys the Thing and remains as the only human survivor – except, as the post-credit sequence reveals, for one of the Norwegians, and yet another incarnation of the Thing as a sled dog, which lead right into the opening scene of 1982's *The Thing*.

As the plot summary shows, the story progression closely resembles *The Thing* (1982), with some elements reminiscent of *The Thing from Another World*. The alien Thing is brought into the base and then proceeds to kill and absorb the crew, whose struggles with distrust hinder their attempts at mounting a defense. Some key roles seem to be repeated: the scientist Dr. Sander Halvorson, who is obsessed with the scientific discovery, fills a similar role as Carrington in the 1951 film and, to a lesser degree, Blair in the 1982 version. Key scenes play out similarly: the Thing being brought into the base and breaking out the ice follows the 1951 film, while the testing scene follows the 1982 one, only with fillings replacing blood samples. Even the film's title is identical to the 1982 version, which suggests a replacement, not an enhancement or addition to the existing film.[13]

If not for the epilogue that bridges the gap to *The Thing* (1982), the 2011 film could easily pass as a remake. A brief survey of reviews and online comments confirms this assessment, as a large number of critics and viewers insist on calling *The Thing* (2011) a remake, in spite of the studio's labeling. A reviewer for *film.com* suspects a ploy to avoid the negative reputation of remakes and asserts that the studio "went ahead and did the remake — but they're *calling* it a "prequel" (Snider). The sentiment is shared by several reviewers, including one for the *Miami Herald*, who warns his readers not to be "fooled" by the label prequel, as "[t]his is essentially the exact same movie" (Rodriguez), and the *New York Times* likewise lines up *The Thing* (2011) in the "annals of redundant remakes" (Catsoulis). The narrow definitions of *remake* mentioned in chapter 2 would still exclude *The Thing* (2011) on the basis of its continuity with

---

13 The opening credits, by contrast, quote the literary source, not the previous film, even though everything about the 2011 film takes its cues from the film, not the novella.

the 1982 film, but these reviews demonstrate Verevis's position that *remake* is not just one fixed industrial or critical category, but also located in "cinematic (and general) discursive fields" (Verevis, *Film* 29). *The Thing* (2011) may be intended as a prequel, but as evidence shows, it may be read as a remake.

The survey of reviews for *The Thing* (2011) yields another insight into the complex workings of the sequence of *Thing* films and its reception. The vast majority of reviews compare the 2011 film unfavorably to the 1982 one. Of course, the latter had itself been widely reviled by critics upon its release, but is now commended as a horror classic in 2011 (e.g. by Snider). The 2011 film demonstrates the canonizing function of remakes by elevating its predecessor, reacting to, confirming and furthering its status as a canonical horror film. It serves to finally counter the negative critical reception 1982 film upon its release, if only by making the 1982 film look better in comparison.

Nationalities, Gender and Dental Care

Since *The Thing* (2011) consciously strives not to deviate from the 1982 film, it offers fewer intriguing changes than other film-remake sequences. The attempt at homage thus subdues the remake's potential for the updating of cultural fears that would lie in a complete reconceptualization of the story from a contemporary point of view. Nevertheless, *The Thing* (2011) makes subtle alterations in the dynamics of gender, groups and structures, as well as the Thing itself.

The adjustment of gender roles is a common trend in remaking, as newer versions of films tend to expand the number and agency of female roles in accordance with social change. By contrast, *The Thing* (1982) cut down the number of women from two to none, which may be explained by its re-adaptation stance: perhaps in the interest of fidelity, the 1982 film reverted to the all male cast of the novella. The 2011 film, then, has no such reservations and introduces a new set of characters to better match the gender politics of its time. The adjustment seems slight, with just two women among more than a dozen men, and oddly enough returns to the level of the 1951 film. As the undisputed protagonist, however, Kate enjoys a much larger significance. For Glasberg, the recasting is "crucial, yet underdeveloped" and "offers a devastating assessment of liberalism and postcolonial feminism" (208). Unfortunately, Glasberg fails to elaborate on that assessment.

In the 2011 film's narrative, Kate takes over much of the MacReady role, in that she gradually takes charge of the group, but unlike him, she is not a maladjusted loner. A combination of character types that had been clearly separate in the 1951 and 1982 films, Kate is a scientist woman of action that comes up with a practical means of identifying the Thing, a method that also saves her life in the end, and she is handy enough with a flamethrower to save her male colleagues from distress. At the same time, she embodies the Hendry role from the 1951 film, acting as opposition to Sander's dangerous scientific ambition.

As mentioned earlier, Sander resembles a more subdued version of Carrington from the 1951 film, the ambitious and reckless scientist, and personifies authority and detached expert knowledge. Sander asserts his own authority as leader of the expedition, reminding Kate that she is "not here to think," and suppressing the spread of information via radio. He repeatedly endangers the crew, as he orders the Thing to be preserved as an important discovery instead of being destroyed. He does not share Carrington's tendency towards monologues, but his insistence that "we have to rely on science" in finding out the Thing comes close to Carrington's platitudes. Unlike Carrington, though, Sander does not develop an unhealthy admiration for the Thing, so his obsession with scientific discovery may be reckless, but not monstrous. Still, Sander aligns with the monster at the film's climax, albeit unwillingly, when a hybrid of Sander and the Thing confronts Kate, in a manner similar to Blair in the 1982 film. Therefore, Sander combines the head scientist characters from both previous films. He is arguably a throwback to the suspicion of pure scientific rationality found in the 1951 film, but that position is tempered by the fact that his opposition Kate is not a military figure like Hendry in 1951, but a fellow scientist.

In fact, there is no military presence whatsoever in *The Thing* (2011), not even the commander in name only found in the 1982 film. The only approximation may be the pilot Sam Carter, a rugged American everyman interested in sports and quick to call for the Thing's destruction. While his practical and aggressive attitude matches the military characters of the 1951 film, Sam wields no state approved authority, and ultimately, he too falls victim to the Thing. Even though conflicts between experts and more practical minds develop, the main divide in *The Thing* (2011) is between nationalities, Norwegians and Americans, those native to the base and the newcomers, with the language barrier raising suspicions for outsiders. The fact that there are at least temporary groups, allegiances, and somewhat clean lines of conflict already makes the group of characters more structured than that of the 1982 version. Nevertheless, the only clear authority (Sander) is a liability, and any others are absent, leaving the well-rounded individual Kate to resolve the problem.

When it comes to the film's monster, all key motives of horror found in the predecessor remain in place, from the body horror, the subversion of identity and the denial of clear categories, to the paranoia. Even the comparison to a virus is now explicitly part of the dialogue. The special effects take advantage of current digital technologies to allow for smoother mutations, but rarely depart from the variations set by 1982's Thing. If anything, the 2011 Thing is more comprehensible. It has more defined tactics, luring people off to catch them alone and then absorb them, as Kate quickly realizes. It also has slightly more defined limitations, specifically, its inability to duplicate anorganic matter like tooth fillings and earrings, which is again found by Kate's scientific reasoning. While the possibilities of ceramic fillings and dental hygiene keep the Thing's shapeshifting advantage from being completely undone, Kate succeeds because she checks for Sam's piercing, and thus ends up with an effective means of stopping the Thing.

Even though the characters should be doomed from the start, *The Thing* (2011) comes off as less pessimistic than the 1982 film it is designed to lead into. Through a combination of practical common sense and expert knowledge, Kate manages to defeat the Thing, stop its spaceship, and make for the safety of a nearby Russian base, which was not available to the characters of the 1982 film. She prevails through hardship, similar to the final girls of the slasher film (discussed in more detail in chapter 8). The conclusion to Kate's plotline is quite definite, with a relatively happy ending and a return to normality in sight, and more conventional than the 1982 film's uncertainty. In that sense, the 2011 film reads as affirmative of predominant social and generic structures. For the film to function as a prequel, though, the Thing must of course survive to haunt the occupants of the American base featured in the 1982 film, and it does in an epilogue unrelated to Kate's recent struggles. The film is therefore split between the neat conclusion of a remake and the open ending of a prequel, which defers the final resolution to the other film. This poses a challenge for reading the monster's interaction with normality, because the Thing is defeated, and then it is not. Taken on its own, Kate's success exceeds that of MacReady, proving that humans can indeed handle the shapeshifting Thing better, which retroactively undercuts the nihilistic terror of *The Thing* (1982).

Overall, the sequence of *Thing* films is an intriguing case study for the winding paths of remaking and the ways it loops back to itself. The first film is a liberal adaptation of a literary source, the second a readaptation with a hint of homage, and the third declared as a prequel to the second film, but with a heavy element of homage. Especially if the novella is considered as part of the narrative cycle, the sequence problematizes traditional notions of originality. Chronologically, of course, the novella should be the primordial source, with the 1951 film taking the first spot when it comes to the films. However, the significance of each iteration shifts over time, with the 1951 film devaluing the novella with its radical departure, and the 1982 film revaluing it. More importantly for the discussion of film remakes, the 2011 film establishes the 1982 version as the lead text, the "true" version of the *Thing* narrative. It may not be labeled the original in a conventional sense, but it is the iconic iteration that serves as the source of further works.[14]

Despite the massive changes in the Thing's capabilities, the basic relationship between monster and normality remains similar. The Thing is an incomprehensible, implacable threat from the outside. Fear of the Other is warranted, and the destruction of the monster, if at all possible, is the only solution. Following the political categorizations of Wood and Biskind, all versions of *The Thing* should fall in the conservative or even reactionary spectrum, even though the 1982 film is almost as hard to grasp as its shapeshifting monster, thanks to its refusal of closure. The preference of action as opposed to pure scientific rationality is a recurring theme, with the 1951 film endorsing a compromise in the shape of group cooperation, and the 2011 film endorsing a balance of the two in the character of Kate.

---

14 E.g. the aforementioned video game sequel, comic books, or the short story "Things" by Peter Watts.

4. Conformity and Doppelgänger Horror

Invasion of the Body Snatchers (1956) and its remakes seem like an inevitable inclusion in this study of horror film remakes. Not only is the 1956 film one of the most lauded examples of its genre and period, a reputation confirmed by its inclusion in the US National Film Registry at the Library of Congress (Grant 7), it is also renowned for its social relevance and the multitude of readings its paranoid scenario about subversion and conformity enables. Moreover, and crucially, it has proven to be exceptionally fertile ground for remaking, with a remarkable total of three new versions in 1978, 1993, and 2007.[1] Consequently, *Invasion of the Body Snatchers* (1956) and its remakes have received a considerable amount of attention in critical and academic circles, including book-length studies of the 1956 film by LaValley (1989) and Grant (2010). This film sequence is one of the textbook examples for remakes, so much that that Loock and Verevis's recent anthology on film remakes bears a screenshot from *Invasion of the Body Snatchers* (1978) on the cover.

Considering the abundance of studies, the *Body Snatchers* sequence may seem like it has been done to death, but there is still plenty of ground to cover. The more recent remakes have received much less attention than the earlier films, partly due to a general critical bias towards the initial version as the original. As one of the goals of this study is to elevate the discussion of remakes by

---

1   There is also another recent derivative, *Invasion of the Pod People* (2007), which does not qualify for the narrow definition of remake used in this study. Even though it is clearly a reworking of the *Body Snatchers* story, the film is a so-called mockbuster, an unauthorized film designed to resemble its official counterpart (see footnote 20). The title appears to exploit the fact that the term "pod people," while coined in reference to *Invasion of the Body Snatchers* (1956), is not trademarked or otherwise restricted from public use, and the timing suggests an attempt to take advantage of *The Invasion's* (2007) release.

viewing them as iterations in a continuously developing sequence, as opposed to a fading trail of lesser copies, this chapter will aim to give equal consideration to all four films instead of prioritizing the one "true" version. While a number of more recent publications feature all versions, the first film is still privileged as the subject of monographs and the only canonical iteration of the story.

In the *Body Snatchers* films, humans are secretly replaced by alien duplicates, the pods or pod people, who are indistinguishable from their originals, except for a complete lack of emotion. Unlike other film monsters, the pods are quite articulate and able to make a case for their point of view. Each iteration of the *Body Snatchers* story features at least one scene in which the pods make an argument for the human protagonists to join them. These scenes serve to focus each film's monstrous metaphor within the context of historically specific cultural anxieties, and therefore offer a crucial point of comparison for the following analysis.

INVASION OF THE BODY SNATCHERS (1956)

Despite its current reputation, *Invasion of the Body Snatchers* (1956) came about as yet another entry in the wave of science fiction and horror hybrids that dominated the genre in the 1950s, produced as a low budget B-movie.[2] The adaptation of Jack Finney's serialized novel *Body Snatchers*, directed by the then barely known Don Siegel, proceeded at a brisk pace, but ground to a halt in post production (LaValley 3-4). Studio executives were confounded by the film and unsure how to market it, an impression they found confirmed by test screenings. During a lengthy reworking process, and after heated debates between studio, producer and director, the film was recut, excising humorous scenes; a voiceover narration by lead actor Kevin McCarthy was added, and additional framing scenes were shot by a reluctant Siegel (LaValley 15-16). The term "invasion" was included in the title in order to firmly locate the film in the then-popular genre of alien invasion films, and also to distinguish the film from 1945's unrelated *The Body Snatcher*. The finished film enjoyed only moderate critical and

---

2   The term "B-movie" originally referred to the lesser half of a double feature, although it would later be used for any low budget or lowbrow film. One of the upsides of B-movies, according to Bogdanovich, was greater creative freedom (173).

commercial success upon its release, but would rise in popularity over the following decades.[3]

The film begins with a framing scene set at a police station, where the seemingly mad protagonist Miles Bennell tells the following story in flashback. Returning to his home town of Santa Mira, California, Miles finds the town subtly changed, with citizens complaining that their loved ones have been replaced by impostors. Miles does not believe these reports and goes on to rekindle his romance with his old high school girlfriend Becky, until he is called in by his friend Jack Belicec, who has found a body at his home. At closer inspection, it turns out to be an unfinished duplicate of Belicec, and Miles also finds a duplicate of Becky at her place. Both bodies disappear when the authorities are involved, but the next evening, more duplicate bodies are discovered at the Belicecs' greenhouse. Miles's attempts to warn the outside world are frustrated, as the town has already been thoroughly infiltrated by impostors. Miles learns that alien beings have landed at Santa Mira, grow human duplicates from plant pods, replace the townsfolk while they are sleeping, and systematically spread to neighboring towns. Discussion with the emotionless pods is futile, and Miles and Becky attempt to flee the town on foot. While Becky, too, is taken over by the pods, Miles manages to reach the highway, where he madly tries to alarm motorists. At this point the film shifts back to the present. The police are inclined to disbelieve Miles's story, but an accidental piece of evidence launches them into action; the FBI is called and a quarantine of Santa Mira is ordered.

The narrative frame and the ending have been a major point of controversy in discussions of *Invasion of the Body Snatchers* (1956). Since these additions were made at the command of the studio and against the wishes of the screenwriter and director, many critics and fans are inclined to disregard the frame.[4] In that

---

3   In a footnote, Mann suggests various factors in the film's rise in popularity, including "film distribution within the television market, the directorial reappearance of Don Siegel in the early 1970s and the rise of auteur theory in academia and critical audiences, the 1978 remake of the film, the resurgence of UFO sightings in the 1970s, and the rise in popularity of cult science fiction and horror films" (Mann 66).

4   Reportedly, some cinemas would later remove the framing scenes and show *Invasion of the Body Snatchers* (1956) as a "director's cut" (Kaminsky 153-154) – not in the sense of a cut officially authorized by the director, but one made autonomously in the expectation of better matching the director's vision. Strangely enough, the discontent with the studio-mandated ending has (to the knowledge of this author) not yielded an alternate cut on DVD, BluRay, or other format. Given that director's cuts and alternate versions are commonplace on DVD and BluRay releases, it would appear that in-

case, the story would end with Miles standing in the middle of the highway, waving at passing cars and yelling that "they're here," with the last shot being Miles looking straight into the camera and screaming "You're next!" at the audience. Obviously, that scene would end the film on a far more pessimistic note, especially since Miles spots a pod-filled truck spreading the invasion even further. Miles would be powerless to stop the pods from taking over (presumably) the world, erasing human emotion forever. In comparison, the added ending marks a radical change by bringing in helpful authorities (Grant 14), yet the final outcome remains ambiguous at best. The viewer does not get to see the success of the police and FBI efforts, and given the speed and subtlety of the pods' infiltration, stopping them seems like a questionable proposition.

The debate over the ending of *Invasion of the Body Snatchers* (1956) raises questions of textual ownership and authority – after all, who owns a film's story, and therefore gets to determine what the "real" ending is supposed to be? Film critics who adhere to auteur theory, which seeks to privilege the director as the main or sole author of a film, are naturally inclined to prefer Siegel's intention. Those interested in how the film industry as a system reacts to, channels, and shapes cultural trends, by contrast, would be ill-advised to disregard the studio's point of view, and any speculation on how the film resonated with contemporary audiences of course has to deal with the film as it was shown. As the following analysis will show, however, the question of the ending is not of central importance to interpretations of the film. Even if the film ends on a more positive note, enough ambiguity remains for wildly divergent readings.

Body Snatching Politics and the Cold War

The hybrid science fiction/horror films of the 1950s, with their colorful titles and outlandish creatures, may have been dismissed as lowbrow entertainment in their day, but have since been reevaluated as revelatory works expressing American anxieties of the Cold War and the nuclear age (Grant 24-25). In sharp contrast to earlier genre traditions rooted in the literary Gothic, these films set their threats in the here and now, from alien invasion and infiltration scenarios to monsters created by nuclear tests (Jancovich *Rational* 2). *Invasion of the Body Snatchers* (1956) marks no exception to this trend; in fact, among the canon of 1950s genre films, it is held as one of the key examples for Cold War paranoia in film. Intriguingly, the film has yielded contradictory interpretations. It is widely read as expressing a paranoid fear of communist infiltration, but also as an indictment of

---

terest in the filmmakers' original intention is not that great after all, or at least not enough to sway the film's current owners.

the anti-communist witch hunts of Senator Joseph McCarthy and the House Un-American Activities Committee (HUAC) (cf. LaValley 4; Jancovich, *Rational* 64). The Cold War is not the only context invoked for the film either, as it may also serve as a critique of a general social transformation towards conformity (cf. Samuels; Jancovich, *Rational* 64ff.), and as an expression of male anxiety over changing gender norms (cf. Mann; Grant 77-92).

The post-WWII era gave rise to a range of anxieties that went on to shape perceptions and policies in 1950s America, and LeGacy describes "a new feeling of paranoia, a new fear of scientists and intellectuals, of foreigners and subversives, fear even of one's next door neighbor" (289). Between the late 1940s and the early 1950s, LeGacy argues, a number of events escalated a sense of American vulnerability into paranoia, including the Hollywood blacklist of alleged Communist sympathizers, the spy trial of former State Department official Alger Hiss, the loss of China to Mao Zedong's Communist Party instead of the American-favored Kuomintang, and the development of a Soviet nuclear bomb thanks to nuclear espionage, all of which culminated in McCarthy's allegations of widespread communist conspiracy (289-90). Even though McCarthy's influence had waned by the mid-fifties, *Invasion of the Body Snatchers* (1956) still reflects these conspiracy fears in the pods' subversive mode of operation. On the surface, Santa Mira appears like a perfectly normal American small town, but underneath, the pods are spreading until every citizen is one of them. The conspiracy goes all the way up to the town's authorities, and Miles observes a clandestine meeting at a family home, in which the pods coordinate their further actions. The pods use their positions of power to remove evidence of their activities, and effectively silence Miles by cutting off communication to the outside world. The extent of the conspiracy brings to mind McCarthy's claims to have uncovered a vast, unprecedented conspiracy at the heart of American life (McCarthy; LeGacy 290), and the takeover of individual citizens' bodies and minds also resonates with fears of brainwashed POWs returning from the Korean War (LeGacy 290).

The conspiratorial method of the pods is not the only parallel to anticommunist anxieties. The pod state itself also resembles a particular stereotype of communists as a rationalistic, godless collective. The pods act as a group with a single purpose, with no room for individuality. In the following dialogue, the pod spokesperson Kauffman explains the process of becoming a pod:

KAUFFMAN. Your new bodies are growing in there. They're taking you over, cell for cell, atom for atom. There's no pain. Suddenly, while you're asleep, they'll absorb your mind, your memories, and you're reborn into an untroubled world.
MILES. Where everyone is the same?

KAUFFMAN. Exactly.
MILES. What a world!

The notion of sameness is unacceptable for Miles, but as the scene continues, it is the pods' inability to "love or be loved" he finds most revolting. Kauffman disagrees: "Love, desire, ambition, faith – without them, life's so simple, believe me." Not only do the pods have no emotions, they also have no use for faith, and their society is characterized by total equality. It adds up to a "familiar mechanistic utopia usually (and rightly) taken as a metaphor for Communism" (Biskind 141). The most striking argument comes not from the pods themselves, but from Miles, who compares them to "a malignant disease, spreading through the whole country." The disease analogy repeats the anticommunist rhetoric of the 1950s. Miles's line reminds some critics of presidential candidate Stevenson (Sayre) or again McCarthy (Grant 65), but a closer match is a 1947 speech by J. Edgar Hoover, in which communism is described as "an evil and malignant way of life" which "reveals a condition akin to a disease, that spreads like an epidemic" (quoted in Underhill 149). Whether or not Miles's diagnosis is a conscious quote, the script repeats the heated political rhetoric of its time and thereby projects fears of communist subversion, well-established during the Korean War, spy trials and HUAC hearings, onto the pods. Miles's frantic cries in the film's penultimate scene ("They're here already!") would thus issue a warning of communist subversion, a counterpart of sorts to the rallying speech from *The Thing from Another World* (1951).

At the same time, the pods still appear to maintain a model small town community, with social roles largely intact. Their attempts to bring Miles and Becky in line with the group consensus ("Tomorrow you'll be one of us!") can also be viewed as a repressive society persecuting dissenters in its own ranks and thus as a metaphor for either the excesses of anticommunist hearings or, more generally, fascism (cf. Braucourt 75). By rendering anticommunist forces, and the mythical American heartland they sought to defend, as the monstrous opposition, *Invasion of the Body Snatchers* (1956) would then position itself on the opposite side of the political spectrum. However, the textual evidence for this interpretation is slightly more oblique. While Miles draws on anticommunist rhetoric to describe the pods, the pods themselves do not make recognizable quotations from said rhetoric. Even though they may be read as crusaders against everything un-American, their rhetoric does not mark them as such.

Instead, this line of argument is supported by Miles's musings about the pod state. During a brief moment of respite, he concludes that the pods are not that alien after all: "In my practice I see how people have allowed their humanity to drain away... only it happens slowly instead of all at once. They didn't seem to mind. All of us – a little bit – we harden our hearts, grow callous." Miles observations suggest that humans can arrive at the same point without alien interference, and that the potential for Otherness resides within everyone. For LaValley, this scene clearly expresses that "we are the villains," and therefore "there was no anticommunist message in the film" (8). The pods are not the Other, but Us, "everything we feared and everything we were becoming" (8). The film may still be read as a warning, but not as one from an outside threat.

These readings suggest contradictory political stances for the film. For Biskind, at least, the case is fairly clear. He considers *Invasion of the Body Snatchers* (1956) as "right-wing scifi" (139), with the pods standing in for the political center as much as communism. LaValley, by contrast, attempts to resolve the question of the film's ideology by investigating the stances of the filmmakers. He characterizes scriptwriter Daniel Mainwaring as a "onetime strong leftist" despairing over 1950s America (6), director Siegel as less political, but fiercely individualistic (9), and producer Wanger as a liberal and only reluctant anticommunist (12-13; 15). Calibrating his reading to these positions, LaValley concludes that the film's ideology "stays well to the left of center" (15). LaValley's approach may be more measured than Biskind's, but it relies on extratextual information and possible intentions instead of the text itself. Ultimately though, despite LaValley's insistence to the contrary (4), it is perfectly possible for a film to contain contradictory ideas, or at least the material to enable such readings, and given its complicated production history, it should come as no surprise that *Invasion of the Body Snatchers* (1956) carries ambiguous meanings. In fact, the very scene that LaValley uses to argue against the film's alleged right-wing leanings is also the launching point for a more sociological reading.

More Pod Perspectives: Conformity, Masculinity

For some critics, anxieties related to the Cold War are not of central importance for *Invasion of the Body Snatchers* (1956). Samuels admits that the film may "perhaps" work as a metaphor for communism, but finds that more directly, "podism spoke to a society becoming more massified, more technological, more standardized" (212). The move towards mass production and rationalization marks the post-WW2 restructuring of society according to Fordism (cf. Jancovich, *Rational Fears* 18ff.). The pods, their pure rationality, and their smoothly functioning community thus express fears of a Fordist vision for the future, in which individuals would be reduced to working in as cogs in a finely tuned system of mass production and consumption. One of the key references for this reading is David Riesman's *The Lonely Crowd*, a 1950 study that perceived American society as transforming from independent "inner-directed" individuals, into conformist "outer-directed" individuals who depend on validation by others (Samuels 208, Jancovich 21). Another reference for the same pattern of social change is William H. Whyte's *The Organization Man*, published in the same year as *Invasion of the Body Snatchers* (1956) (Jancovich, *Rational* 22; Grant 67).

Miles's already quoted thoughts about the gradual loss of humanity is crucial for this reading. Since humans are prone to let their humanity drain away by everyday life, the threat is not purely external, but "only the inevitable outcome of developments within American society and culture" (Jancovich, *Rational* 65). This interpretation is based on the same observations as LaValley's rejection of anticommunism, only it attributes the pressure to conform to a change in society and the working environment instead of a political movement. The pervasive effects of this social transformation are mirrored by the subtlety and inevitability of the pods' takeover. The people of Santa Mira are replaced in their sleep, unable to resist or even realize the magnitude of the change taking place around them. It is also significant that the pods mostly rely on a non-violent approach and try to persuade Miles and Becky to join them. There is no doubt that the pod spokesperson Kauffman, still performing his human role as a psychiatrist, genuinely thinks of the pod state as an improvement over human flaws and insecurities. His arguments are to be taken seriously, and Siegel remarked that there is "a very strong case for being a pod," even though the end result is a "very dull world" (Kaminsky 154).

Miles, however, is able to resist the pods' advances thanks to his strongly independent character. Unlike the emotionless, outer-directed pods, Miles is inner-directed and passionate. Like many of Don Siegel's protagonists, he is a rugged individualist who must be odds with the group (Gregory 8). In fact, the underlying conception of individuality is so radical that it is ultimately incompatible with any form of society or human bond. Miles appeals to "friends, the law, the system, his woman", but is betrayed by all, as "All are part of the group, the enemy" (Gregory 8). Samuels repeats Gregory's assessment and concludes that despite the invasion theme, the film is more about being an outsider (Samuels 213-14).

From this perspective, the pods stand for pervasive social change that threatens an inner-directed, individualist lifestyle, which boils the film's central conflict down to individual versus group. However, Miles may also be considered as a representative of a whole group afraid of displacement by other groups. According to Mann, for example, *Invasion of the Body Snatchers* (1956) reflects "hegemonic white patriarchy" feeling besieged by racial and gender difference, whose changing status in the 1950s she considers more important for the film than communism and bureaucrats (Mann 49). Crucially, Miles's warning to the audience includes the phrase "They're after all of us – our wives, our children," which suggests a particular definition of "us" – married men and fathers. The ideal viewer is thus "presumed to be a white heterosexual (benevolent) patriarch whose way of life was imminently threatened by invasive outsiders" (Mann 50). Mann places *Invasion of the Body Snatchers* (1956) in a historical continuum of xenophobic fears, and with the pods as a focus, finds parallels to a wide range of "popular postwar tropes surrounding racial migration, immigration, white flight, mass society, technocracy, brainwashing, aggressive female sexuality, and concerns about racial integrity and miscegenation" (Mann 51). Like the anticommunist interpretation covered earlier, this reading casts the pods as *Them*, not *Us*, that is, as an outside threat as opposed to the realization of a tendency found within. Consequently, the same criticisms that yielded contradictory political interpretations may apply here as well. At the least, claims regarding the pods as an assault on patriarchy or "whiteness" (Mann 52) need to consider the fact that the pod society, despite all claims of total sameness, is evidently still run by the same white men as before (Kauffman and police chief Grivett).[5]

Nevertheless, a distinct fear of femininity and sexuality permeates the narrative arc of Miles and Becky. Becky, like Miles a divorcee and therefore already a bit of an outsider in the community of Santa Mira, starts out with an unusual degree of independence and confidence. As her relationship with Miles progresses, though, Becky quickly submits to traditional gender roles, from making breakfast for Miles to wishing to have his children (Grant 82). Her transformation into a pod and subsequent loss of interest in Miles is presented as the film's most terrifying moment, with Miles asserting "I've been afraid a lot of times in my life, but I didn't know the real meaning of fear until... until I had kissed Becky" (see fig. 3). Miles's voiceover continues to emphasize Becky's irreversible change in-

---

5   Admittedly, Mann's case for racial difference as a theme in the *Body Snatchers* story is much stronger for the novel. Her reading of the pods as "lazy immigrant" stereotypes finds ample evidence there, but is somewhat less compelling for the pods of the film, who display quite the protestant work ethic in spreading the seed pods that expand their control. Mann's link from produce trucks to migrant workers and hence Mexicans is also rather tenuous (57). She is of course correct in locating an underlying fear of invasion and takeover, but I would argue that the film largely disconnects those xenophobic fears from their established symbols and instead projects them onto the idealized self.

to "an inhuman enemy bent on my destruction." Becky's turn also marks a significant departure from the novel's source material, where Miles and Becky allied to successfully repel the pods.[6] The film's take on Becky and its misogynist
overtones can be explained with its director's brand of rugged individualism.
Kaminsky finds that in Siegel's films, women are no help at all, but "tempting,
deceitful creatures", that "can't be denied, but must never be trusted" (178), and
according to Gregory, Siegel's female characters are "a constant source of pain
and betrayal", as they "represent commitment to the group" (8). Accordingly, the
struggles of Miles would represent a particular masculine individualism threatened from all sides.

Incidentally, the transformation of Becky is frequently named as a plot inconsistency, as it completely contradicts what the film has so far established
about pod duplication. Up to this point, a fairly clear sequence is in place. Judging from the growing duplicates at the Belicecs' and Becky's home, as well as
Kauffman's explanation, alien seed pods would have to be placed in proximity to
the target to grow into their likeness. The exact timeframe is not defined, but going by the precedents, the process seems to take more than a few minutes. Once
the original has gone to sleep, the duplicate copies its mind and takes its place.
The fate of the original body is not clarified, and Miles can only speculate that
"probably the original is destroyed or disintegrates." Becky, however, is left
alone in a mineshaft, far from any vegetation, and after the change, her body appears exactly the same as before. Therefore, it appears that a replacement by a
duplicate body did not take place; instead, Becky had a change of mind when she
went to sleep. The remakes take great care to avoid such contradictions, yet for
Grant, the narrative lapse "makes sense as a masculine hysteria made manifest in
the text" (88), since Becky as an independent woman is monstrous to 1950s male
sensibilities (89). The breakdown of causality thus represents the degree of male
panic. In a similar vein, Mann argues that Miles's terror over Becky's change is
actually rooted in his loss of reproductive control (62), and Nelson likewise
reads the pods' "asexual reproduction" as fear of change in women's roles and

---

6 Jancovich counters gender criticism of the story by pointing out that the novel's critique of conformity targets gender conformity as well (Rational 71-73). The film adaptation drops that point, and Jancovich speculates that the absence of a gender revelation in the film "prevents any effective solution to the crisis" (75). In addition,
Jancovich views Becky's transformation as her embracing conformity, including conformity to gender roles (75), whereas Mann reads the same scene as expressing a fear
of female resistance to such conformity (62).

loss of sexual difference post-WW2 (60).[7] At any rate, the nuclear family is directly threatened by the pods, and Becky's contested body (or mind, depending on how the plot inconsistency is accounted for) is the site of the conflict.

Normality and the Pods

At first glance, Wood's basic horror formula of normality being threatened by the monster can certainly be applied to *Invasion of the Body Snatchers* (1956), as the normality of Santa Mira (and specifically, that of Miles Bennell) is threatened and ultimately destroyed by the alien and therefore monstrous pods. Yet, the subtle method of the pods is not so much an assault on normality as a gradual subversion, which in turn renders any of the film's displays of normality insecure and unstable. The film defines normality as the small town community, where everyone knows everyone else; there are families with children, people mowing their lawns, barbecues in the garden and so forth, all the hallmarks of idealized small town or suburban communities. Deviant behavior is only marginal at first – a boy runs away from home, insisting that his mother is not his mother, and Becky's cousin Wilma feels the same about her uncle Ira. When these individuals return to their normal patterns of behavior, Miles begins to question what "normal" even means ("How could Jimmy and Wilma seem to be normal now?" cf. Biskind 138). However, once doubt in the authenticity of the town's normality is instilled, "all forms of normalcy are inverted" (Samules 209), meaning that markers of normality instead serve as markers of monstrosity. The film thus generates a paranoid attitude which renders any otherwise "normal" patterns of behavior suspicious. Normality and monstrosity become so tightly interwoven as to be inseparable.

As Jancovich remarks, the horror is not in the aliens' difference, but their similarity to normal Americans (*Rational* 66). Grant further claims that *Invasion of the Body Snatchers* (1956) is the "first postwar horror film to locate the monstrous in the normal" (7), even before *Psycho* (1960).[8] While the dialogue and

---

7   Technically, the pod duplication does amount to "asexual reproduction," yet while the pod growth involves monstrously distorted childbirth imagery, it has rather little to do with human procreation, as the numbers and identities (though not the loyalties) of Santa Mira's population remain exactly the same.

8   "The normal" applies in two meanings here. First, the setting, a small and intact town in the contemporary US marks a departure from horror conventions, which typically located the monster on the edges of civilization or as relics of the past. Second, the monsters themselves take the guise of "normal" people, although normal is relative

Miles's narration stress the difference of the pods, their appearance and actions mostly project sameness. The film employs very few visual markers that conventionally signify monstrosity in genre films; only the growth process of the pods, their ejection from oversized seed pods in bubbling foam, represents a visible violation of natural categories, as a grotesque parody of human childbirth and a transgression of the boundary between plant and human. The remainder of the pods' monstrosity is entirely intellectual in nature. The soft-spoken pod representative Kauffman would barely register as monstrous, were it not for the horror associated with the unwilling loss of all human emotion, and even this downside needs to be weighed against the perks of the pod state. As quoted earlier, Siegel saw a strong case for being a pod, and further stressed that the dull world of the pods "is the world that most of us live in" (Kaminsky 154), which would equate it with normality.

The institutions designed to maintain the normality of Santa Mira, from the police to the mental health expert Kauffman, are all revealed as part of the pod conspiracy. In fact, it is the police chief who gives orders regarding the distribution of seed pods to neighboring communities, which suggests that despite the pods' supposed equality, the social hierarchy of Santa Mira is not upended. In addition, the infiltrated authorities demonstrate the abusive potential that society might mobilize against deviants (cf. Warren 290). Regardless of the degree of pod infiltration, society's structural inertia favors the pods. Kauffman's task as a psychiatrist is enforcing conformity, and whether he is a pod or not is unlikely to alter his approach (Jancovich, *Rational* 66-67). Even Miles unwittingly suppresses his patients, advising Becky's cousin to subordinate her perceptions to those of others (essentially, asking her to be outer-directed) and diagnosing that "the trouble is inside you." Later, Kauffman appeals to Miles as a scientific man, suggesting that scientific-rational mindset would be in favor of the pods. In short, Santa Mira's institutions are a liability, rationality leaves the town defenseless against the pods, and experts prove to be useless (Jancovich, *Rational* 66-68). This is where the film's added epilogue marks a significant change: the psychiatrist and police outside of Santa Mira appear trustworthy, and take action when Miles's story is verified, even though that takes a near-miraculous coincidence. The conclusion turns around from a broad suspicion and dismissal of all authorities to presenting them as potential saviors. Still, Jancovich concludes that even the added ending "cannot finally erase the distrust of experts which the film has encouraged up to this point" (*Rational* 76).

---

here – the pods are, after all, alien invaders with fantastic origins, as opposed to *Psycho's* still human, if schizophrenic killer Norman Bates.

The contexts of the Cold War and of American society's post-war development are layered throughout *Invasion of the Body Snatchers* (1956). The film is loaded with the fears of its time and blends them into a dystopia of subversion, conformity and dehumanization, and it is precisely this ambiguity which has kept the film interesting for a spectrum of critics.

INVASION OF THE BODY SNATCHERS (1978)

The first remake was still produced on a moderate budget, but the appearance of recognizable actors, with Donald Sutherland in the lead, definitely represented a step up from the first film's B-movie roots. Compared to the 1956 film, the production of the remake was fairly smooth, with no drastic changes in post production, and the reception by critics and audiences was quite positive.[9] While the film was well-received at the time, it has drawn less academic interest than its predecessor and is mostly discussed in relation to that film and others in the *Body Snatchers* remake sequence. The adaptation to the vastly different setting of 1970s urban America brings about thematic changes, and the fears of the Cold War are replaced by a profound sense of urban alienation and paranoia, which is rooted in a distrust of both institutions and human relationships.

The story remains fairly close to the previous film, and even though the running time is about 30 minutes longer, the key plot points remain mostly identical with the exception of the ending. As the most obvious change, the action is moved from the small town to the city of San Francisco. All key roles are preserved, but the characters' names and occupations are reshuffled. Miles becomes Matthew, a public servant instead of a medical practitioner; Becky goes by Elizabeth and has a career of her own, and while Jack Bellicec is still a writer, he is struggling and runs a mud bath with his wife Nancy. Kauffman is now called Kibner, perhaps to avoid confusion with the film's director (Grant 95), and publishes celebrated self-help books. The central relationship between Matthew and Elizabeth is reframed as a triangle with the introduction of Elizabeth's partner Geoffrey. There is also a certain narrative tightening, in that Elizabeth fuses the roles of Becky (male protagonist's love interest) and Becky's cousin Wilma

---

9 Muir quotes a number of positive contemporary reviews, including an ecstatic Pauline Kael (*Horror 1970s*, 544-545). Exact documentation on box office numbers is harder to come by, but *Box Office Mojo* offers a lifetime gross of 25 million $ on a budget of 3,5 million, which is decent at any rate, and mentions that the film debuted at number 1 ("Invasion of the Body Snatchers").

(character who feels that a loved one has been replaced, thus setting the plot into motion).

Invasion of the Body Snatchers (1978) dispenses with the framing device. The opening scene follows the departure of spores from an alien planet, their travel through space and landing in the city of San Francisco, where they grow into small pods tipped by a flower. One of the pods is picked up and brought home by Elizabeth Driscoll, a lab technician at the city's Department of Public Health. When Elizabeth's partner changes behavior, she asks her friend Matthew Bennell, a health inspector at the same department, for advice. Matthew introduces her to psychiatrist Kibner, who suggests social changes as the root of the alienation between the couple. However, Matthew's friends, the Bellicecs, find an unfinished duplicate body at their business, and Matthew finds a duplicate of Elizabeth at her place. They alarm the authorities, but the bodies vanish, and Matthew's further attempts to warn about the pod infiltration lead nowhere. After he finds and destroys more pods in his garden, Matthew and Elizabeth go into hiding, but are found by Kibner, who reveals himself as a pod. Matthew and Elizabeth again escape, ending up at the harbor where pods are grown and shipped worldwide. Elizabeth is replaced, and Matthew attempts to destroy the facility, but as the ending reveals, he too is ultimately replaced by a pod.

The 1978 film is not only a remake that restages the same story in a different time and place, it also works as a homage that "contains elements of sequels" (Leitch, quoted in Loock 138), and the director Philip Kaufman even claimed that "his film is not so much a remake as a sequel" (Grant 94). The crucial scene for this claim follows Matthew and Elizabeth on a drive through the city. At an intersection, their car is approached by a seemingly crazed man who yells incoherent warnings and runs away to be killed off screen, presumably by another car. For viewers unfamiliar with the 1956 film, the scene is yet another in a long line of disconcerting events that hint at the pod conspiracy. However, the crazed man is played by Kevin McCarthy, Miles Bennell in the 1956 film, who repeats the frantic warnings which concluded that film's main narrative: "They're coming . . . You're next!" (see fig. 4). As the scene quotes the earlier film, using the same actor, it implies continuity between the two narratives (Grant 93, Loock 138), and Kaufman suggests that the character of Miles has been on the run since the first film (Kaufman, cf. Holston and Winchester 288).[10] Viewing the two films as one continuous narrative also erases the added framing scenes of the 1956 films, which imposed a more hopeful ending on Siegel's deeply pessimistic cut. Instead, the 1978 film takes the ending point intended by Siegel and trans-

---

10 The 1978 film credits name McCarthy's character as "Running Man," which leaves his relation to 1956's Miles Bennell unclear.

plants it, segueing the narrative of the first film into the remake and adding a new conclusion – the unceremonious death of Miles Bennell.

However, this is only one short scene in a 110 minute film, and the hints toward continuity are contradicted by the rest of the narrative. After all, the opening scene tracks the journey of the pod spores from an alien planet, not from a pod-laden Santa Mira produce truck. The progress of the pod subversion is noticeable over the course of the film, and given the speed of the pods' spread, it would seem impossible for that process to have dragged on for the 22 years between the two films. On an extratextual level, an insistence on continuity would require the audience to negotiate two similarly named, yet slightly different casts of characters going through the same story, and a dedicated sequel would of course avoid that kind of awkwardness. Reading the 1978 film as a literal sequel, then, does not work out.

This does not mean that McCarthy's scene should be dismissed as a simple in-joke for fans, even though it serves that purpose as well. More importantly, his appearance acknowledges and honors the previous film, serving as a tribute (Loock 138), and adds legitimacy to the potentially controversial project of remaking a well-regarded film. A cameo by Don Siegel as a cab driver later in the film serves the same purpose and implies Siegel's blessing for the remake. In more general terms, these appearances also foreground the fictionality of the story and the exchangeability of actors and characters. For a brief moment, the remake admits that it is not unique and unprecedented, but acknowledges that it is a derivative.

In Leitch's terms, *Invasion of the Body Snatchers* (1978) should be classified as a true remake, since it uses the 1956 film as its primary source while updating the setting and themes to the late 1970s (cf. Leitch 49). Only Matthew's attempt to destroy the pod greenhouse towards the end of the film alludes to Finney's novel, which means that the triangular relation between the remake and its sources is still massively skewed in favor of the 1956 film. At the same time, the 1978 film also displays a distinct drive towards improving on its predecessor. The remake not only intensifies the horror generated by the scenario and individual scenes, it also corrects plot inconsistencies, and even seeks to rectify the much maligned studio decision to amend the ending of the 1956 film. Instead of letting the protagonist alarm the well-meaning authorities, the remake turns him into a pod and cements the defeat of humanity by having him betray the last human survivor. Thereby the remake not only restores the pessimistic conclusion planned by Siegel, which would have had Miles as a crazed last survivor, it actually tops it. That narrative turn also assures a climactic shock moment for viewers familiar with the 1956 film. As the podification of Becky's counterpart Elizabeth is to be expected, the remake ups the ante by also turning Matthew into a pod. The 1978 film thus aims to realize what the 1956 film should have been, at least in the minds of the director and a vocal segment of critics and fans, and then to outdo it.

Paranoia and Alienation

While the first *Invasion of the Body Snatchers* (1956) sparked lengthy debates about its ideology, the 1978 remake has yielded far less controversy. Nevertheless, the remake is just as attuned to its historical context and contemporary cultural anxieties as its predecessor. An intense sense of paranoia permeates the film, but its objects have shifted from the 1956 film. The Cold War, frequently invoked as a frame of reference for the 1956 film, no longer plays a role in the remake. Over the course of the 1970s, the Cold War had simmered down again after events like Nixon's visit to China in 1972 and the conclusion of the Vietnam War in 1975. Consequently, Muir sees fears of communism replaced by fears of a "domestic crisis," in light of a self-absorbed "me" generation, the (perceived) fragmentation of society, and a general distrust in the wake of Vietnam and Watergate (*Horror 1970s,* 548). In the film, these concerns manifest in two objects of fear: government conspiracy and emotional alienation (548).

The pods' creeping takeover is explicitly called a conspiracy in the dialogue, and government institutions are inevitably involved, from the police that cover up evidence of the pods and isolate humans to the garbage trucks that work day and night to dispose of human remains. For the more counterculture-attuned Bellicecs, the revelation fits into a worldview already dominated by conspiracy theories. Even when evidence of the pods' activities is still thin, Jack Bellicec is already convinced of a "big conspiracy" that involves "everything." Matthew, as a more trusting government employee, still attempts to use the system against the pods, but his efforts are futile. A montage of phone calls to shows the extent of Matthew's struggles, and also the nebulous complexity of government institutions. It is unclear whether Matthew is blocked by pods inside the agencies, or whether existing structures are simply incapable of reacting to the threat. Considering the film's paranoid stance, it would seem to make little difference. The pods' use of existing government structures is essential to their ultimate victory over humankind, and even though a distinct distrust in authorities was already present in the 1956 film, it is more pronounced in the 1978 version. Where the first film added an epilogue to restore hope and trust in the authorities, the remake never strays from its portrayal of government authorities as either suspicious or downright threatening.

The pods may successfully employ government structures, but their takeover is also facilitated by urban anonymity and emotional alienation (Muir, *Horror 1970s* 548). As people lead increasingly shallow relationships and instantly distance themselves from any sort of problem, they are unable to realize the pod takeover going on around them. The aforementioned scene with Kevin McCarthy's running man is just one example for this tendency. Matthew and Elizabeth are reluctant to get involved, and as soon as a policeman appears on the scene, they gladly depart. Their apathy and trust in authorities keep them from learning about the pods. As Kibner explains to Elizabeth with regard to a different incident, as a response to shock "you wanted to shut your feelings off, withdraw. Maybe make believe it wasn't happening, because then you don't have to deal with it." The tendency towards emotional disengagement and apathy already prefigures the pod state, which is characterized by a total lack of emotion.

Kibner's observations on emotions and relationships are the closest equivalent to Miles's speech on human callousness ("we harden our hearts...") from the 1956 film, in that they insinuate a link between common human patterns of behavior and the pods. Since the pod state is merely a continuation of human tendencies, the pods are not an absolute Other, and monstrosity is therefore located in normality. However, the realization is not as clear as in the 1956 film, and its impact is therefore much lower. Kibner does not draw a direct comparison between humanity and the pods, knowledge of whom is not confirmed at this point. The uncertainty whether or not Kibner is a pod at this point offers another complication, as it is impossible to tell whether Kibner truly believes what he says or merely tries to keep Elizabeth from learning the truth. Nevertheless, his points still amount to the film's thesis statement regarding the human condition in late 1970s urban America.

The lives of Americans, pod or not, are characterized by bland conformity and thoughtless consumerism. When the pods capture Matthew and Elizabeth, Elizabeth's partner Geoffrey claims that podification makes no difference whatsoever: "Nothing changes, you can have the same life, the same clothes, the same car." The stress on clothes and cars implies that life is defined only by material possessions. Tellingly, Geoffrey spends his free time watching television commercials (cf. Kaufman).[11] The emotional emptiness that accompanies this lifestyle is presented as another perk. Kibner promises that "You'll be born again into an untroubled world. Free of anxiety, fear, hate." The first sentence is an exact quote from the 1956 film, but the second sets new priorities. Where the 1956

---

11 Notably, the same year sees the release of *Dawn of the Dead* (1978), which tackles consumerism more directly (cf. chapter 6)

pods promised sameness and overcoming "love, desire, ambition, faith," their 1978 counterparts merely aim to get rid of unpleasant and unwanted emotion.

The protagonists' hopeless struggle against pod conformity works as a general metaphor for social trends, but it can also be read as a more specific commentary on the decline and dissolution of post-1960s counterculture. Hoberman calls Matthew and Elizabeth "ex-hippies" (30), and while these two may already have given in to conformity by taking government jobs, the Bellicecs remain more clearly part of the counterculture. Jack's worn-out US army jacket and his deep suspicion of FBI and CIA suggest a (past) involvement in protest movements, and Nancy's familiarity with pseudoscientific literature (Immanuel Velikovsky's *Worlds in Collision*) and belief in UFO mysticism hints towards some sort of New Age esotericism. For the Bellicecs, the revelation of an inhuman, all-encompassing conspiracy that enforces mindless conformity is hardly a paradigm shift – it is the world they already live in. Consequently, the Bellicecs and Nancy in particular adapt to the new situation rather quickly. Nancy's belief that plants have feelings may be an unwitting punchline (after all, the pods are born from plants and do not have feelings), but she is quick to develop a somewhat accurate working theory on the origins of the pods, based on esoteric UFO beliefs. Nancy also develops a method for escaping the pods' notice by hiding her emotions. In the end, however, the Bellicecs' countercultural background gives them only a slight edge. They cannot escape assimilation by the pods, they just see it coming.

It is not quite clear how much the film laments the decline of the counterculture into bland conformity and consumerism, and how much it blames it for its own demise and a crumbling social fabric in general. Director Philip Kaufman stresses that he saw the 1960s as a brief period of Americans waking up from a "conforming, other-directed" lifestyle (Hoberman 30), which implies some degree of appreciation for the 1960s counterculture movements. However, Hoberman suggests that the "pop-sociological context" for the 1978 film is found in Christopher Lasch's 1979 book *The Culture of Narcissism*, a distinctly conservative work that blames the decline of the traditional family in favor of self-centered personalities on counterculture movements (30).[12] Grant draws the same connection and considers the 1978 film "an ironic critique of me-generation hedonism and the culture of narcissism" (94). The references to Lasch seem to insinuate a somewhat conservative viewpoint for the 1978 film. If

---

12 Even though Lasch's book was published after the film, Hoberman views it as an indicator of a late-1970s zeitgeist that, in light of the Moscone-Milk assassinations and the People's Temple mass suicide in Guyana, suggested that "the wages of lifestyle might be death" (30).

the fact that, in Kibner's words, "the whole family unit is shot to hell" is partly responsible for the pod takeover, then it stands to reason that the film would favor a return to the family unit and more traditional relationships. Yet, the role of Geoffrey as a malevolent boyfriend puts suspicion on such relationship arrangements, and the romance between Matthew and Elizabeth never develops into a traditional or alternative relationship model. Compared to the romance in the 1956 film, which drives both Miles's and Becky's actions throughout the film, it appears more subdued, and remains limited to a timid kiss and unanswered declarations of love. Notably, no intentions of having children are uttered, nor is any concern for "our wives, our children" expressed. Family is not on the table for Matthew and Elizabeth.

Regardless of the protagonists' ambitions, their relationship still ends with the female lead being replaced by a pod. Becky's transformation in the 1956 film has been read as the focal point of anxieties of sexuality and women, and the same still applies to the corresponding scene in the remake (cf. Nelson 58). However, the altered sequence of Elizabeth's replacement and reveal subtly shifts the scene's impact. Where a shocking kiss revealed Becky's apparent change of mind in the 1956 film, followed by Miles's lamentations about the "death" of her soul, the remake shows the graphic disintegration and unambiguous death of Elizabeth's body, followed by the rise of an immaculate pod copy in her image. By foregrounding the replacement process, the remake effectively divorces human Elizabeth and her pod replacement. Since Matthew, along with the audience, can clearly track the switch from original to Other Elizabeth, the sense of betrayal is arguably lessened; after all, Elizabeth evidently does not turn on Matthew, only her pod impostor does. In addition, the scene's shock effect is soon overshadowed by the film's climactic twist, the revelation that Matthew, too, has been replaced by a pod. The ultimate act of betrayal, attributed to Becky in the 1956 film, is now committed by Matthew.

The procedure and context of Elizabeth's replacement would seem to deflate the menacing femininity embodied by 1956's Becky, but new complications arise instead. Most importantly, pod Elizabeth appears in the nude, which charges her with a physical sexuality that stands in sharp contrast to her mechanical mannerisms (her appeals to Matthew sound impatient rather than seductive; contrast with a similar scene in *Body Snatchers* (1993)) and blends with the monstrous threat conveyed by her pod origins. Nelson views the scene as a reversal in gender roles, with pod Elizabeth revealing a "dominating, uncontrollable and fearsome female sexuality" (58) that threatens Matthew's masculinity. Still, that threat hits Matthew less intimately than Miles, as he rarely feels the need to reassert his masculinity in interactions with women.[13] For comparison, the pervasive suspicion of women in the 1956 film was partly traced to Don Siegel's radical conception of rugged individualism (cf. Gregory 8), which has largely vanished from the 1978 remake. Matthew may follow the same trajectory of isolation from society, but unlike the self-employed physician Miles, he is comfortably part of a bureaucratic structure, and seems to relish in the authority given to him by the health department. Since the more radical anti-social and anti-government positions are voiced by the Bellicecs, Matthew hardly registers as a social outsider, of the rugged individualist type or any other.

In *Invasion of the Body Snatchers* (1978), normality is characterized by fragile human relationships and a general social trend towards conformity and self-absorbed consumerism that increasingly marginalizes outsiders like the Bellicecs. The state of late 1970s America leaves it vulnerable to the pods, which capitalize on these trends and lead them to their ultimate conclusion, a society that is utterly numb and apathetic. This correlation is already insinuated early in the film, when Elizabeth tries to identify an alien pod-flower and finds references to dangerous crossed plant species that thrive on devastated ground (cf. Robinson 30). The success of the pods can thus be explained by contemporary San Francisco being fertile ground, but the prerequisite devastation is limited to human relationships.

Pod and Body Horror

The previous section has already gained some insight on the pods' relationship with normality, but a closer look at the pods themselves is required to fully appreciate their potential meanings. Among the various changes and updates of the 1978 remake, a clear tendency towards the dehumanization of the pods is evident. The pods' growth process is more grotesque and repulsive, their lack of emotion is more pronounced and threatening, and they are clearly marked as inhuman and monstrous. In contrast to the 1956 film, there is "little argument in favor of podification" to be found (Hoberman 30).

The 1978 film pays much attention to the technical aspects of pod reproduction. Thanks to advances in special effects and a larger budget, pod growth is shown in more vivid and unpleasant detail, which follows the contemporary genre trend towards body horror. During the lengthy pod duplication/birth sequence

---

13 Miles is not only flirtatious with Becky; even his interactions with his receptionist Sally are heavy on innuendo, and he leaves no doubt as to his seductive powers: "My interest in married women is strictly professional, or yours would have been a lost cause long ago."

at Matthew's house, pods are shown as oversized, slime-covered embryos that writhe about while slowly growing into the likeness of their human counterparts. Familiar images of human bodies and childbirth are recombined to evoke disgust and drive home the point that the very formation of the pods is already a monstrous offense against the natural order. Not only are categories like *plant* and *human* violated, the growth process also contradicts human stages of development by skipping from an adult-sized embryo to the fully formed adult. At the same time, the integrity of the human body is subverted by the effect the process has on the original body, as demonstrated by Elizabeth's graphic decay. The human body thus cannot be trusted for two reasons: it may be fake, or it may easily fall apart after being sucked dry by a pod.

In addition, the film strives to develop a consistent model of podification and avoid the logical flaws of the first film. Seed pods are not only placed in proximity to their targets, they also grow fine tendrils that establish a physical connection through which the duplication is enabled. The 1978 film also confirms Miles's speculation about the fate of the original bodies by showing the complete disintegration of Elizabeth as she is replaced by a pod. The increased concern for pod bodies serves two purposes. First, it serves to increase horror and monstrosity, exploiting the pod growth for shock effect and reinforcing out the inhumanity of the monsters. Second, it expands on the first film, and corrects its most blatant inconsistency, the change of Becky, in order to improve on that film.

In their fully developed form, pods remain physically indistinguishable from humans. Even though the remake upholds this element of the story, it still finds a way of marking the pods as monstrous by having them utter a scream whose piercing sound would be impossible for humans to generate. As the film progresses, the pods operate more openly and frequently discard human speech in favor of pointing and screaming, which effectively drops the human façade and signals their alien nature. The scream is remarkably effective as a symbolic act of exclusion from the now pod dominated community, and therefore, as a metaphor for othering processes. It also functions as a reminder to the audience that the pods are not human after all – an auditory marker of monstrosity.[14] Moreo-

---

14 The film's final shot of Matthew pointing and screaming at Nancy Bellicec is still an iconic genre image, and has gone on to serve as a minor in-joke (or *meme*) among particular internet fan communities. For example, when posters express their dislike of an otherwise sacrosanct work, others would post said image of Matthew to (jokingly) mark them as outcasts from the fan community. While localized, this behavior illustrates the lasting impact of the 1978 film and the effectiveness of its othering metaphor.

ver, the dehumanization of the pods extends to their behavior. Their characteristic lack of emotions is expressed as a total lack of compassion and performed more consistently compared to the 1956 film. For instance, pod Becky's performance is still a theatrical display of spite, whereas pod Elizabeth acts with a mechanical indifference that is inverse to the dramatic importance of the scene and thereby accentuates her lack of humanity. As with the pods' biology, the consequences of their mental state are realized more thoroughly.

As another example for the revision of the pods, the contrast between the two pod spokesmen, 1956's Kauffman and 1978's Kibner, is striking. Where Kauffman is calm and smiling, and attempts to persuade Miles using reason, Kibner and his fellow pods immediately use brutal force on Matthew and Elizabeth and sedate them to speed up pod takeover. The arguments for being a pod are more incidental to Kibner's approach; his cold rationality leaves no regard for individual choice. Matthew's pleas ("David, you're killing me!") are met with indifference, and Elizabeth's expression of hatred prompts Kibner to explain, "We don't hate you. There's no need for hate. Or love." Perhaps paradoxically, even though the 1978 film depicts the pods as more monstrous throughout, it still refrains from equating that monstrosity with malevolence. Admittedly, part of Kibner's ambiguity can be traced not to the character itself, but also to an extratextual factor – his casting. Grant commends the casting of Leonard Nimoy as the "ideal pod spokesperson" (96), since Nimoy's defining role as Spock on *Star Trek* is renowned as the embodiment of pure reason. In a variation of what Verevis calls "celebrity intertextuality" (*Film* 20), Nimoy's personal intertext of positively connoted rationality is subverted by his casting as the personification of a menacing and inhumane rationality, thus generating tension between audience expectations and the story unfolding on screen (cf. Muir, *Horror 1970s* 549).

Kibner acts as the film's main antagonist, and as the face of a monstrous threat otherwise characterized by its impersonal collectivity. Yet according to Robinson, the problem with Kibner is "not so much his post-pod personality, but our suspicions about his pre-transformation character" (33). Early in the film, before evidence of the pods solidifies, Jack Bellicec accuses Kibner of trying to "change people to fit the world" with his brand of pop-psychiatry self-help books. As it turns out, Jack's assessment is spot on: the objective of the pods, after all, is turning people into emotionless replicas that can function more easily in a dull world, and therefore, the pods represent the logical continuation of Kibner's work as a psychiatrist. The character of Kibner reverberates with a general distrust of psychiatrists, but more specifically, the film voices a critique of an ideal of mental health that is viewed as a limitation of human experience and a prerequisite for a disaffected materialism or consumerism.

Essentially, this interpretation is fairly similar to some of the approaches discussed in regard to the 1956 film (e.g. Samuels and Jancovich, *Rational*), except for the replacement of Fordist society with a slightly adjusted, contemporary form of social conformity. For a close remake of the same story, such an update to contemporary social contexts is the expected outcome. However, the question remains whether the marked dehumanization of the pods in the 1978 film undercuts these points. In order for the pods to function as a metaphor for contemporary social trends, they still need to register as basically human. With their more monstrous origins and behavior, and without Miles's reminder that all humans may follow the same path, 1978's pods are clearly less human than their 1956 counterparts. With reference to Wood, we may even read the depiction of a more inhuman monster as a shift towards a more conservative viewpoint that vindicates the status quo (cf. Wood 192). Nevertheless, the pods only thrive because of social trends already in place, because normality is already flawed and headed in their direction. The heightened callousness of the pods does not serve to distance them from an idealized normality; it serves to raise the tension and the remake's effectiveness as a horror film.

Finally, while *Invasion of the Body Snatchers* (1956) is rated as the original film by critics and scholars, and remains the prime subject of monographs and articles, the 1978 version seems to have attained a secondary position as the original remake (e.g. on the cover of Loock and Verevis, eds.). The fact that the most recent remake, *The Invasion* (2007), makes references to the 1978 film also suggests canonization. Yet even though the 1978 remake is widely lauded as highly accomplished, it still cannot eclipse the original. At least as far as academic attention is concerned, this seeming lack of appreciation need not be based on an unfair preference towards supposed originals. A more accomplished film by standards of filmmaking craft does not necessarily hold more interest for academic studies, and the confusion of clashing ideologies in the 1956 film, combined with its slice of unabashed 1950s zeitgeist, may just yield more material for debate than 1978's more refined picture.

BODY SNATCHERS (1993)

The second remake perhaps rates as the most obscure film of the *Body Snatchers* sequence. Even though the film shared its producer with the successful 1978 remake and was directed by Abel Ferrara, who had previously gained recognition for his independent films, it was plagued by a difficult production. Due to the studio's lack of confidence and complex internal politics it "barely made it into cinemas" (Stevens 173, 180). As a result of a very limited run, the box office take was abysmal, despite somewhat positive reviews.[15] Academic interest also appears rather limited, and the film mostly features in retrospectives on Ferrara's work or the *Body Snatchers* sequence. While a minor canonical position may be argued for the 1978 film, the same does not apply to the 1993 version, nor is it acknowledged by the next remake in the sequence, *The Invasion* (2007).

The 1993 film reverts to the title of the source novel, *Body Snatchers,* yet the tagline "The Invasion Continues" seeks to link up with the previous filmic adaptations of the story, even though no narrative continuity is suggested in the text. In fact, the narrative takes significant departures from all of its source materials by swapping the cast of characters and moving the action to a military base. The basic story remains similar – a dwindling group of characters uncovers subversion by alien impostors and subsequently has to take flight – but plot points, character roles and motives are rearranged, with a nuclear family now at the center of the story.

The Malone family, consisting of Steve, a chemist for the US Environmental Protection Agency, his teenage daughter Marti (from his first marriage), and his new wife Carol and son Andy, travels to a military base in the American South, where Steve is to verify the safe storage of biochemical weapons. While Marti gets romantically involved with Tim, a helicopter pilot, evidence of strange happenings at the base slowly mounts. The chief medical officer, Major Collins, tells Steve about a wave of paranoia among the personnel. Andy witnesses the decay of his mother's body and the emergence of a duplicate, but his reports are not taken seriously. Soon thereafter, the pods attempt a simultaneous attack on the Malone home. Marti and Steve are covered in plant tendrils and duplicate bodies begin to grow, but Marti is saved by chance and escapes with her father and Andy. Halfway through the chase, a firefight erupts between pods and humans. Steve attempts to warn the outside world, but is told by an exhausted Mj. Collins that it is futile. Caught by the pods, Collins chooses suicide, whereas Steve is replaced by a pod and killed by Marti when she finds out. During the escape, Marti is captured and rescued again, and Andy, too, is revealed as a pod and killed. Marti and Tim finally manage to take off in a helicopter and proceed to destroy convoys leaving the base and the base itself with rockets. With the destruction complete, they fly to Atlanta. Over the closing scene, a distorted voice-over repeats the pods' earlier threats and leaves the ending ambiguous.

---

15 *IMDb* gives a gross of 428,868 $ at an estimated budget of 13 million $ ("Body Snatchers (1993)," *IMDb*). Review aggregator sites tend to be less accurate pre-2000s, but *Rotten Tomatoes* records 71% positive reviews ("BODY SNATCHERS (1993)," *Rotten Tomatoes*).

While the 1978 film mostly relocated, updated and expanded the events that made up the narrative of the 1956 film, the 1993 version attempts a more extensive reconception of the story and cast. Steve Malone bears a few similarities to Miles and Matthew Bennell of the 1956 and 1978 films respectively, in that he has a scientific profession, tries to methodically investigate the pod infiltration, and is betrayed by his love interest. However, Steve is not the film's uncontested primary character; that role is filled by his daughter instead. Marti's central role is emphasized by her voiceover narration, which opens and closes the film, delivers exposition, and foreshadows the coming horrors. Since her narrative arc of teenage rebellion has no precedent in any other version of the story, some of the previous protagonists' key scenes are transferred to minor characters. Now Andy is the one to witness the traumatic decay and replacement of a loved one, and Collins debates the pods and tries to call the outside world. The phone call, during which the operator on the other end of the line reveals herself as part of the pod conspiracy by referencing Collins by name, plays out almost identically in all four *Body Snatchers* films. In short, the role of Miles/Matthew Bennell is broken up and distributed over several characters, while the new protagonist Marti mostly follows her own narrative arc. Therefore, the narrative of the previous films is arguably preserved, but frequently confined to the background. This remaking strategy might also be read as an element of homage in a film otherwise bent on distancing itself from its predecessors.[16]

Like the previous remake, the 1993 remake is set in the present day, which means that it inevitably invokes a new set of contexts specific to its time period. For a start, the mention of biochemical weapons and Steve's role as an EPA inspector introduce a discourse on infection and chemical contamination that touches on contemporary fears (cf. Huygens 58). While the 1956 film compared the pods to disease, the 1993 film also associates them with environmental contamination. Taking the military setting into account, the contamination discourse may furthermore connect to Gulf War syndrome, the mysterious condition that afflicted many veterans of the 1990-1991 Gulf War (Muir, *Horror 1990s* 318).[17]

---

16 For example, in contrast to the 1978 and 2007 remakes, the 1993 film is devoid of any cameo appearances that could serve as a playful nod to the earlier films.

17 As with the link between AIDS and *The Thing* (1982), the Gulf War syndrome link might be something that colors later readings, but did not yet inform cultural anxieties at the time of production. In addition, the specific nature of the condition and its limitation to war veterans would seem to limit its potential as a widespread cultural anxiety. Reading it as a permutation of a general suspicion of returning war veterans, which might be traced back to the Korean and Vietnam Wars, might work better for *Body Snatchers* (1993).

Collins's inquiries about the possible psychological consequences of exposure to chemicals may be read as a commentary on that phenomenon as well as post-traumatic stress (PTSD). The Gulf War is subtly established as background for the military characters, as Marti's love interest Tim Young mentions having shot at people in Kuwait, and the conclusion's aerial bombardment might well be read in that context.

More historical readings abound. In a moderately compelling interpretation, Muir reads the pods' drive towards conformity as a reflection of 1990s "political correctness" (Muir, *Horror 1990s* 318). Hoberman draws a broader historical parallel and concludes that "the movie collapses the whole of baby-boomer history – from the Cold War through Vietnam to the New World Order – into a single package" (30). An even wider range of possible associations is offered by Brenez, who reads *Body Snatchers* in context of Ferrara's other works. She sees three "dimensions of human experience" in the film: "family romance," industrial pollution and global militarization, and a "retrospective meditation on 'Hiroshima man'", by which she means the shadow-like residue of atomic bomb victims (6).[18] She goes on to claim that the film asks three questions, the historical question of what the use of nukes on Japan tells us about the society responsible, the political question what to do against "industrial standardization of the entire world", and the biological question about the "life-drive"(7). Brenez's multifaceted and at times rambling analysis finds few concrete answers to any of these questions, however.

Director Ferrara himself offers another take on the theme of infection and suggests a parallel to AIDS in the 1990s, but remains vague on both details and other possible meanings: "Obviously it's a metaphor for *something*" (quoted in Stevens 174). Ferrara's statement is mostly a general claim for relevance, but hardly conducive to an in-depth analysis. AIDS had certainly reached the public consciousness at that point in time, and reinforced fears of lethal infection, especially through sexual contact. The relative increase in sexualized horror in the 1993 film may be viewed as an expression of these fears. Between the seduction attempts of pod Carol and pod Marti, sexual temptation is represented as highly dangerous. Ultimately, though, two other thematic clusters are more pronounced in the film and therefore merit closer examination: first, the role of military culture and conformity, and second, the disintegration of the nuclear family at the center of the narrative.

---

18 To Brenez, the use of atomic bombs on Hiroshima and Nagasaki qualifies as "the most violent act of aggression ever inflicted on humanity" (6), an assessment which is at least debatable.

Military Authority and Conformity

In the two previous films (1956 and 1978), the pods targeted perfectly ordinary sites of American life: the small town and the city, respectively. The 1956 film in particular derived much of its impact from the idealized normality of its setting, and as the previous sections have shown, the pods have consequently been read as a commentary on general social trends pertaining to that normality. By contrast, *Body Snatchers* shifts focus to what might best be described as a subculture by moving the action to a military base. The base represents a closed community, united in purpose and controlled by a single governmental authority, the US Army. All of the base's regular inhabitants are more or less part of this structure, which enforces different social rules and conventions than the outside world. Therefore, the pod community on base reads more narrowly as a commentary on military culture, and less as a commentary of broader social trends.

According to Grant, the pods mainly function as "a metaphor for the military mentality" (Grant 99). That mentality, the military mindset and organizational structure, turn out to provide ideal conditions for the pods' typical pattern of duplication and gradual takeover. Grant states that the "military mentality . . . makes it impossible to distinguish professional soldiers from those who are pods" (Grant 98),[19] and Stevens makes the same point (Stevens 177). After all, the soldiers on base are already trained to act as part of a collective and to execute orders without emotion getting in the way, and the suppression of the soldiers' individuality is even marked by their uniforms. Put bluntly, the pods go unnoticed because soldiers are pods already.

Whereas the previous films employed the pods towards a more general critique of perceived increases in social conformity, *Body Snatchers* is sharply focused on military conformity. Accordingly, the portrayal of military characters is almost overwhelmingly negative, and Stevens summarizes its attitude in drastic words: "It is perhaps an oversimplification to say that *Body Snatchers* . . . treats America's armed forces with the complete and utter contempt they deserve, but to a large degree this is the case" (177). There are only two exceptions, both of which appear to distance themselves from the Army structure. Major Collins is an outsider due to his medical profession, and Tim Young is critical of his own role and quick to align himself with the civilian Marti. A handful of resistance fighters against the pods appear too briefly to make an impact, as the rest of the soldiers are portrayed as suspicious or menacing from the very start, from the warnings of a fugitive soldier to the hostile reception by General Platt. To sup-

---

19 Grant also draws a comparison to *The Crazies* (1973), which in his estimation used the same approach "to better effect" (Grant 98).

port that portrayal, the film strategically uses lighting and perspective to obscure soldiers' faces, diminishing their humanity and individuality.

Grant suggests that the thorough subversion of the base picks up on Jack Bellicec's suggestion from the 1978 film that "the government is controlled by pods" (98). Without a doubt, the 1993 film is permeated by a deep distrust of the military, and it shows all appointed authorities as working for the pods. However, due to the film's narrow focus on the military base, its paranoia never reaches the scale of the 1978 film. The pod hierarchy duplicates the base hierarchy, and that is headed by General Platt. No other institutions are revealed to be part of the conspiracy, and since Platt sends pod transports to other bases, the contagion is (still) limited to the infrastructure of the US Army. By contrast, the 1978 film implied a vast network of government departments and agencies that might plausibly be in on it, and thus conjured up a total conspiracy. Even though it is possible to read the portrayal of the military in the 1993 film as a synecdoche, the text itself hardly supports the same totality. In addition, 1993's Steve is also a government employee imbued with a certain amount of power, and the first round of his clash with General Platt also represents tensions between civilian and military authorities (EPA and US Army).

Investigating this conflict further, *Body Snatchers* may be read as a bit of a return to a dynamic that characterized the monster movies of the 1950s. As mentioned in the previous chapter, the central conflict between science and military in many of these films has been used as an indicator for their ideological positions (cf. Biskind 131). Applying this approach to the 1993 film, we find that the distrust of experts and intellectuals that was noticeable in the 1956 film in particular has shifted. The male lead Steve is a scientist, and Collins fits that mold as well. Furthermore, the main representative of the pods is no longer a psychiatrist (and thus an intellectual), but instead a military leader. The change underlines that the hierarchical structure of the military is stated as a problem in the film, whereas the psychiatrists in the previous films stood for a softer social pressure to conform.[20] Still, the decrease in anti-intellectual suspicion does not mean that the 1993 film puts its trust in science and experts. If that were the case, Steve and Collins would be more prominent and effective characters. Instead, the shift may be an inadvertent result of the film's distinct anti-military stance, as it deemphasizes the pods' pure rationality (associated with science and

---

20 This is also evidenced in the casting for the pod spokesman and its (mild) celebrity intertextuality. The 1978 film was arguably subversive in casting an actor associated with benevolent rationality; the 1993 film instead casts an actor associated with abusive military authority (R. Lee Ermey, whose acting career was built on his performance as a Marine drill sergeant in *Full Metal Jacket*).

intellectualism) in favor of making a point about conformity (associated with collectivity).

This change in focus becomes evident during the debate between Collins and General Platt. In a scene closely recreated from the previous films, the pods are given the opportunity to clearly articulate their positions. As they encircle the exhausted Collins, Platt tries to convince him of the pods' cause: "When all things are conformed, there'll be no disputes, no conflicts, no problems any longer." The other pods support him in a detached chorus, adding that "it's the race that's important, not the individual" and that "the human race left to its own devices is doomed." Collins counters that the individual is "always important" and chooses suicide before assimilation. Platt identifies human conflicts as the pods' main concern, with the added irony of having soldiers working for an end to conflict, and Collins's reaction elevates the question of collectivity versus individuality to an existential issue. While the pods promised a simpler life without love and anxiety in the previous films, they now seem determined to specifically end strife at the cost of individuality. Grant calls the pods' ideology, with its stress on race and the collective, "fascist" (99), which may point out the core of the film's critique of the Army's conformity: the suspicion that the military mindset engenders fascism and general repression.

Brenez takes a few steps further and reads the film as a much broader critique of the system the military stands for. In the depiction of the military and the pods, she draws connections to a variety of "collective evils" from the Gulf War (1990-91) to Nazism and Hiroshima (7). She also leaps to find the capitalist system "figured as a toxic military base" (10), and views the dissolution of bodies as a reflection on how, among other things, "the American Way of life – this terrifying economic Moloch – exacts, every morning, a toll of human lives viewed as anonymous and of no value" (150). The details of some of Brenez's interpretations may not be obvious from the text alone, considering that the film never offers a perspective outside the military context. The basic sentiment, though, that the pods and the military fuse into some general monstrous evil, certainly amounts to a valid observation.

The conclusion of *Body Snatchers* escalates matters and replaces lingering paranoia with all-out war. Even though the film has spent over an hour subtly or explicitly linking all things military with monstrosity, a military approach appears to be the only effective means of stopping the pods. Thanks to Army equipment and training, Tim is able to wage a one-man war against the base and appears to succeed where 1978's Matthew failed. Even though the film disavows the structure and mindset of the military, it seems to embrace its methods. Marti comments on the attack in voiceover: "Our reaction was only human. Revenge, hate, remorse, despair, pity and most of all fear. I remember feeling all those things as I watched the bombs explode." Marti makes a sobering claim, that violence is human, whereas an absence of conflict, as offered by the pods, would be monstrous. Like its predecessors, *Body Snatchers* postulates anxiety and suffering as inevitable parts of the human experience and brands any attempts to eliminate those as dehumanizing.

Still, any satisfaction from the violent finale is complicated by the by the depiction of wounded pods in the ruins of the base, who appear just as helpless as any human war victim. Considering the final scene – a shot of Atlanta ground crew mechanically guiding in the landing helicopter, while pod Carol's voiceover claims that there is "nowhere to run" – the attack on the pod convoys may be an empty gesture. For Grant, the ending is as ambiguous as the conclusion to the 1956 film (100). A resolution of the pod problem is implied, but its success remains to be confirmed. According to Stevens, though, whether or not the pods succeed makes little difference: "We need not literally assume the soldier has been taken over, since that spirit of conformity represented by the aliens is already present in American life" (Stevens 180).

Family Disintegration

Parallel to the theme of military conformity, *Body Snatchers* dramatizes the collapse of the nuclear family. That narrative strand is driven by the pod infiltration as much as the military one, but the two largely remain separate, which leads to some disagreement about their relative importance. For Stevens, the "decreasing importance of the family unit" is central to the film (Stevens 176), and even though Grant acknowledges that the pods "vaguely represent family tensions," he assigns more importance to the military metaphor (Grant 99). Obviously, the film allows for several plausible readings, and establishing a hierarchy is not necessary in this case. The simple fact that the 1993 film replaces a middle-aged male protagonist and his love interest with a nuclear family of four implies a significant shift that warrants further investigation.

In the previous section, I mentioned Grant's link between *Body Snatchers'* (1993) attitude towards the military and a line of dialogue from the 1978 film (Grant 98). I would suggest that the 1993 film instead expands on another quote from that film, namely Kibner's claim that "the whole family unit is shot to hell." The collapse of the nuclear family is described as a growing social disaster in the 1978 film, but it plays out in the 1993 film. Alternatively, I might as well invoke Miles's warning that "[t]hey're after all of us – our wives, our children" from the 1956 film, because it is a lot more accurate for 1993's Steve, a husband

and father. The family has been threatened by the pods in every iteration of the *Body Snatchers* story, but what has been a hypothetical becomes explicit in the 1993 version.

The Malone family is a fragile conglomeration from the start. Steve's remarriage is a constant source of tension with his daughter Marti, whose alienation from her new family, her stepmother Carol and her half-brother Andy, is established in the expository narration. Marti refers to Carol as "the woman who replaced [her] mom," which already anticipates Carol's replacement by a pod (cf. Stevens 176). The replacement of Carol and later Steve by pods literalizes the estrangement felt by Marti (Nelson 65). Carol is indeed not Marti's real mother, but not only because she is her stepmother – she is not the real Carol, either. Likewise, Marti's fear of being pushed out of the family (she accuses Steve of wanting her out) is realized when all family members betray her, one after the other, and turn out to be pods. Marti then metaphorically enacts her resentments against her family by shooting Steve and dropping Andy out of a helicopter (Grant 99). Once her family ties are cut, she has nothing left but to depart with her boyfriend Tim, after what amounts to a particularly traumatic coming of age narrative.

The portrayal of Marti also echoes a trend towards young female horror protagonists which proliferated in the horror films of the late 1970s and 1980s. Clover famously labeled this emergent character type the "Final Girl" (35), and even though *Body Snatchers* does not follow the slasher paradigm which gave rise to the type, Marti at least shows a few parallels to the Final Girl. Most importantly, she manages to fight back against the pods and survive. Tim may handle the bombardment, but Marti is responsible for dispatching the pod versions of Steve and Andy, and she fully approves of violent revenge against the rest of the pods.

Body Snatchers follows the horror formula that "normality is threatened by the Monster" (Wood 78), but normality is not an idealized state of harmony for the Malone family and especially Marti. Their relationship is already strained by everyday events, the move to a new location, and once the monstrous pods come into play, their patched up nuclear family falls apart under the pressure. Again, the pods continue and exacerbate existing trends and divisions by exploiting rifts inside the family (cf. Nelson 65). This still raises the question how much the film attributes the dissolution of the family to external pressures, and how much it portrays the family itself as inherently dysfunctional. Robinson at least seems to support the latter. She argues that the film "focuses on the oppressive nature of family conformity in the face of dysfunction" (36), and she reads the bombing as Marti's rebellion against oppressive motherhood, family, and military lifestyle (37). The Platt family offers a counterexample: initially, General Platt is only seen at work, his wife is an alcoholic, and his daughter Jenn rebellious. As pod duplication proceeds, Mrs. Platt exchanges alcohol for playing bridge, and Jenn works along with the pod community by trying to trap Marti. The association of traditional family with pod conformity is also brought up by Tim, who supports his pretend change into a pod with the claim that "we're a happy family now." Tellingly, family is the closest analogue for the oppressive and emotionally repressed pod community that Tim is able to come up with.

By contrast, Nelson views the film as an expression of contemporary anxieties about the "changing American family" and gender roles, which would place it more in support of traditional family concepts. She finds that the film assigns clear responsibilities, as it "portrays the breakdown of the nuclear family, largely at the hands of female characters" (64). Marti and Carol are assigned the blame, since "Marti's teen angst fractures the family," while Carol actively undermines it by attempting to convert the other family members (65). In this scenario fueled by heightened popular anxieties, Steve takes the place of a "beleaguered male" who loses his position as head of the household (65). While the film does reflect these anxieties, the narrative perspective arguably reduces their importance. Since the opening narration establishes Marti's point of view as privileged, Steve functions as her antagonist throughout much of the film. He may be a beleaguered male, but the film is not on his side (as opposed to 1956's Miles), it is on Marti's.

Nevertheless, there is a noticeable undercurrent of monstrous femininity and sexuality throughout the film, more so than in the previous versions. As mentioned, Carol is replaced by a pod early on, and even though General Platt is revealed as the leader and spokesman of the pods, Carol acts as the face of the pods and primary antagonist throughout much of the film. Along with the other housewives of the base, she is a primary vector of infection (cf. Robinson 36). Carol's use of manipulation and seduction to sinister ends evokes Becky's betrayal from the 1956 film, as does her farewell monologue to Steve, but pod Carol plays a far more important role in the narrative. Her witch-like performance recalls a host of myths and stereotypes of feminine monstrosity (cf. Brenez 84). Another example of a monstrous seductress is the short-lived pod duplicate of Marti. Appearing nude before Tim, she tempts him to pick her over the real Marti. With her blatantly sexualized mannerisms, pod Marti is "paradoxically desirable and horrifying" (Nelson 58), and Nelson interprets the "fine line" between desire for and fear of female bodies in the *Body Snatchers* films as an expression of male sexual insecurity (58).

The pod duplication process is also charged with sexual overtones. The basic process follows the model of the 1978 film very closely: a seed pod, placed in close proximity to the target, establishes physical contact once the target has fallen asleep and then grows into an exact duplicate. More refined special effects again render the growth process more repulsive than in previous films and emphasize its physicality. At the same time, it is depicted as more invasive, especially in case of the first attempted replacement of Marti. The scene shows Marti nude in a bathtub, while tendrils crawl over her bare chest and into her mouth and nostrils, strongly suggesting sexual violation. Combined with the seductiveness of the female pods, *Body Snatchers* features a much closer association of sexuality and horror, a far cry from 1956's shocking kiss with Becky.

In conclusion, Abel Ferrara's 1993 remake approaches the familiar themes of the *Body Snatchers* narrative from two angles. Both the military and the family are systems that facilitate the pod takeover, as both are predisposed towards conformity and emotional alienation. The pods cannot be distinguished from soldiers because soldiers are conformist drones anyway, and they cannot be distinguished from family members because the family, or at least a patched-up family like the Malones, breeds resentment anyway. The general point remains the same: the pods and their unstoppable pattern of duplication serve as a metaphorical continuation and therefore critique of human tendencies and social trends. The pods may technically be an external threat, but they only succeed because they latch onto an already existing, internal threat; as Stevens puts it, the pods represent "the final triumph of an internal menace" (177).

However, not everyone falls victim to the pods, and *Body Snatchers* leaves two human survivors, Marti and Tim, to reach the dubious safety of the outside world. When it comes to the logic of pod duplication, Kiefer and Stiglegger observe that those who have given themselves up already (e.g. Mrs. Platt) are the first pod victims and seamlessly fit in the new society (28). Stevens makes a similar point, concluding that General Platt and his daughter are unwilling to think for themselves and therefore transformed into pods (178). Stevens draws a parallel to Romero's *Dawn of the Dead* (1978), in that "only individuals who transcend societal structures can successfully resist becoming 'zombies'" (178). In both films, he sees a black man (Collins/Peter) and a white woman (Marti/Fran) as such individuals. The fact that Tim, a white male, is also along for the ride would seem to contradict that argument, but Stevens makes a somewhat awkward exception by rating Tim as a "feminine white male" and an outsider (178). That last point may be more accurate than aiming for racial/gender lines. Both Marti and Tim completely cut their ties to the social structures that constricted their lives, the Malone family for Marti, and the US Army for Tim, and therefore manage to escape as individuals.

THE INVASION (2007)

The first three films in the *Body Snatchers* sequence had all been produced on low to moderate budgets and were, with the exception of the 1978 film, released in moderately respectable channels. The 1956 film was part of a B-movie double feature, the definition of a second-rate film, and the 1993 version was left to the home video market after a negligible theatrical run. The 2007 remake, by contrast, marked a far more ambitious project, at least in terms of production budget and effort. Hollywood stars Nicole Kidman and Daniel Craig were hired as the lead actors, in the case of Kidman at considerable expense. Nevertheless, the release was delayed for over a year, as the first cut from director Oliver Hirschbiegel proved so discouraging to the studio that it staged extensive reshoots with another director, James McTeigue, who was not credited for his work.[21] Despite these efforts, *The Invasion* still ended up as a critical and commercial failure.[22]

The film takes some unprecedented departures from its sources, especially in regard to the pods, which are replaced by a functionally similar alien virus. The characters bear names familiar from earlier iterations, but their occupations are again reshuffled. The protagonist is now Carol Bennell, a divorced psychotherapist and mother based in Washington DC Carol's friend Ben Driscoll is a physician, and Carol's ex-husband Tucker is a government official in the field of public health. TV and radio newscasts are a constant presence in the film and firmly locate the story in the media and political landscape of the mid-2000s.

When a space shuttle disaster spreads debris across the US, CDC official Tucker Kaufman is infected with an alien virus that takes over his body. Kaufman not only uses the CDC's resources to spread the infection under the guise of flu inoculations, he also seeks contact with his estranged ex-wife Carol Bennell, who has custody of their son Oliver. By the time Carol learns of the creeping alien takeover, Kaufman has already abducted Oliver and has her forcibly infected as well. Carol struggles to escape the aliens while trying to find Oliver, a task in which she is aided by her friend Ben Driscoll. In the meantime, the alien takeo-

---

21 Thanks to internet news sites and film blogs, reports of the delay appeared quickly, accompanied by rumors surrounding the reasons for the reshoots and their extent (cf. Sahota).

22 Review aggregator *Rotten Tomatoes* lists only 19% positive reviews ("THE INVASION (2007)"), and box office tracker *Box Office Mojo* puts the film at 15 million $ domestic, plus 25 million foreign, for a total that is only half the estimated 80 million $ budget, a costly failure by any measure ("The Invasion").

ver ushers in an unprecedented era of world peace, as infected leaders bury human conflicts. Keeping the takeover of her own body at bay, Carol finally tracks Oliver down in Baltimore and learns that he is immune against the alien virus and thus presents the key to a cure. Posing as one of the infected, Carol frees Oliver and overcomes the also infected Ben to finally be rescued by a special military unit, who then engineers the cure to be spread across the world. The alien infection is eradicated completely, with everyone affected being returned to their previous state.

The Invasion puts severe strain on Leitch's triangular model of sources for the remake, as it potentially has one literary and three filmic sources to draw from. At this point, the complex network of hypotexts and hypertexts makes it exceedingly difficult to weigh the relative influence of each source. The 2007 film of course repeats general motifs, and still restages specific scenes from earlier films. A child insists that a parent is not their parent, or a married adult insists that their partner has been replaced by an impostor; the alien pods make their case for an emotionless state, a friend turns out to have been replaced, the last humans try to pass for pods by suppressing emotions, and so forth. Since these key scenes have already been remade several times, it may not be possible to determine a clear lineage to one specific iteration of the scene. Instead, the previous films may be considered to merge into one *Body Snatchers* hypotext, containing a pool of themes and plot points that have been severed from individual textual iterations, to be freely rearranged. Therefore, *The Invasion* embodies Verevis's notion (drawing from Stam) that later remakes as "new hypertexts do not necessarily refer back to original hypotexts, but rather encompass the entire chain of remakings that form a 'larger, cumulative hypotext'" (*Film* 83).

Nevertheless, there are still elements of *The Invasion* that point towards particular source texts. The title only repeats one part of the 1956 and 1978 film title – invasion – and neglects the novel *Body Snatchers*. The choice of character names – Bennell, Driscoll, Kaufman – points to the novel and the 1956 film. At the same time, the urban setting and a cameo appearance align the film with the 1978 version. Washington and Baltimore in the 2000s of course look different than 1970s San Francisco, but the sense of urban anonymity is still similar and a far cry from the Californian small town of 1956 or the Southern military base of 1993. An appearance by Veronica Cartwright, who played Nancy Bellicec in the 1978 film, marks the perhaps strongest reference and homage to the earlier film. Cartwright does not resume her role as Nancy, but appears as one of Carol's patients, in a role comparable to 1956's Wilma. Nevertheless, her appearance is a direct "celebrity intertextual" link to the 1978 film, whereas no such connections are made to the 1956 and 1993 films.[23] Cartwright's inclusion aims to legitimize *The Invasion* as a remake, and it also excludes the 1993 film from the sequence. McCarthy's appearance linked the 1956 and 1978 films, and Cartwright's appearance does the same for the 1978 and 2007 versions.

Intriguingly, Kevin McCarthy's scene as the "running man" from the 1978 film also finds its way into the 2007 version. While going through a tunnel, Carol's car is stopped and a seemingly crazed woman warns her, "They're coming! They're here!" before running off to be hit by a car. In the 1978 film, the scene teased a connection between the first two films, but it does not serve the same purpose in the 2007 version. There is no hint towards continuity, and the woman (credited only as "panicked woman in tunnel") is just another chance encounter to set the mood, or at best, a moment of foreshadowing for Carol's coming woes. The 2007 film quotes a quote, but deprives it of the meaning generated by the casting of the role. As is, the scene only serves as further proof that *The Invasion* heavily draws from the 1978 remake.

The Current Crisis and the Failure of Government

While the previous films in the sequences contain more or less subtle hints at their socio-historical contexts, *The Invasion*, makes very conscious efforts to be relevant to a particular historical moment. This is not a film that (only) inadvertently reflects the socio-historical circumstances of its production; it delivers blatant commentary on what it perceives as contemporary concerns. The presentation already hints at the urgency and currency of events. The film is interspersed with TV newscasts that track the global spread of the alien infection, and great care is taken to ensure that these news clips appear as credible as possible, including the use of actual network logos and graphics from CNN, MSNBC, and Fox. The story moves at the pace set by 24 hour news networks, and the intimate horror of gradual isolation is always put in perspective by news reports that connect to a bigger world. Notably, *The Invasion* is the first film in the *Body Snatchers* sequence to realize the concept of the pod takeover on a global scale. Previously, the world beyond the protagonists' community was only implied through outgoing pod shipments, but in the 2007 film, live updates about the rest of the world are inescapable. This foregrounds a concern with global biopolitics,

---

23 Since *The Invasion* was shot a full fifty years after *Invasion of the Body Snatchers* (1956), there were also obvious practical limitations to cameo appearances. Most of the principal cast of the 1956 film was dead by 2007 or shortly thereafter.

with the intersections of political power and human life being played out through the pod infection scenario.[24]

Accordingly, the plot points of the alien invasion draw from recent headlines. The Shuttle crash that brings the alien virus to Earth is reminiscent of the Space Shuttle Columbia disaster in 2003, including the search for fragments spread over the US and attempts to sell them on ebay. The shuttle is named "Patriot," not in keeping with NASA nomenclature, but perhaps as a comment on the political mood. Furthermore, Kaufman's fabrication of a flu epidemic as a pretense for his vaccination/infection program evokes general fears of infection, but likely plays on the "bird flu" (avian influenza) scare of the early 2000s as well. The newscasts spread throughout the film focus on contemporary international hotspots, including North Korea, Afghanistan, Iraq, Iran, and Sudan's region of Darfur, along with brief clips of recognizable figures like George W. Bush and Hugo Chavez.

The choice of news stories, locations and political figures not only serves to date the film and support a sense of recognizable normality, against which the invasion can play out. It also establishes a frame of reference for its political commentary. *The Invasion* reiterates the distrust in government institutions that could be found to varying degrees in all of the films in the *Body Snatchers* sequence. Yet even though the dialogue claims to make observations about a general human nature, the film's critique of government is specific to its historical moment, the US in the post-9/11 era and the George W. Bush administration. Brief references to that administration's actions and failures, from Iraq to New Orleans, are strewn around the dialogue and the ever-present news media that busily generate a sense of global crisis.

The US government is met with criticism from the start. Early in the film, the characters still assume incompetence rather than malevolence. Ben mentions resignations of scientists because the government is handling the shuttle disaster wrong. Later, biologist Dr. Galeano reports that the contagion is treated more seriously in Europe and Japan, while the US response is again lacking. The failure to formulate an effective response may be explained by the activities of Kaufman and his fellow alien conspirators, but since the film also brings up New Orleans as a point of reference during the Belicecs' party, it also invokes the failures in the management of Hurricane Katrina in 2005.

As the narrative proceeds, the US government takes on an increasingly sinister role. The setting, Washington DC, already suggests a political focus, as the infection is spread from the seat of government. The main antagonist and face of the aliens, Tucker Kaufman, is a high-ranking official for the Centers of Disease

---

24 See chapter 5 for a discussion of biopolitics in the context of *The Crazies*.

Control and Prevention, a federal agency. Control over the CDC's resources is crucial for the success of the aliens, especially since there appear to be few limits or safeguard mechanisms to the agency's powers. Kaufman can pressure the pharmaceutical industry into furthering his goal, which suggests that government can easily enforce its will on private enterprise. Notably, the CDC is also a favorite bogeyman of American conspiracy theorists, often in conjunction with the Federal Emergency Management Agency (FEMA). Likewise, the spread of the alien infection through a mysterious vaccine plays into current vaccine scares that assume a link between vaccinations and autism or other conditions, based on mostly pseudoscientific research. None of these fears are entirely new phenomena exclusive to the 2000s, of course – drinking water laced with mysterious chemicals is a conspiracy standby from the 1950s, and AIDS conspiracy theories from the 1980s onwards are too plentiful to list. However, *The Invasion* maps its scenario of infection and subversion onto current iterations of those fears, and invokes fringe positions in the process.

As the alien takeover proceeds, more authorities get involved. That a man claiming to be a census worker tries to force his way into Carol's house may be of little consequence to the plot, but it adds another level of government to the alien conspiracy (and the US Census is again a favored target of conspiracy theorists). More importantly, the police and National Guard are instrumental in spreading the alien infection and asserting control over the cities. That turn of the story matches the previous films, where police forces, whether civilian or military, are always working for the pods. The 2007 film ups the ante by introducing a military quarantine, but does not develop the role of the military enough to invite a comparison to the 1993 film. Again, the 1978 version is the closest parallel, and even though the 2007 film does not spend as much time on the labyrinthine structure of city government, its portrayal of government subversion is more far-reaching, all the way up to the presidency. It appears that all levels of government in *The Invasion* are turned into instruments of oppression, but there is a surprising exception.

Even though the film shows the National Guard in the streets and President Bush on TV as parts of the alien conspiracy, a mostly unseen and vaguely defined group of elite scientists at Fort Detrick, home of the US Army medical research arm, delivers a solution to the problem. They manage to stage a special forces operation to rescue Carol and her son from a rooftop, and proceed to not only develop a cure for the alien infection, but to distribute it across the world. Why Fort Detrick remains operational even though the aliens are in full control of all world governments is not explained, and the details of the cure are glossed over in an expository interview scene. While the film repeatedly mentions the existence of this elite group, the extent of their capabilities strains credibility and contradicts the portrayal of institutions up to this point. *The Invasion* spends most of its running time building a massive distrust of government institutions, but then has remnants of that same apparatus, scientific experts working in a military structure, resolve the problem. The ending thus "attests to the belief in scientific and technological solutions" and "restores stability" (Loock 137).

It may be tempting to dismiss the conclusion and point towards extratextual factors to account for seeming flaws or contradictions. As mentioned, the film's production was quite problematic, and the originally intended, more ambiguous ending was reportedly replaced during the extensive reshoots. This is, however, the same process of revision and reconstruction that *Invasion of the Body Snatchers* (1956) went through. In both cases, dissatisfaction by the studio led to a more optimistic ending that attempts to restore some degree of trust in experts and institutions. Still, whereas the 1956 film developed a growing following that aimed to restore Don Siegel's vision and incorporated questions of authorship in the critical discourse on the film, there has been no such movement for the 2007 film. Even though media technology has made it easier to release alternate versions of films, or to add material cut from theatrical releases as bonus content, it is doubtful whether *The Invasion* is capable of generating the interest required for such a reconstruction. Ultimately, there is little point in discussing a text that was never fully formed, when there are plenty of intriguing and puzzling questions left for the text that has found official release.

The Invasion is not only anxious to appear up to date, but also to appear relevant to a particular moment in US and international political history. The film's constant media reports of suicide bombings and disputes with "rogue states" (as defined by the George W. Bush administration) firmly place it in a post-9/11 world. The global alien takeover solves a long list of international problems, and the news reports mention North Korea agreeing to nuclear disarmament, an end to bomb attacks in Kabul, Afghanistan, a cessation of hostilities in Darfur, the withdrawal of American troops from Iraq, and George W. Bush signing a deal with Venezuelan president Hugo Chavez. That last scene relies on the audience's perception of Bush and Chavez as implacable enemies: the handshake can only work as a sign of alien control if the viewers are certain that these two political leaders would never make peace. The same applies to the next snippet, positioned as the punchline to the world news segment, which shows Bush working with Hillary Clinton to implement universal healthcare.

As a downside to the film's efforts to be current, half of these shocking developments already seem dated and therefore less effective at the time of this writing. Furthermore, the film not only inserts contemporary political references to appear up to date, it also advances a deep suspicion of political structures and state institutions, only to completely revert to the status quo again. In order to speculate about the possible political stances of *The Invasion*, a closer look at the aliens that drive its political upheaval is required.

Disease Revisited

As the most radical departure from its sources, *The Invasion* does away with the pods. There are no longer giant seed pods from which duplicates grow; instead, people simply contract an intelligent virus of alien origin. Human bodies are taken over by alien minds, not replaced by doubles. This is a somewhat neater approach for the narrative, as it removes complications and sources of plot inconsistencies. The previous films had to account for the presence of seed pods and the time required for a duplicate to grow, or risk contradictions, as in the case of Becky in the 1956 film. Once the infection is contracted in the 2007 film, the change can occur whenever and wherever the subject goes to sleep, and given the plethora of ways to catch a disease, no particular attention has to be paid to causality.

Consequently, the word "pod" never comes up, and the aliens are instead referred to as "alien virus," "entity," or simply "they." Given that "pod people" is a term with some recognition among genre fans, this marks an act of disavowal that stands in contrast to the homage paid in character names and Cartwright's appearance. Nevertheless, even though the term "pods" is technically no longer applicable, the difference is largely negligible when it comes to the monster discourse at the core of the *Body Snatchers* story, and several authors retain the term "pod" for discussion of *The Invasion* (e.g. Grant, Loock, Nelson). After all, People are still taken over when they fall asleep, and replaced by emotionless versions of themselves. The stress on collectivity is likewise retained, as is the horror of losing one's self. Since the previous films never allowed for humans and their pod duplicates to be active at the same time – the human original would be destroyed once the pod gained full consciousness – the 2007 film basically takes a shortcut to the same result.

With the viral nature of the aliens, the infection discourse pervading the *Body Snatchers* scenario becomes more concrete. Not only do the aliens spread *like* a disease, as Miles noted in the 1956 film, they *are* a disease. That change invokes a wide range of cultural fears regarding infection and pandemic, and it also opens up an unprecedented possibility: thanks to a complicated earlier case of chicken pox, Carol's son Oliver is immune and thus holds the key to an easily mass-produced cure. This twist marks the most radical departure from the earlier films, which held the pod takeover as irreversible. The best case scenario for the 1956 and 1993 films was containment of those lost to the pods, and the 1978 film ended with the utter defeat of humanity. Now, the fact that the alien control is reversible strips the story of much of the horror, as the loss of humanity is only temporary, and drastically changes possible readings.

The development of a cure as a resolution marks the end point of a reassessment of science over the course of the *Body Snatchers* sequence. Where the 1956 film was still suspicious of scientific rationality (Kaufman's appeal to Miles's scientific mind aligned science with the pods), and the following two remakes portrayed science as helpless (the analyses pursued by 1978's Elizabeth and 1993's Steve led nowhere), the 2007 film casts a mostly unseen group of scientists as saviors of humanity. Even though Yorish, the film's voice of harsh truths, mocks Carol for her supposed belief in curing every condition with pills, the film's conclusion is a resounding affirmation of the idea that medication can solve any problem. In addition, the mere fact that the alien virus can be fully understood and combated using scientific methods reduces its monstrosity; it is, after all, not an incomprehensible supernatural force, but just another sickness, foiled by chicken pox. In short, then, *The Invasion* puts its trust in science even when it is suspicious of government authorities, or at least finds science capable and credible enough to employ it as a *deus ex machina*.

As with the previous films in the *Body Snatchers* sequence, the aliens are given opportunity to explain their point of view, and matching *The Invasion's* (2007) general efforts to be relevant, their statements are charged with topical references. For example, Carol's ex-husband Tucker Kaufman draws a comparison between the alien state and psychotherapy: "You give people pills to make their lives better. How is that so different from what we're doing?" Indeed, the alien infection removes the need for therapy, as Carol finds all her appointments cancelled. Both the 1956 and the 1978 film expressed a suspicion of psychotherapy and clearly aligned it with the pods. Not only did therapists serve as the pods' spokesmen, the 1978 version prefigured a parallel between the work of the pods and Kibner's brand of therapy, which allegedly aimed to "change people to fit the world." The 2007 film reiterates that suspicion, but makes it more explicit as part of the dialogue. At the same time, the fact that *The Invasion* casts its therapist character not as the main antagonist, but as the protagonist would seem soften the force of its critique.[25]

---

25 The film's stance on psychology is complicated by a one-off remark from its chief scientist character. Explaining the alien infection, Dr. Galeano asserts that people are (to 80%) defined by genetic expression, and that altering genes alters minds. His

The main argumentative thrust comes from Ben, however. In a scene again familiar from previous films, he reveals his transformation, corners Carol with a group of fellow aliens, and tries to persuade her to give up resistance. His opening lines ("Have you seen the television? Have you read the newspapers? Seen what's happening here, and what we're offering?") establish the state of the outside world, not Carol's personal experiences, as a frame of reference, and invoke the news media as crucial mediators. Ben goes on to offer "A world without war, without poverty, without murder, without rape, a world without suffering. Because in our world, no one can hurt each other, or exploit each other, or try to destroy each other, because in our world, there is no other . . . our world is a better world." The constant repetition of "world" underlines both the completeness of the aliens' utopian promise as well as the global stakes. Furthermore, Ben concentrates on massed human suffering, which distinguishes him from the more personal focus of his 1956 and 1978 counterparts. The argument is closest to the pods of the 1993 film, who promised an end of all conflict through total conformity. Compared to the previous films, Ben makes a fairly compelling case, supported by a stream of televised evidence – the utopian alternative society is not only a promise, but quickly materializing outside.

The most remarkable part of Ben's monologue is his claim that for the aliens, "there is no other." I might as well capitalize "Other" here, as the wording strongly suggests an awareness of the academic term and thus a reaction to critical and academic readings of the previous films in the *Body Snatchers* sequence. The 1956 film in particular has been a popular subject for analysis, and the resulting discourse on alterity, on the negotiations of Self and Other that take place in the pod subversion scenario, is now directly written into the film's dialogue. This would mark an example of film remaking not only weighing a hypotext, the previous film(s), against current genre developments and audience tastes, but also taking metatexts, critical readings of those hypotext(s), into account. Nevertheless, the film's heightened awareness does not result in a more sophisticated discourse on alterity or any other issue; it merely makes its points more obvious.

This tendency is also evident in *The Invasion's* (2007) debate on human nature. The positions are made plain in the dialogue between Carol and Russian ambassador Yorish: while Carol believes in the continuing evolution of the human mind, Yorish insists that civilization is only a façade and that atrocities, war and violence are inevitable unless "human beings cease to be human." The global alien takeover puts Yorish's what-if question to the test, and in case the resumption of terror attacks after the cure was not clear enough, the final scene al-

---

statement is mostly inconsequential for the progression of the story, but it expresses a firm belief in genetic predetermination.

so repeats Yorish's words in voiceover to vindicate his position. Yorish and Ben voice a blatant thesis statement about human nature that the invasion narrative seeks to support. The aliens no longer function as a continuation of current social trends, but purely as a counterpoint to the film's conception of humanity. Once that point is made, the aliens are removed without trace, and the explanation that the victims of takeover experienced the whole affair "as if asleep" further reduces their impact to that of a dream (of world peace, that is).

The previous films in the *Body Snatchers* sequence always posited humanity as flawed, but in 1956 and 1978, that merely required dealing with heartbreak and anxiety, whereas efforts to do away with those were cast as dehumanizing. The 2007 film, by contrast, asserts that hoping for humanity to become less violent is naïve, and that there must always be deadly terror attacks because humans are human. That stance can be explained as an expression of despair and helplessness over a sense of constant world crisis, perhaps tied to a post-9/11 news cycle, but it may also turn the whole narrative into a parable on the necessity of violence, which could in turn be used to dismiss responsibility for cynical or immoral attitudes and policies. Deducing a political stance for the film therefore requires the balancing of potentially contradictory readings. On the one hand, the presence of George W. Bush as an alien puppet and the mention of Hurricane Katrina in line with atrocities read as attacks on the by then fairly unpopular Bush presidency, which might hint at a vaguely liberal point of view. On the other hand, the intrusion by external monsters and the unambiguous restoration of normality are fundamentally conservative story elements, according to Wood (75), and the 2007 film far exceeds any of its predecessors in this regard. Normality may be deeply flawed in *The Invasion*, but the only conceivable alternative is evidently inhuman.

"A post-modern feminist": Gender in *The Invasion*

Among a number of unprecedented changes made by the 2007 remake, the choice of protagonist stands out as one of the most significant. The 1993 remake already featured a female protagonist, but Marti never functioned as a full replacement for Miles and Matthew Bennell. *The Invasion* emphasizes the gender swap by assigning Carol the last name Bennell, and by turning Becky/Elizabeth Driscoll into the male love interest Ben Driscoll.[26] Like Miles, Carol is a self-

---

26 The importance of Carol as the protagonist is also reflected in the casting of Nicole Kidman, whose salary for the role alone exceeded the entire budgets of the 1956 and 1978 films, and comes close to that of the 1993 version, adjusted for inflation ("The Invasion (2007)," *IMDb*).

employed practitioner, financially independent and divorced, yet unlike Miles, she is also a parent and appears to be the primary caretaker of her son. Carol also describes herself as a "post-modern feminist," and even though the meaning of that designation is not explained, it vaguely positions her as an intellectual progressive. In several regards, Carol is an update and an inversion of the fairly traditional, rugged individualist Miles.

Like her male counterparts, Carol is ultimately betrayed by her transformed love interest, but it is her divorced husband Tucker Kaufman who acts as her main antagonist throughout the film, forcibly infecting Carol and abducting their son. As Nelson remarks, the conflict between Carol and Tucker is "an extension of their custody battle," and the alien involvement only changes the stakes of a "pre-existing family conflict" (Nelson 66). As the fight over the possession of Oliver escalates, the parallels become more evident, and Tucker finally blames the failed marriage on Carol's priorities, which placed him third after career and child. "That can't happen in our world," he adds, and asks for them to be a family again, which suggests that the alien utopia is based on a more reactionary nuclear family model. Tucker's complaints are hard to reconcile with his supposed lack of emotions, as he is clearly driven by frustration, and they put an entirely different spin on the relationship between the aliens and normality. The discourse on global violence, as laid out by Ben, stresses the difference of the aliens, yet the conflict between Tucker and Carol only continues petty human disputes. *The Invasion* thus employs the aliens in contradictory roles. In this case, they represent the protagonist's fear of patriarchal control (Grant 102).

While Carol struggles to resist external control over her life, her top priority remains Oliver's safety. For Nelson, her devotion to her son above all else even "borders on sociopathic" (69). Indeed, Carol proves capable of violence in desperation, and guns down numerous aliens who (in retrospect) could have been cured – only in the case of Ben does she shoot to wound. Carol's role as a "supermother" (Nelson 70) can be read as a repudiation of her own claims to postmodern feminism. According to Nelson, at least, Carol is "reifying gender roles even as she challenges them" because she struggles between roles and male and female traits (69). Ultimately, Nelson views Carol as submitting to traditional gender roles by moving in with Ben, thus rejecting single motherhood as "unnatural" and affirming the nuclear family (Nelson 71).

Grant, however, offers a slightly different reading of the conclusion. He argues that the film implicates "aggressive masculinity as the root of human conflict and misery" (Grant 100), and in that context, Carol shooting the alien-controlled Ben in the kneecap functions as a "metaphoric castration of the husband" (104). This reading suggests that only once Ben's destructive masculinity is symbolically removed is he capable of forming a healthy relationship, as opposed to the repressive family envisioned by Tucker Kaufman. Either way, the film at least affirms *some* form of nuclear family, even as it despairs over human nature in general. Amidst *The Invasion's* (2007) efforts to be up to date, the casting of a female protagonist is without doubt a sign of and tribute to changing social roles, yet it also exposes remaining constraints. Neither 1993's Marti nor 2007's Carol can fully take the place of their male predecessors in the manner that 1978's Matthew took over from 1956's Miles.

Overall, *The Invasion* exhibits competing drives familiar from most remakes: on the one hand, to honor at least two of its predecessors with character names, quotes, and a cameo, and on the other hand, to reinvigorate the familiar narrative by reconceptualizing the pods and protagonist and by bringing it firmly into the current day. The conclusion marks a drastic departure from the previous films, and mostly discards the anxiety of conformity in favor of constructing a parable about the inescapable violent undercurrents of humanity. With their threat dissolving without trace at the end, the aliens ultimately serve as a tool to make that point.

COMPARING POD DUPLICATES, 1956 TO 2007

The sequence of *Body Snatchers* films offers the opportunity to compare four takes on the same story, with over fifty years between the first and the most recent film version. For the purposes of critical analysis, the number of repetitions becomes a convenient device that helps to distinguish the themes and fears that remain current from those whose relevance is inextricably tied to a specific historical moment. As this chapter has shown, the fear of collectivity erasing individuality, and of the dehumanizing effects of social conformity, remains constant. What is associated with that collective, however, changes. In all four films, any social structure that promotes unthinking conformity and emotionless detachment is a breeding ground for the pods, because it allows their subversion to go undiscovered until it is too late. This applies to the small town as well as the big city, and to consumer society as well as the military; institutions of any kind do not fare well along the way. In the end, each film makes a plea for beleaguered individuality, which it equates with an essential quality of humanity. A less favorable reading may interpret that stance as a paranoid close-mindedness, as arbitrary social developments are cast as dehumanizing and monstrous infection.

At the same time, the *Body Snatchers* narrative proves surprisingly adaptable to different settings and capable of accommodating thematic shifts. At the beginning of this chapter, I suggested the pods' recurrent sales pitch to their human captives as a point of comparison. By explaining the advantages of their state of being, the pods spotlight what the film conceives as the downsides of the human condition at its respective historical moment. While the 1956 film starts out with the fairly innocuous complications of love, desire, ambition, and faith, the remakes progressively escalate the stakes with anxiety, fear, and hate in 1978, war and conflict in 1993, and the combined horrors of rape, murder, terrorism, and war in 2007. Yet, even though each film takes a dimmer view of humanity, the case for the pods only gets weaker as well.

This analysis has focused on comparing repeated scenes, but the complicated intertextual relationship between the various iterations of the *Body Snatchers* narrative also becomes evident at the margins of the texts. The credits, the peritext in Genette's terms, invariably mention the literary source, but not the previous film(s) that usually had a larger influence on the remake in question. The filmic hypotexts are instead invoked in titles or subtitles: *Invasion of the Body Snatchers* (1978) repeats the title of the 1956 film, not the novel's, and even as *Body Snatchers* (1993) reverts to the novel's title, its tagline "The Invasion Continues" again invokes the previous films (Knöppler, "Intertextualität" 132-33). The films' peritexts thus illustrate the triangular relationship between sources and remake as described by Leitch (39). A similar negotiation of sources and their different canonical weight takes place in the epitext of DVD packaging or online blurbs. Moreover, while this study is limited to films and their remakes, it is still interesting to consider the literary source, Jack Finney's novel *Body Snatchers*. Numerous editions of the novel were marketed with the film title *Invasion of the Body Snatchers*, and their back cover blurbs likewise invoke the film adaptation. In terms of marketing at least, the original source appears subordinate to its better established film adaptations, and perhaps the significance of the *Body Snatchers* complex is more accurately located in the web of relations between the texts (cf. Knöppler, "Intertextualität" 134).

At this point, the question remains why *Invasion of the Body Snatchers* (1956) would be remade so many times. The commercial argument is often considered the only relevant factor in remaking: film studios try to minimize the financial risks inherent in the production of films by relying on proven concepts, and a remake of a film that has worked before is both easier to produce (thanks to a pre-existing script) and to sell (thanks to an already known title) than a new project. At least the second half of this assumption is challenged by the performance of the of the *Body Snatchers* films, however. The 1956 film was only a moderate success, doing decent business relative to its low budget, while the 1978 remake performed better. A moderate success may appear safe, if not too inspiring, but the 1993 remake failed to achieve even that. Nevertheless, its dismal box office take did not discourage the production of another remake a mere fourteen years later. The 2007 remake also underperformed at the box office, failing to recoup its considerable budget despite having recognizable stars attached to it. Therefore, it would seem that the supposed safety of remaking cannot be the sole explanation for the continued reissuing of the *Body Snatchers* story, simply because it has not proven to be a safe money maker.

Even though the above may read as a gross oversimplification of the complexities of Hollywood film production, it is vital that we consider the properties of the text itself in this pattern of reproduction. As Loock puts it, the story of *Invasion of the Body Snatchers* possesses a "particular suitability for cinematic remaking" (124). Its central paranoid conceit, that the people you know are replaced by duplicates, is adaptable to a wide range of contexts, as long as these involve social interaction. Accordingly, Grant explains the film's enduring popularity with "a combination of a central metaphor for the monstrous that, like the vampire or the zombie, is sufficiently flexible to accommodate multiple interpretations, with a style and structure that is admirably economical even as it is highly expressive" (8-9). He further quotes Durgnet about the story's simplicity intersecting with "all sorts of suggestions and themes" to enable a multitude of interpretations (104), and later concludes that it should remain relevant in light of many new technologies of reproduction (104). After a close examination of four iterations of *Body Snatchers*, I am inclined to agree that the core story is likely to remain relevant, but not because it deals with reproduction. Instead, it holds a potent metaphor for alienation and social pressure, and expresses a fundamental tension between individuals and communities. The fear of being absorbed by a collective will likely remain relevant because it is, at its most general, part of the human experience.

Fig. 1. The UFO crash site in The Thing From Another World *and* The Thing *(1982)*

Fig. 2. The grotesque mutations of The Thing *(1982)*

Fig. 3. "The real meaning of fear" in Invasion of the Body Snatchers *(1956)*

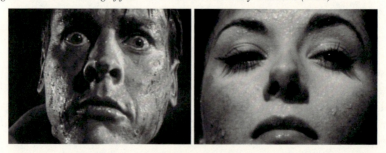

Fig. 4. "They're here!" Kevin McCarthy in Invasion of the Body Snatchers *1956 & 1978*

5. Contagion and Social Collapse

Since its failure at the box office, *The Crazies* (1973) has enjoyed the same fate as the rest of George Romero's non-zombie films (J. Russell 75). It has remained rather obscure, and distributors have relied on invoking the director's more famous works to attract any interest at all.[1] Likewise, it has received rather little scholarly attention despite the many thematic similarities to Romero's main works (cf. Williams 59). This is likely to change, as the 2010 remake has elevated the status of the original film, albeit only slightly. More polished re-releases on DVD, coinciding with the release of the remake and intended to cash in on it, confirm the canonizing function of remaking.

The Crazies (1973) is a film that is highly charged with the politics of its time, in particular the Vietnam War. The remake, then, shows a process of adaptation and substitution of Vietnam with the discourses surrounding terrorism and the Iraq War. The concepts of monstrosity change, losing ambiguity and becoming less a symptom of systemic problems. Thanks to the relative obscurity of the original and the novelty of the remake, the two films form a very limited complex, with little obvious impact on other works, but they still demonstrate the workings of remakes, in particular the adaptation of cultural fears, in this case both of losing control over the self and of oppressive state power. The latter ties into a distinct biopolitical element that runs through both films.

---

1   For instance, paratextual references on the 2010 DVD version distributed by Anchor Bay firmly tie the film into an authorial canon. The front cover labels the film as *George A. Romero's The Crazies*, adding "from the director of *Night of the Living Dead*" to further drive home the point. The back cover emphasizes those cast members who played parts in *Dawn of the Dead* (1978) and *Day of the Dead* (1985), even though their parts are minor in both cases.

THE CRAZIES (1973)

The fourth film by George Romero marks a partial return to the horror genre, but offers a more low-key scenario than the director's zombie films. The accidental spill of a contagious biological weapon, codenamed "Trixie" by the US military, gradually turns the inhabitants of rural Evans City, Pennsylvania, into homicidal maniacs, or "crazies." The military scrambles to establish a quarantine, yet miscommunication and incompetence quickly add up to escalate the situation. The town's slide into open violence is mainly shown from two alternating points of view. On the one hand, a group of townsfolk struggles to evade the military and escape the town. On the other hand, the military command on location works to overcome lacking manpower and information to maintain the quarantine.

The townsfolk are represented by the fire fighters and war buddies David and Clank, who catch the first glimpse of the "crazy" epidemic when they are called in on a fire set by an infected farmer. They are joined by David's pregnant wife Judy, a nurse who learned about the outbreak when the military began to set up a base of operations at her doctor's office. All three are already suspicious of the quarantine measures when they are apprehended by a military patrol. Along with two other townsfolk, Artie and his daughter Kathy, they escape when given the opportunity. With David as a tentative leader, the group takes to the woods to shake any pursuers. While David is initially reluctant to use violence, he and Clank soon find themselves exchanging fire with soldiers.

It also appears that several of the group are affected by the contagion: Clank becomes violent and unhinged, murdering a group of unarmed soldiers during a nighttime raid on a farmhouse, while Kathy is increasingly disconnected. Her father Artie's affection, too, takes a turn for the worse as he rapes her. David, however, shows no symptoms of the contagion, and Judy speculates that he might possess a natural immunity. Still, David cannot keep the group from falling apart: Artie is found hung to death, Kathy wanders off to be shot dead by panicked soldiers, and Clank, realizing his decline into insanity, throws himself into a hopeless fight against the army and dies. Finally, Judy is killed by a marauding band of crazed town youths, which prompts David to simply give up and turn himself in.

The side of the military is represented by the commanding officer in town, Colonel Peckem, and his subordinate, Major Ryder. Ryder is first seen in command, with Peckem only arriving when the quarantine operation is already under way. Despite his frustrations with the slow buildup of personnel and materials as well as lacking information, Peckem implements the strategy that his superiors decided on. This strategy is containment, and Peckem is instructed to have his men herd the townsfolk together in one place to better control them. While Ryder already expects resistance to this measure and prepares for small-scale war, Peckem tries to limit civilian casualties, albeit with little success. Local authorities are quickly disposed as soldiers break down doors and arrest the townsfolk with little explanation. As expected, the situation escalates to open rioting.

In the meantime, Dr. Watts, a military scientist from the Trixie project responsible for the contagion, is brought to Peckem's headquarters against his will. While repeatedly protesting the flaws of the entire operation, he begins work on a cure, but is constantly hindered by complicated hierarchies and security protocols. When Watts finally makes a breakthrough discovery, he rushes out to Peckem's headquarters, only to be caught between soldiers and a riot of "crazies." Watts dies by accident, and his cure is lost. Peckem's mission, however, is judged a success: in the end, his units have completed the internment of the town's surviving population, and Peckem is reassigned to command the quarantine of another possible outbreak.

The command level above Peckem deserves separate mention. As the situation in town deteriorates, a group of political and military leaders develops military and information strategies from a safe distance, already preparing cover stories while persuading the President to have nuclear weapons in the air and ready to strike as a last measure. A man named Brubaker appears to be in charge, even though his office or function is never revealed.

In order to analyze the policies of army and federal government in *The Crazies* (1973), and the discourses of contagion and quarantine that inform them, it may be useful to consider the concept of biopolitics as defined by Foucault:

Foucault's concept of biopolitics assumes the dissociation and abstraction of life from its concrete physical bearers. The objects of biopolitics are not singular human beings but their biological features measured and aggregated on the level of populations. This procedure makes it possible to define norms, establish standards, and determine average values. As a result, "life" has become an independent, objective and measurable factor, as well as a collective reality that can be epistemologically and practically separated from concrete living beings and the singularity of living experience. (Lemke 5)

This notion of biopolitics, Lemke continues, ties into "specific political knowledge" and disciplines such as demographics and (relevant for *The Crazies*) epidemology, which "make it possible to analyze processes of life on the level of populations and to 'govern' individuals and collectives" through a number of practices including correction and exclusion (5). The coercive quarantine measures depicted in the film line up with these practices of governance, enabled by disciplines like epidemology and specialized knowledge displayed by the leading group around Brubaker.

From this perspective, the scenario of the film serves to illustrate multiple aspects of biopolitics. The population of the town with its bio-warfare-induced insanity is the object of the military action; it is to be managed and controlled, with the survivors measured as a percentage (in terms of demographics) to determine the success of the quarantine strategy. Individuals like David and his companions are utterly insignificant from this perspective. By using multiple points of view, *The Crazies* (1973) shows the scope of the collision between individual life and political power (executed by the military) and its consequences.

A Failure of Communication

While *The Crazies* is marketed as horror, no doubt thanks to its director, it plays out more like a disaster movie, depicting the impact of a catastrophic event on several levels of society. At the bottom, the common people around David experience the catastrophe first hand, from the effects of the contagion to the brutal military response. In the middle, the military and scientific authorities around Peckem try to manage and solve the problem with the means available to them. At the top, the leaders around Brubaker pursue the same goals, but focus on the national instead of the local level and, more importantly, control the flow of information to cover themselves. While the infected people's slip into insanity and ensuing graphic acts of violence can be named as generic horror elements, it is mostly confusion, lack of information, unclear goals, and constant infighting that characterize all levels of the film's narrative.

A failure of communication between the several groups of actors or institutions as well as between individuals makes any sensible solution to the problem impossible. Necessary information is passed out too slowly, if at all, thanks to systemic flaws. The leadership orders a "blackout operation," that is, an operation under secrecy, with no unauthorized information getting out. This attempt to control information has disastrous results throughout. The first commander on the ground, Major Ryder, is told that the Trixie contagion is a deactivated vaccine and acts accordingly. Only Colonel Peckem informs him that Trixie is in fact a biological weapon, and Peckem himself is later corrected by Dr. Watts, in that the contagion is "often lethal, always debilitating" with no cure in sight. This exchange of information is more accidental than controlled by the top-level leadership, and obviously, the outbreak cannot be handled effectively on incomplete information. As another example, Dr. Watts's cure is lost thanks to several failures of communication: First, Watts does not explain his findings to his assistant, despite her inquiries. Second, the system in place to ensure secure radio communications fails to connect Watts to his superiors. Third, the military guards in front of Watts's laboratory cannot identify him, and give him no chance to prove his identity. Instead, they assume he is one of the crazies, and Watts dies in the ensuing chaos.

None of the characters in this scenario feels qualified to handle the situation. All three insist, at various points, that they are in the wrong place. Early on, Ryder complains about having to make decisions on his own and insists "I'm not an infantry man, I'm chem-corps. I can't hold a perimeter and fight a small scale war at the same time." Peckem later remarks that he is a "combat man" himself, and is also not the right man for the job. Watts is literally dragged to Evans City against his will by military police, who assure him that they will carry him if necessary. Watts is brought in because Peckem wants "someone from Trixie" on the ground, and his political superior Brubaker simply gives orders to send the first man that shows up – Watts. Watts's insistence that he is useless without a lab are irrelevant, and while Peckem sees the problem, protocol does not allow him to let Watts go. In this case, Brubaker and the system he represents send in the wrong people from the start.

The characters at the bottom of the hierarchy find themselves with even less information. David and his fellow fugitives have to puzzle together the picture from their own experiences and what little information Judy learned from the doctor. The lack of information gives rise to speculation: "Maybe we are in some kind of war," David guesses. The interrogation of captured soldiers yields little new information, as the army patrols are just as ignorant as the townsfolk they round up. One of the soldiers sums up the experience: "You never know what you're doing or why you're doing it. You just do it because you're told to." In fact, this ignorance may just be required for the operation to work, as Peckem explains: "If those men know the truth, they'll be breaching the perimeter themselves."

"It's a police action": *The Crazies* as Vietnam Allegory

A number of critics view Romero's earlier *Night of the Living Dead* (1968) as a commentary on the Vietnam War, which reached its climax in the year of the film's release. While there are no explicit references to Vietnam in *Night,* the mindless brutality of the authorities and their "shoot 'em in the head"-attitude as well as the "anxious discourse of contagion and containment" taking place on TV (Russell 69) have been read as reflections of the Vietnam War's representation in the media. While the war thus forms part of the "political unconscious" of

Night (Williams, Hearths 100), the references become far more explicit in the case of *The Crazies,* which was released while US involvement in Vietnam was drawing to an end.[2] The bluntness of Romero's allegory may be distracting for some viewers, and Maddrey calls the film an "all-too-obvious comment on the Vietnam War" (125).

The discourse of contagion and containment mentioned by Russell becomes the main theme of *The Crazies* (1973), with the weaponized disease Trixie as the cause of violent madness. The logic of the army's quarantine replicates the Cold War strategy of containing communism. Likewise, the ad-hoc nature of the military operation, the sudden build-up of men and materials as the local situation escalates, only to move out again when it is declared as resolved, follows the pattern of US counterinsurgency operations in Vietnam and the lack of clear frontlines that characterized the whole conflict. Despite a questionable result, Colonel Peckem's efforts are lauded as he is flown out to the next site of Trixie activity in Lousiville, Kentucky, where presumably the story will repeat itself. The rounding up of the Evans City population, intended to ease communication and end the spread of the contagion, likewise resembles relocation strategies in Vietnam, which saw communities forcibly removed from their homes for their own protection and to cut off support for the Viet Cong (Williams, *Knight* 60). Like in Vietnam, the military loses the battle for the townsfolk's hearts and minds, as one of *The Crazies'* political leaders predicts: "Look, you put martial law on a town, drop a sneak perimeter on them like that, and you're just polarizing the situation. That army becomes an invasionary force; those people are going to resist!"

While these examples may still be filed under the film's "political unconscious," as Williams puts it, *The Crazies* (1973) also features more explicit references to the Vietnam War in both imagery and rhetoric. In protest of the military's actions, a priest sets himself on fire, in a close replication of the famous photograph of Thich Quang Duc's self immolation in Saigon on June 11, 1963 (see fig. 5). Likewise, a soldier calls the Evans City quarantine a "police action," quoting the US government's euphemism for the war. In a discussion of the military's trustworthiness, David states that "They can turn a campus protest into a shooting war," referencing the Kent State shootings in 1970, during which National Guard fired at student protestors, killing four. As these examples demon-

---

2   The release date for *The Crazies* is given as March 15, 1973 on *IMDB* ("The Crazies (1973)"). The Paris Peace Accords were signed in January of the same year, signaling an official end to US military involvement. While ground troops were soon evacuated, the US Air Force was involved well into 1973, and the possibility of further American interventions was still debated in the same year.

strate, the worldview of *The Crazies* is firmly rooted in its period and its contro-versies.

A number of other elements can be read as allusions to the Vietnam War. One scene has David's group fleeing through the woods while exchanging gun-fire with army soldiers and a helicopter, putting them in a position vaguely com-parable to that of the Viet Cong. As another example, the leaders around Bru-baker use deception and media manipulation to sell their strategy to the public from the very start, which can be read in the context of the Johnson administra-tion's misleading of the American public, as revealed in the Pentagon Papers. Williams also considers a scene in which an infected resident spits into the face of a soldier as an allusion to the treatment of US soldiers returning from Vietnam (*Knight* 61). According to Williams, the depictions of war crimes and body bags allude to the Vietnam War as well (69), and Russell sees the Trixie project as an analogue to Agent Orange, the highly toxic defoliant dropped on the jungles of Vietnam in vast quantities (75).

While some of these examples are subjective, stronger connections can be found in the character back stories and dialogue. The Vietnam War directly in-forms two of the main characters: both David and Clank are disillusioned Vi-etnam veterans. This fact is mentioned explicitly only once, in dialogue between David and Judy: "The whole time I was in 'Nam, I figured you were Clank's girl." David at least distances himself from his former role as a Special Forces soldier: "Action, adventure, Evans City's only Green Beret. Christ, I can't be-lieve that was me." From their experience, both David and Clank derive a clear distrust of the US military. When Artie proposes cooperating with the army pa-trols, Clank quickly dismisses the idea: "The army ain't nobody's friend. We know, we've been in."

Their negative view of the army is actually shared by its members. A group of soldiers, frustrated about being kept ignorant by their leaders, resolves to "sit it out, let someone else do the dirty work." Peckem himself, as the operation's commanding officer, agrees with Dr. Watts criticism of the military's efforts. When Watts expresses amazement at "how shoddy this operation is," Peckem replies: "Nothing amazes me anymore, doctor. Nothing in this god-damned army amazes me." The term "anymore" suggests that Peckem's past experiences have shaped his outlook, just like they did for David and Clank. For all involved, it is established well before the mishandling of the quarantine becomes evident that the US military is inherently flawed and incapable of handling the situation with any kind of regard for the local population. In fact, securing just two thirds of the population, with the rest most likely dead, qualifies as a success for the leadership and causes little introspection among the higher-ups. This perception of the military apparatus is of course informed by the conduct of the Vietnam War.

By staging a containment scenario in a small town in Pennsylvania, *The Crazies* (1973) transports the whole conflict into the center of America and demonstrates the systemic flaws that led to its failure. The film works as an "ironic inverse allegory of American involvement in Vietnam with Americans playing the roles of occupier and occupied, soldier and civilian, exploiter and exploited" (Williams, *Knight* 60-61). This strategy undermines the divide between the war's sides, complicating identification with categories like "Us" and "Them."[3] This is key to the next section.

"How can you tell who's crazy?": Indistinguishable Monstrosity

The Crazies (1973) is remarkable insofar as the monsters play a relatively minor part. The fugitive group around David spends more time evading the military than battling aggressive crazies, and the military kills roughly as many fleeing unarmed townsfolk as aggressive attackers. The problem, and the intriguing part, is that monstrosity is not easily distinguishable from regular behavior in *The Crazies* (1973). The infection with the Trixie contagion expresses itself only in changed behavior, gradually worsening from quirks and agitation to very dramatic displays of psychosis. The exact effects seem different from case to case. Some turn into stereotypical psycho killers: a farmer murders his wife and sets fire to his house, then rambles and screams as police arrest him. A grandmother repeatedly stabs a soldier with a knitting needle, only to return to knitting with a smile. The transformation can be observed more closely in David's group, as all members except David succumb to the infection. Kathy becomes increasingly unconcerned about events, giggling about death and wandering off into danger, which leads to her demise. Her father Artie turns both aggressive and overprotective, and finally succumbs to incestuous desires. Clank turns violent, killing soldiers without inhibition, and tries to upstage David's status as a former Green Beret. Judy turns more sentimental and clings to David, but is killed while still in a relatively early stage.

From these examples, it appears that the contagion does not generally induce violent behavior. Instead, it appears to increase perhaps unconscious tendencies and remove inhibitions. The monstrous behavior of the crazies is thus fully rooted in their normal personalities, as Wood points out: "The continuity suggested

---

3   This approach matches that of anti-war science fiction writers, as examined by Franklin in "The Vietnam War as American Science Fiction and Fantasy": "Here American troops are both victimizers and victims . . ." (177).

by the opening between normality and craziness is sustained throughout the film," as the "boundary between the two is continually blurred" (116). Monstrosity in *The Crazies* (1973) is then not diametrically opposed to normality, but a consequence of the same attitudes and patterns of behavior. Wood explains the relationship further:

The hysteria of the quarantined can be attributed equally to the spread of contagion among them or to their brutal and ignominious herding together in claustrophobically close quarters by the military . . . The crazies, in other words, represent merely an extension of normality, not its opposite. The spontaneous violence of the mad appears scarcely more grotesque than the organized violence of the authorities (117).

In line with Wood's psychoanalytic theory of horror, then, the crazies enact a "return of the repressed," exposing tendencies that are already present, but not commonly acknowledged.

Consequently, the film's characters struggle to distinguish insanity and normality. When made aware of the contagion, David remarks: "Some of the rednecks that live in this area, they could be shooting each other and not even care why." In David's experience, pointless violence is already part of everyday life around the small town. As mentioned in the previous section, one of the political leaders names resistance as a natural consequence of the quarantine measures. Given the inherent brutality of both military and "rednecks," the actual effects of the contagion are only of minor relevance – the scenario might play out much the same if the outbreak were imaginary, including the shootings and the massive loss of human life. Put bluntly, *The Crazies'* American society, from the rednecks to the president, is already dangerously insane.

A closer examination of the spread of the Trixie contagion leads to the core family as the first site of this violent insanity. The film's opening scene shows a boy teasing his sister, followed by their father demolishing the house in a fit of rage. During his rampage, he inadvertently sets the house on fire, while the children discover their murdered mother. This scene of domestic violence sets the stage with the "acting out of tensions dramatized within the family" (Wood 116). Following Wood's psychoanalytic reading of horror films as the return of the repressed, this scene brings underlying conflicts within the family to the forefront. The contagion, then, merely acts as a catalyzer for the violence inherent in the family unit itself. The same applies to the incest and rape committed by Artie, which marks the end point of a slow escalation.

Williams picks up Wood's thesis and takes a stronger focus on gender, interpreting much of *The Crazies* as the dramatization of patriarchal repression

(*Knight* 62). Partly, the contagion causes a repressive system to step up its measures, while it also reveals hidden tensions against patriarchy (63). For instance, Williams reads a knitting grandmother's attack on a soldier as a rebellion (63), even though the woman in question returns to the knitting activity that would seem to be in tune with traditional gender expectations. Likewise, he concludes from the deaths of Kathy and Judy that masculinity represents danger to females in *The Crazies* (68). And only by rejecting "macho values" (69), that is, his attitudes as a soldier in Vietnam, does David stand a chance to survive. Williams even suggests that David's rejection of "patriarchal violence" is the reason for his immunity to the contagion (71). While that is not strictly supported by the text (there is no causal relationship between infection and a person's value system, whereas a simple physical immunity is at least mentioned in the dialogue), Williams's reading is at least plausible: since the contagion brings out repressed violence and exacerbates harmful patterns of behavior, a character completely without any of those would seem to feel no symptoms.[4] It is questionable whether this argument pans out to the end, though. When the random death of Judy breaks David's spirit, he becomes indistinguishable from the crazies. During their only encounter, Peckem asks a soldier whether David had been tested for the contagion (which could reveal his immunity), and the soldier replies "do you need to ask?" The soldier is right in the sense that it makes no difference if an infection is confirmed or not, as sanity is under threat from a number of directions in *The Crazies* (1973), not only from those outlined by Williams.

Family and gender roles are just one angle as *The Crazies* (1973) moves to a "more generalized treatment of social disintegration" (Wood 116). Still, the symptoms of the contagion appear to roughly go along with stereotypical social roles and traditions. In addition to the examples already mentioned, several men become violent, matching the description of rednecks given by David. One woman absent-mindedly sweeps the fields with a broom as she follows a violent mob, the town priest turns martyr via self-immolation as another woman watches, gleefully clutching her cross pendant.

Despite the fact that there is no easy way of distinguishing healthy and infected individuals, Peckem issues an order that anyone "obviously infected or resisting is to be treated as the enemy." There is no "obvious" sign of infection, but the inclusion of all those resisting makes the distinction moot anyway. Holding the perimeter is the only objective, the human element is utterly neglected. Watts summary is correct: "The whole thing's insane. How can you tell who's

---

4   This pattern recurs in *Dawn of the Dead* (1978), where Roger's and Stephen's descent into obsession prefigures their later death and return as zombies (cf. chapter 6).

infected and who isn't?" His question remains unanswered, as Peckem deals with the next urgent issue.

Attempts to determine monstrosity are obviously frustrated by the film's deliberate blurring of all such distinctions between the sane and the infected. Perhaps it is more helpful to return to Wood's formula of horror, "normality is threatened by the Monster" (78). At first glance, the film's monsters seem easily located: normal townsfolk, transformed into psychotic murderers, who disrupt the normality of small town life. The army, then, works as an agent of normality, aiming to contain and remove the monsters in order to restore normality. However, the army's methods cause equal or greater harm to the normality of Evans City than the crazies themselves. A third of the population are "lost," and given the orders to fire at all who resist or try to break the perimeter, combined with the fact that identifying the infected is impossible, it is likely that a significant part of the dead were not infected at all. The film's conclusion does not restore normality, as the survivors are crammed into the high school, which now serves as a makeshift madhouse. The normality of Evans City has ended and cannot be restored, which is as much the fault of the army as that of the contagion (which is, in turn, caused by the army). Thus, the army, too, works as an outside threat disrupting regular life, as the initial source of the monstrous outbreak (developing and losing the Trixie contagion) and by completing the destruction it inadvertently began.

This line of argument does not end with the military, though. As mentioned before, David attributes as much violent madness to the local rednecks. The triangular model Wood posits for *Dawn of the Dead* (1978) and then applies to *The Crazies* (1973) is, in the end, obsolete. While the film turns into a three-way struggle between crazies – besieged – military (cf. Wood 117), it arguably ends up with one normal man (or perhaps two, if we count Peckem) in a world of monsters. If the world is already insane in *The Crazies* (1973), then the world is also monstrous. Normality is not only disrupted and irrevocably destroyed; it has never existed as distinct from the monsters.

In regards to genre discourse, *The Crazies* (1973) still has many elements of 1950s monster B-movies. The conflict of military and science plays out between Peckem and Watts, with Watts possessing a more accurate view of the situation. While Peckem is still concerned about civilian lives, he puts those concerns below his goal of completing the mission. Watts works much more as a representative of reason, but he is not without flaws. His empathy for human beings is limited, as he speaks of "human guinea pigs" and people as "vectors" for the contagion. The film does not present Watts, and thus science, as the "better" side. As mentioned, Watts fails to communicate his work (to his assistant) and explain his discovery, thereby completely wiping out any progress through his extremely ill-advised escape attempt. Where films like *The Day the Earth Stood Still* (1951) put their trust in scientists as the voice of reason, *The Crazies* (1973) is disillusioned with all sides of the establishment.

While the conflict between science and military is at the forefront in *The Crazies* (1973), other authorities enjoy a similar fate of reluctant collaboration, followed by being deposed by the army. This applies to the doctor, the mayor, and the sheriff. The latter shows a brief burst of violent resistance, but the pattern is the same: the town authorities all cooperate, due to their belief in higher authorities. When they realize that the army is not serving the town's interest at all, it is too late. The mayor is seen in one of the final shots as one still sane individual among the imprisoned townsfolk. Local authorities are depicted as less destructive and ignorant, but are helpless to influence events.

THE CRAZIES (2010)

Released to theaters in February of 2010, the remake of *The Crazies* enjoyed relatively positive reviews and moderate box office success, at least doubling its production budget.[5] While still an independent release, the budget and promotional campaign far surpassed those of Romero's 1973 film. Due to its recent release, *The Crazies* (2010) has been given very little scholarly attention as of this writing. However, it represents an interesting case for the purposes of this study, as it updates a film charged with the politics of its period. The fact that the remake was produced by a company which, according to its mission statement, "seeks to entertain audiences first, then to invite them to participate in making a difference" ("Our Mission") also promises insight into the calculated use of horror narratives as part of political discourse. It seems likely that Participant Media, better known for its documentaries including the Al Gore feature *An Inconvenient Truth*, saw a potential in Romero's 1973 film that matched its sociopolitical outlook (cf. Anderson).

The remake is set in Ogden Marsh, a rural community in Iowa, and focuses on the town sheriff David and his wife Judy, who serves as the town's physician. Both notice a rise in unusual behavior among the townsfolk, from general ab-

---

5   *Box Office Mojo* reports a domestic take of $39 million, plus an international take of $15 million, at a budget of $20 million ("The Crazies"), whereas Anderson lists the budget at only $12 million (Anderson). As for reviews, *Rotten Tomatoes* records an average of 71% positive ("THE CRAZIES (2010)").

sent-mindedness to a farmer's inexplicable murder of his family. Investigating the discovery of a dead body in the woods, David finds that a military aircraft has crashed in the nearby river. He concludes that the plane's cargo may have contaminated the water supply and shuts it off, but unknown to David, the army has already initiated a quarantine protocol. Phone and internet connections are cut off just as violence among the townsfolk increases. Before David and Judy can leave town, they are captured by soldiers and brought to a hastily erected internment camp without further explanation. There, the couple is separated as Judy is diagnosed as infected. David is set for evacuation, but when riots break out, he returns to save Judy as the army leaves the camp behind.

After the rapid failure of containment, David and Judy, together with David's deputy Russ and Judy's nurse Becca, again attempt to leave the devastated town, evading the hostile army and the infected "crazies" alike. Both groups appear to attack indiscriminately, such as when a gang of crazies kill Becca, or when an attack helicopter destroys the group's car. Both the nature of the contagion and the army's goals remain obscure, until a captured intelligence officer gives a short summary: the plane contained a biological weapon on its way to disposal, and now the army tries to keep it from spreading by any means. Russ, suffering from the contagion as well, murders the officer and, realizing his slip from sanity, sacrifices himself at an army checkpoint to allow David and Judy to sneak by. At a truck stop, David and Judy find evidence of a mass execution by the army, and after surviving yet another attack by crazies, they commandeer a truck and leave the area before it is destroyed by a nuclear explosion. As they head to Cedar Rapids, Iowa, on foot, on-screen text informs the audience that the containment protocol is still ongoing and that the military will move on Cedar Rapids next. During the end credits, a short newscast relates that the destruction of Ogden Marsh has been covered up, and that the contagion is still spreading.

The most basic plot points of the original film remain unchanged: a plane crash releases a biological weapon upon a rural community, turning its inhabitants violently insane. As the army botches its containment efforts, a group of townsfolk around a main couple struggle to escape. The biopolitical dimension of the narrative is still present in the attempted management of the population and the ensuing collision of political power and individual life. The most notable change in the remake is the change of perspective. Instead of exploring the catastrophe and containment from three different points of view (townsfolk, army, and higher leadership), the remake focuses exclusively on the first group, whereas the motivations of the army, not to mention the political leadership, remain almost completely unknown. This renders the story far more straightforward, as the two main characters and two supporting characters make their way from one life-threatening obstacle to the next. Considering this structure, as well as the increase in suspenseful escape scenes and graphic violence, it is easier to firmly locate *The Crazies* (2010) in the horror genre. This shift towards a more effective horror film also significantly alters the dynamic of monstrosity and normality, compared to the 1973 film, as the following section will show.

The Army as Monstrous

As explained in the previous section, *The Crazies* (1973) is characterized by an utter failure of communication at all levels, between individuals as much as institutions. The remake's narrowing of perspective gives a different twist to this fundamental problem: instead of the internal inefficiency of military structures, it showcases the struggles of individuals dealing with a faceless, incommunicative opposition. The first hints of the military's presence are completely depersonalized. A satellite view marks the first as well as the last sign of their involvement in the film. A conspicuous black SUV is seen in the street, only to disappear with screeching tires when approached. Most soldiers wear NBC gear, that is, gas masks and protective suits, leaving no human face to empathize with. Communication is limited to barking orders to "keep moving;" questions from Dave or Judy are never answered.

Only two counterpoints to the faceless authority appear throughout the film. One soldier is unmasked at gunpoint and explains himself as following orders. He appears to be a terrified young man, who is as ignorant as the populace. He only knows that there was "some kind of accident" and says that his unit only realized where they were when they read the road signs. Towards the end, a captured intelligence officer offers full information, revealing that the virus, codename Trixie, got lost on its way to a disposal plant. Still, he is totally unapologetic: "It was designed to destabilize a population, in this case the wrong one. Look, fella, we lost a plane. What do you want me to say?" He insists he came to help, but before that claim can be verified, he is murdered by the increasingly unstable Russell. On screen for barely a minute, the intelligence officer is the closest analogue the remake has to the original's Peckem and Watts. While short, this appearance is key to determining the army's attitude and role in the film.

According to the officer, the Trixie contagion was designed as a weapon to destabilize populations, a revelation which outrages the group and Judy as a medical professional in particular. This suggests a military, or rather a military-scientific complex that has, or at least had at one point, an interest in causing precisely the sort of mass violence and murder that the town Ogden Marsh has suffered to this point. To what end is left to speculation, but the idea itself suggests a leadership that either accepts or wants to cause civilian casualties on a massive scale. Given that Trixie was on its way to incineration, the doctrine behind Trixie might have changed, but its accidental spread demonstrates that even abandoned attitudes still cause harm in the present. Even if we assume that the current military leadership disposed of Trixie for ethical reasons, the mass executions of townsfolk regardless of infection still show little care for the civilian population. The manufacture of a behavior-altering virus may be the stuff of fantastic genres, but *The Crazies* (2010), like its predecessor, suggests that in extreme circumstances, the US army would in fact be ruthless and clueless enough to massacre American citizens.

Beyond this small part, the military's efforts and decision making process remain completely obscure. The only communication between military and civilians are orders to keep moving. The 1973 film had the military perform an information blackout; in the remake, that blackout also hits the audience. In the first film, the military is a destructive force thanks to the flaws in its own organization and leadership. It's not so much bad intent as incompetence, confusion and disregard of civilian suffering in favor of larger scale security and image concerns. The military in the 2010 version is a destructive force, and also utterly incomprehensible and unfathomable. The viewer gets no insight how we get from a plane crash to a quarantine and a nuclear weapons drop on American soil. The most telling image is the distant, mechanical satellite view. That is the military's perspective in the remake. It might be a more competent force than in Romero's film, but it's distinctly less human. On this point, Anderson quotes the director Breck Eisner:

"In Romero's movie," Mr. Eisner said, "there's a bifurcated point of view, between the military and the townsfolk. In our version the military's still a force, but the story's not told from their point of view." Which is more frightening, he said. "You or I wouldn't have the advantage of knowing the military's thought processes. Giving the audiences the military's view lessens the impact of the movie and, in a way, lessens the message of the movie." (Anderson)

Eisner may be correct if we focus on "impact" as the creation of suspense and mystery. An unknown, invisible enemy may generate more tension than one whose motivations and movements are known and understood at all times. These techniques of obscuring are used in the construction and depiction of monsters, and by applying them to the military, it functions as a monster in the narrative of *The Crazies* (2010). If we are concerned with the "impact" or "message" of the

1973 film in regards to the flaws of institutions, however, then obviously the absent military is not going to provide as much insight.

Is the army monstrous in *The Crazies* (2010)? The problem with this decision, whether the army is depicted as well-meaning, but flawed and overextended, or whether it is simply callous as an organization, is that the film offers very little insight into its internal workings. Romero's 1973 film shows exactly where the handling of the outbreak goes wrong, and that is, at all levels. Colonel Peckem is driven by a genuine desire to protect civilians and has serious doubts about his mission, but performing his function in the system by following orders inevitably leads to failures at tremendous human cost. The army in the 1973 film is arguably monstrous in its incompetence, short-sightedness and its adherence to harmful structures and procedures, provided that human failings qualify as monstrous.

The remake, however, offers the viewer only the same limited information obtained by the protagonists. That includes traces of atrocities, an unapologetic intelligence officer, and a lone private putting a human face on the otherwise faceless military machine. The identification of monstrosity and normality in the 1973 film was frustrated by the film's continuous blurring of these distinctions, yet the remake keeps its actors and concepts fairly separate. Compared to the 1973 film, the military seems more powerful and omniscient, as evidenced by the total communications blackout and the satellite surveillance capable of picking up two individuals walking across a field in the final scene. It also appears more coherent and disciplined, from what little the film shows. There are no scenes of internal disagreements or looting, for instance. The unnamed private does his duty even in complete ignorance, yet he helps David on nothing but his word.

While the remake was evidently designed with a particular political position in mind, it is rather reluctant to insert direct references to current US wars or security policy. While the first film was rife with imagery and rhetoric from the Vietnam War, the remake makes no mention of terrorism, or of national security. None of the characters involved relate their experiences in Iraq or Afghanistan, and the short-lived prison camp is never compared to GTMO at Guantanamo or other infamous military prisons in dialogue; in fact, the characters talk very little about matters larger than their immediate survival concerns. Where the 1973 film had its characters loudly wonder whether they were in a war or explain their attitude towards the army, the remake's cast limits itself to wondering "who are these fuckers?" Even Judy's discovery that "they exterminated everyone, not just the sick" leads only to a debate about the chances of survival and a reaffirmation of the main couple's relationship. Given the political consciousness of its source, and abundant contemporary criticism of related security policies, the remake appears oddly understated and even reactionary.

Instead, only more general comparisons can be drawn: an airstrike on a car may recall drone attacks on suspected terrorist leaders, the makeshift open-air prison camp may evoke GTMO, both satellite imagery and night-time army raids of civilian houses are reminiscent of US military actions in Iraq and Afghanistan. Even without the direct references of the original, the depiction of the army in *The Crazies* (2010) naturally draws on media images that have been omnipresent throughout the 2000s, and any readings of the film are likewise shaped by the extensively covered engagements US forces have had over the past decade. Overall, the army's performance in the film boils down to this: it fails at handling an insurgency, and not having learned from this, its destructive containment policy targets the next bigger American town.

In summary, even without insight into the military's organization and decision making process, it appears that the criticism in broadest terms remains the same as almost four decades earlier: in its attempts to solve the problem that they themselves caused, the military will do more harm than good. It is, however, far more drastic in its measures. The threat of nuclear bombing that constantly hung over the 1973 film is finally realized in the remake, concluding the film with an apocalyptic image, and like all of the military's actions, it comes with no warning to the locals. 2010's *The Crazies* may not offer insight into the workings of government and military, but it expects the worst from them.

Monstrosity of the Crazies

The progression of symptoms from the contagion in *The Crazies* (2010) is fairly straightforward. The infected first appear absent-minded and disconnected, only to become increasingly violent. Invariably, the crazies turn into psychotic murderers who are either unwilling or unable to communicate with their victims. This transformation can be traced on the bodies of the infected: a nosebleed signals the start of the transformation, which progresses through paleness, until it concludes with monstrous bulging veins and visible eye discoloration. In the end stage, the infected appear distinctly inhuman and barely different from the undead zombies in current genre films. Their relentless aggression and lack of speech except for feral screams also match this type, and the crazies' attack in the car wash plays out in a similar fashion as comparable scenes in *Dawn of the Dead* (2004).[6]

---

6 Bishop claims that the 1973 film pioneered "running zombies" as murderous, but not undead cannibals (cf. Bishop, *American* 205). That is a bit of a stretch and incorrect

Not all of the crazies are reduced to a feral state, however. The widow of a farmer David shot in self-defense shows up at his house along with her son to enact her revenge. Despite her grotesque appearance, she is quite capable of explaining her intention, as she remarks to her son that "this is the gun that killed your father." The two are also capable of subduing Judy and tying her up while laying an ambush for David, and the mother responds to David's insults. This suggests that the crazies still possess some human capability for reasoning, at least in certain stages of the infection. In summary, the depiction of the crazies draws on a mixture of established horror film monster types, in particular zombies and the psychotic rednecks of the genre colloquially known as hillbilly horror and described as "urbanoia" by Clover (124; cf. chapter 7).

Following the original film, and typical for horror narratives in which monstrosity is contagious, the progress of the infection is exemplified by one of the characters. David's deputy Russell demonstrates the slide into callous violence, punctuated by occasional moments of clarity. Fiercely loyal to David, he only turns on him when he feels his efforts are not appreciated and takes control of the group. After being disarmed, he realizes the hopelessness of his condition and, determined to not cause further deaths, walks into an army checkpoint with an empty gun to get himself killed.

In the 1973 film, the contagion caused the extreme exaggeration of pathological tendencies already present in its victims and their social roles. The same seems to apply for at least some of the crazies in the remake, who still act in extension of underlying issues and conflicts, as unhinged continuation. In the example above, a mother acts out her frustration over the death of her husband. Likewise, a group of poachers resorts to killing humans, treating them in the exact same manner as game animals. But unlike the 1973 film, the remake shows only murderous crazies. There is no equivalent to Cathy's oblivious curiosity, or the woman sweeping the fields with a broom, or even purely self-destructive insanity like the self-immolating priest. The contagion does not amplify a whole range of behaviors into extremes, but turns everyone into a killer. That diminishes the point Williams makes about the original and its dismantling of particular

---

when it comes to cannibalism. 1973's crazies are living people, infected with a contagion and therefore aggressive and dangerous. Few scenes evoke the zombies of previous and later films, and only the mass uprising in school, where a mindless mass pushes against the soldiers, really works in this way. The comparison is, however, appropriate when it comes to the remake, whose crazies are not cannibalistic, but in many cases indistinguishable from the running zombies of *28 Days Later* or *Dawn of the Dead* (2004).

roles and institutions, as it seems to make no difference what the crazies' former roles, gender and issues were.

As with monstrous behavior, the remake is less ambiguous and more effect-driven when it comes to appearances. There are clear signs, and clear categories. While the first film kept blurring the distinctions between groups, the remake only deals with such ambiguities in the first part. Russell's symptoms are subtle at first, and the army's method of finding the infected produces a false positive on Judy. As the story develops, though, ambiguity makes way to certainty, as a single glance confirms the status of an individual. The threat of the crazies becomes much more evident, which in turn makes the army's excessive action more reasonable: they may have committed atrocities, but did so in the face of a genuine threat. Therefore, while *The Crazies* (2010) appears to disapprove of the army's methods, it creates a scenario in which said methods may just be adequate.

Heartland: The Small Town

As with all horror narratives, monstrosity is contrasted with normality in *The Crazies* (2010). Ogden Marsh is established as a typical American small town in an opening montage: first, the film shows the town as empty and devastated, and then it flashes back to a montage of fields, busy tractors, the sheriff's car on an empty highway, the town's main street with a mother and her children, another couple of children riding bikes and a store clerk sweeping the sidewalk, while "We'll Meet Again" sung by Johnny Cash plays. It is only a brief scene, but it emphasizes the vastness of the fields and the small size of the town. The main street is framed by the American flag and a banner welcoming the local baseball team, while no chain stores or large advertisements are to be seen. Family and cleanliness contrast with the devastation to come, and the choice of song is perhaps ambiguous, but expresses a kind of country flair.

Family, like all institutions, was unstable in the 1973 film, and frequently the site of violence. In the conclusion of the first film, David is helpless as his pregnant wife Judy is killed, leaving him a broken man. The remake is less pessimistic in this regard. Arguably, it affirms the value of the nuclear family, as 2010's David and Judy survive and at least have the possibility of life as a family. Throughout the horrors of their escape, the two remain as a unit, supporting each other both emotionally as well as professionally. Remarkably, the conclusion of *The Crazies* (2010) swaps personal tragedy, the death of Judy and her unborn child, in favor of mass tragedy, the destruction of Ogden Marsh and any possible survivors. In more provocative terms, the remake has no reservations about dropping a nuclear bomb on the town, but it doesn't dare touch the nuclear family.

When it comes to the general population of Ogden Marsh, the remake is likewise less critical. David makes no disparaging remarks about rednecks, and the closest example of redneck stereotypes are a group of hunters who go out hunting even after hunting season has expired. While they offer excuses and moan at the seizure of their guns, they remain respectful of the David as a representative of the law. Later in the film, the hunters reappear as late-state crazies, barely recognizable as human and massacring human beings. Given their appearance and complete lack of communication, they are clearly different from their earlier selves, and it is difficult to read them as a commentary on rural population. As a counterexample, the mother looking to avenge her husband acts in continuation of a sentiment expressed earlier in the film, but again, the visible physical transformation signals a clear distinction from the regular human population. And while both examples appear as monstrous rednecks, they do not confirm the 1973 film's thesis that, like the military and government, the American rural population is already dangerously insane.

The Crazies (2010) features a conflict of local and federal authorities, but only insofar as local authorities are completely ignored along with the rest of the populace. The 1973 film showed cooperation with local government, law enforcement and medical professionals until it broke down, whereas the army in the remake makes no such attempt. In this context, it is worth noting that the main couple, David and Judy, represents authorities, and more so than their predecessors in the 1973 film. 1973's David is a fireman, not in a leading position, and Judy works as a nurse. Their counterparts in the 2010 film take a step up the career ladder as a Sheriff and physician, respectively. While this puts them above most of the townsfolk in terms of authority and ability, they are still represented as average small town inhabitants as opposed to experts. According to Jancovich, experts are distrusted in a number of 1950s monster movies, as a reaction to social change in the post-war era (26). Some traces of this motive can still be found in current horror narratives, especially when they remake earlier films, working as palimpsest. However, while 2010's David and Judy could be cast as experts, they are presented as clearly separate from the representatives of the mostly unseen government-military-scientific apparatus responsible for both the outbreak and the equally devastating response.

Overall, the remake of *The Crazies* appears more drastic in terms of direct horror, but less radical in its politics. Not everything is as fundamentally rotten as in the first film. Not the whole world is insane, but the military machinery may be. The 1973 film was blatant in its political commentary, yet nuanced in the depiction of monstrosity and normality. The 2010 film is reluctant in its commentary, but blatant when it comes to its monsters. The radical quality of the first film, so appreciated by Wood, is absent, whether as a side effect of a retooling as a lean, effective horror film, or as a result of a more conservative film industry. Considering some of the other examples in this study, this should come as no surprise; it does, however, call the mission statement of its producers into question.

6. Consumer Zombie Apocalypse

Far from a localized intrusion of monsters into peaceful normal spaces, the two versions of *Dawn of the Dead* feature an apocalyptic scenario in which a massive zombie outbreak most likely spells the end of humankind. Individually, the walking dead may be less impressive than other horror monsters, but as an ever-growing mass, they not only threaten, but destroy civilization on a global level. While the scale of the *Dawn of the Dead* films is ambitious, the core narratives only focus on the struggles of a handful of survivors who take refuge in a shopping mall. Each iteration takes on a different tone, and where the much celebrated 1978 film satirically casts hapless zombies and humans alike as obsessed consumers, the 2004 version forgoes much of the social commentary in favor of a fast-paced, violent struggle for survival.

Dawn of the Dead (1978)

After a number of less successful projects, George Romero returned to the genre that had launched his filmmaking career with *Dawn of the Dead* (1978). The film was again shot on a fairly low budget, and released without support from major film studios. Nevertheless, it earned remarkable critical and commercial success, ranking as one of the most profitable independent features at the time (Gagne 83, J. Russell 95). Quickly achieving cult status, the film went on to serve as a paradigmatic work for the zombie film genre. Thanks to the efforts of special effects man Tom Savini, it set new standards in terms of splatter, the explicit and excessive depiction of violence, which oddly served to amplify the script's satirical tone. Over the years, the combination of gore and social critique has drawn considerable academic interest. *Dawn of the Dead* (1978) has been the subject of numerous academic articles, and forms a mainstay of book-length studies on Romero's work or the zombie genre in general. The latter has seen a resurgence in production since the early 2000s, and a vast increase in academic interest to go along with it. Amidst this activity, *Dawn of the Dead* (1978) remains a key work in the genre canon, and a launching point for various critical readings of the genre.

At the start of *Dawn of the Dead* (1978), the United States appears to have been crumbling under a zombie epidemic for some time. As the studio of a Philadelphia TV station descends into chaos, female lead Fran attempts to make a difference before abandoning her post and eloping with her partner, traffic helicopter pilot Stephen. Meanwhile, a botched raid on a tenement building leads to numerous deaths as police units open fire on inhabitants and zombies alike. SWAT officers Roger and Peter, both disillusioned by the experience, desert the force and join up with Stephen and Fran. The four leave the city via helicopter and, after a risky refueling stop, decide to land at a shopping mall to load up on supplies. Even though the mall is overrun with zombies, the stores are intact and well-stocked, and the men decide to stay despite Fran's protests. Fran reveals that she's pregnant, but insists on being a full member in the undertaking.

The group develops a plan to shut off and secure the mall, commandeering trucks to block the doors before exterminating those zombies still left inside. The plan succeeds and the group takes possession of the mall, but Roger's overconfidence leads to him being bitten by a zombie. While the group is now free to enjoy the luxuries of the mall, Roger's condition slowly worsens, and once he dies and rises as a zombie, Peter shoots him. Over the following months, the remaining three survivors live comfortably inside the mall, but also grow increasingly bored with it and each other. Their routines are shattered when a roving band of looters appears and breaks into the mall. Stephen and Peter resolve to defend the building, and in the ensuing battle, zombies break into the mall and decimate the looters. Stephen is killed and turned into a zombie, and proceeds to lead the undead into the human survivors' hideout. Peter contemplates suicide, but resolves to join Fran in the helicopter and head towards an uncertain future, while zombies once again roam the mall.

Dawn of the Dead (1978) is part of a cycle of films, and as dawn follows night, the title suggests a continuation of Romero's earlier *Night of the Living Dead* (1968). There is however no narrative continuity between the two films, as *Night* conclusively wrapped up its zombie threat, while it is evidently ongoing and unstoppable in *Dawn*. Neither characters nor events of *Night* are mentioned; therefore *Dawn* may not be a sequel in the strictest sense. Instead, it has been perceived as blurring the line between genre, sequel and remake (Verevis, "Redefining" 17). For some, *Dawn* counts as a straightforward remake of *Night* (cf. Loudermilk 84, Wood 114), since its basic scenario – a group of survivors besieged by zombies – is arguably identical. That reading, however, is based on a rather broad concept of the term remake that again bleeds into what is more productively called a (sub)genre. It requires an essential core of the story, itself unique and original, as the key marker of a remake. Given the complex web of intertextual connections from which cultural products spring, and more specifically, the repetitive nature of popular genres such as horror, that notion becomes rather problematic. Once the story of *Dawn* is condensed far enough, it may indeed match *Night*, or any of Romero's zombie films (Verevis, "Redefining" 17), but at that degree of abstraction, several generic plots will. As a variation of a theme, as opposed to a new version of the same film, *Dawn of the Dead* (1978) does not conform to the narrow definition of remake as employed in this study. It is not a "'conventional' or *direct* sequel" either, but a "serialization" that develops several of Romero's ideas, including zombie consciousness and political commentary (Verevis, "Redefining" 18-21).

Beyond the connection to Romero's earlier zombie film, there is also a certain thematic overlap between *Dawn of the Dead* (1978) and *The Crazies* (1973). While *Dawn* is not a Vietnam War allegory like *The Crazies* (1973), the war and the discourses surrounding it still inform the film. The police raid at the start of the film plays out like a small-scale repeat of the disastrous military action from *The Crazies* (1973), as law enforcement and National Guard enact a policy that does more harm than good to the local population. Williams finds that the film's images reflect the war, in particular the prominent role of helicopters and military weaponry (Williams, *Hearths* 149). Nevertheless, the war, still a pressing issue in 1973, moves to the background in 1978, vanishing behind the distractions of consumer culture as the narrative progresses. Another link to the Vietnam War is frequently drawn on an extratextual level, between Savini's experience as a combat photographer in Vietnam and the spectacular wounds and amputations he modeled for the film. Through the special effects artist, then, the Vietnam War makes its way back to the film, and Bishop echoes Skal's assessment that *Dawn of the Dead* (1978) is the "cinematic version of posttraumatic stress syndrome" (Bishop, *American* 137).

While the progression of consumer culture and the Vietnam War are the primary references for historicizing readings, a few critics also draw connections to other events. For example, Russell quotes Stephen King with the claim that *Dawn of the Dead* (1978) captured a "sense of decay and entropy" sweeping American culture during the late 1970s, with references as diverse as the oil crisis and the nuclear disaster at Three Mile Island (J. Russell 94). While these connections are fairly tenuous,[1] the general idea matches Romero's intention of doing "one of these [zombie films] for every decade and try to reflect the attitude of the times" (quoted in Verevis, "Redefining" 21).

Amidst the general crisis that unfolds in *Dawn of the Dead* (1978), the institutions of American society disintegrate, and the opening scenes in Pittsburgh serve to demonstrate the utter failure of both news media and state authorities (cf. Bishop, *American* 141). First, the TV studio is shown as noisy and chaotic, with the crew loudly commenting on a live interview. The interviewer and the crew are hostile to the guest, who appears to act as an expert on the zombie problem. Meanwhile, the station is still broadcasting outdated information that will endanger the lives of refugees because they fear that ratings will drop if they stop. Neither the interview nor the listings transmit useful information, and the station's priorities are absurdly inappropriate to the emergency situation at hand. The pattern repeats later during the film, when the only remaining television broadcast appears to be the same interviewer arguing with a scientist, again without progress or consensus. In both interviews, the experts being interviewed appeal to reason as the only way to resolve the crisis, but are consistently drowned out. The media, as represented by television, thus produces only noise and no signal.

Next, the response by government authorities, as represented by police and National Guard units, fares just as badly. The raid on a housing project is chaotic, with no effective command structure in place, and with more directly lethal consequences. When one of the SWAT officers goes on a shooting rampage after spouting racist remarks, his unit is incapable of stopping him until Peter opens fire on his fellow officer. Peter has to break the rules of his institution – the police – because of its systematic failure to control its own personnel and prevent civilian deaths. The entire raid is a questionable success, as the inhabitants appear to have their own zombies locked up and under control until the police break in and set them free. Once we factor in that the police has to shoot its way past a group of resistant inhabitants and the ensuing one-man rampage, it should be clear enough that the authorities and their strategy of aggression and escala-

---

1   Not to mention the fact that the Three Mile Island disaster, as well as the second oil crisis King is likely to refer to, took place well after the release of *Dawn of the Dead* (1978). Therefore, these references are examples of audiences projecting their experience of current events onto an already completed work, as opposed to current events and attitudes influencing production (cf. *The Thing* (1982) and AIDS, chapter 3).

tion are responsible for far more damage than the ostensible monsters of the scene.[2]

Russell argues that the headshot "symbolizes everything that's wrong with the authorities' response to the crisis" (J. Russell 93), as it eliminates the rational and encourages the body to take over. Both the mindlessly violent raid, which sees (figuratively) headless police shooting the heads of humans and zombies alike, and the pointless TV interviews are evidence of what Russell calls the "apocalypse of reason" (93). This condition not only leads to the self-destruction of institutions, but of individuals as well, as the avoidable deaths of Roger and Stephen demonstrate (cf. J. Russell 93). However, while *Dawn of the Dead* (1978) opposes base physicality and emotion, it stops short of endorsing scientific rationality. The core of Dr. Rausch's argument is that we have to adapt to changing circumstances without clinging to obsolete preconceptions, a key theme in Romero's works that will also recur later in this chapter.

The raid not only demonstrates the authorities' callous incompetence; it is also charged with racial tensions, as the inhabitants of the building are mostly African American. Before the first zombie even enters the picture, the film is occupied with images of police rounding up African Americans. Waller adds a historical dimension to his reading by calling the raid a "shoot-out reminiscent of a 1960s urban riot" (Waller 299). Notably, the film's first shock effect is the head of an African American tenant exploding when hit by a gunshot, which aligns the police with the extreme degree of violence normally reserved for the confrontations between monsters and humans. At least until zombies enter into the already disastrous scene, it is arguably the police, or at least the psychopathic racist officer, that plays the role of the monster by violently intruding into the inhabitants' normality.

Harper puts a special emphasis on the "SWAT scene" that is supposedly "hardly mentioned in academic analyses." He claims that the scene "provides an interpretative context for the rest of the film" and furthermore "invites the audience to consider zombiedom as a condition associated with both racial oppression and social abjection and, therefore, sanctions socio-political interpretations of the film as a whole" (Harper). While such interpretations would not seem to require sanction, Harper is certainly correct that *Dawn of the Dead* (1978) introduces its monsters into a charged socio-political context and preempts a more

---

2 On its own, the scene only vaguely links to the Vietnam experience, but taking into account the very similar critique of *The Crazies* (1973), the argument becomes much stronger. The zombie apocalypse in Dawn of the Dead (1978) does read as an insurrection that the US government is unable to handle, or rather, is kept from effectively handling due to their faulty preconceptions and ineffective structures.

straightforward positioning as absolute Others. Although racism is implied as a theme of the text, especially with the African American Peter opposing the murderous SWAT officer, it only serves as a departure point and does not reappear – explicitly, that is, because the zombies are now positioned to be read in the contexts of, in Harper's words, racial oppression and social abjection.

The opening scenes set the mood and establish what Wood names as the premise of *Dawn of the Dead* (1978), that the "social order . . . *can't* be restored" (118).[3] The last scene in Philadelphia documents the breakdown of order by showing police officers who abandon their duties and strike out on their own. Out in the country, National Guard and local "rednecks" still fail to appreciate the hopelessness of their fight against the zombies, and beyond that point, only a dwindling number of TV and radio broadcasts maintain a semblance of normality. Even at the height of the emergency, government is still stuck in inefficient rituals, as one radio broadcast mentions the President submitting measures to Congress, which – hardly surprising – are never heard from again. The crumbling institutions of the old social order include the nuclear family. As Wood remarks, the family "as a social unit no longer exists," and is only "reconstituted in parody" later on, with the injured Roger being pushed around in a cart like a child on a shopping trip (118).[4] Wood, always interested in what he views as alternatives to a repressive traditional society, considers the apocalyptic scenario as an opportunity: since the characters are absolved from responsibility to value structures of the past, "they are potentially free people" (118). The realization is expressed in the film by Peter: "We're thieves and we're bad guys. We gotta find our own way." Nevertheless, until the conclusion of the film, Peter and the others are distracted from this goal by the shopping mall and the lifestyle it represents.

Consuming Stuff and People

While the group's stay at the shopping mall is not planned, the well-stocked and undamaged stores quickly capture the imagination of all three men. In fact, the mall seems to have an almost intoxicating effect that impairs rational thought. When Peter and Roger are trapped in a store by zombies, escape is only a secondary concern: "Who the hell cares, let's go shopping first!" While the men

---

3   Williams makes the same point, pronouncing the "old order" as "dead" (*Hearths* 154).
4   Even though the family may be gone, Wood finds that the "male 'buddy' relationship" (118) continues in its traditional boundaries. Wood reads the relationship between Peter and Roger as sexually repressed, with the attraction between the two men instead channeling to violence (120).

load up on goods, Fran is left behind unarmed and barely survives an encounter with a zombie. Still, Stephen hardly cares about her ordeal: "You should see all the stuff we got!" The widespread irrationality observed by Russell is amplified by the mall, and the men become obsessed with owning all the "stuff" the mall has to offer (cf. J. Russell 93). The film leaves little doubt that most of the goods that Peter, Stephen, and Fran hoard in their hideout have little use, from dollar bills to fashion, yet the thought of losing the mall to the gang of raiders is so revolting to Stephen ("This is ours! We took it!") that he starts a shootout that ultimately claims his life.

The living are not the only ones drawn to the mall; it appears just as attractive to the zombies who wander its halls or press against its doors. When Fran wonders about what drives the zombies to the mall, Stephen speculates, "Some kind of instinct. Memory of what they used to do. This was an important place in their lives." The power of consumer culture, then, is so great that it endures even death. Needless to mention, the zombies have even less use for the commodities found inside the stores. One recurring zombie carries a rifle through much of the film, despite being unable to use it, and at the conclusion exchanges it for another one he wrests from Peter. The zombie is so fascinated with his new acquisition that he ignores Peter. For the rest of the zombies, though, the desire to consume now extends to consuming humans as well (Gagne 87), so much that Bishop considers humans as products in a "zombie economy" (*American Zombie Gothic* 138).

The strange power of consumerism is the central theme of *Dawn of the Dead* (1978). As Bishop points out, most scholarship on *Dawn of the Dead* (1978) "rightly focuses on the film's rather overt criticism of contemporary consumer culture" and the film's simple core metaphor, that "Americans in the 1970s are the true zombies, slaves to the master of consumerism" (*American* 130). The point is hard to miss, as Romero stages images of zombies as grotesque parodies of regular shoppers, wandering around the mall with empty expressions, while cheerful easy listening music plays in the background (cf. Williams, *Knight* 86). Russell remarks that casting zombies as consumers may be "too obvious" for some, but insists that the blatancy of the film's central metaphor matches its barely concealed disgust for "the shallow, zombified wasteland that is 1970s America" (J. Russell 94).[5] Shaviro strikes a balance and calls Romero's films both "pop left-wing action cartoons" and "sophisticated political allegories of late capitalist America" (82).

---

5   According to Gagne, the lack of subtlety is part of a conscious strategy, and he quotes
    Romero as balancing the "socially satirical" elements with "obvious jokes" in order to
    keep the film from being a lecture (Gagne 87).

Inevitably, Romero's satire of consumerism is shaped by its historical context, and the choice of location picks up on a contemporary trend in consumption habits. Shopping malls had been invented in 1956, but were proliferating by the 1970s ("Birth, Death and Shopping" 102-03). Harper stresses the relative novelty of the mall setting at the time (Harper), and Gagne locates the intent as historically specific, since Romero's script "describes the mall as a veritable temple to the materialistic 'me' generation of the seventies" (87). Gagne's quote from the script heightens the significance of the mall by comparing it to a cathedral and an archeological dig unearthing "the gods and customs of a civilization now gone" (87). To Bishop, the mall functions as a character in the film's "morality play" (*American* 131), and also as a Gothic structure, the "site of uncanny mystery, suspense, horror, and, ultimately, death" (144). More focused on the theme of consumerism, Harper considers the setting's "dramatic potential" as a "potential site of resistance to the forces that regulate consumerism" (Harper). The mall thus serves as a central symbol of a culture of consumption that is perceived as unsustainable.

The film's stance seems clear, then: Harper considers *Dawn of the Dead* (1978) as "a radical (i.e. oppositional) anti-consumerist text" (Harper). For Bishop, too, the "true problem infecting humanity" is a paradigm of "pervasive consumerism" (*American* 130), and he quotes Marx and Hegel to argue that the characters lose their humanity by losing productive labor (130). However, some critics view the film's critique as broader. For Russell, the target is not only consumerism, but the entire "postmodern capitalist culture" (J. Russell 94). Beard sidelines the obvious and argues that the film is "unaware of its real political significance" (30). Drawing on Fredric Jameson, he claims that the "zombie is a figure of an expanding post-Fordist underclass filtered through a bourgeois imaginary of disgust," a "hysterical class fantasy" (30). While zombies are "de-subjectified" (30), they are hardly different from humans when it comes to the drive to consume. The zombies' ineptitude may be comical, but it is "not a satire on mindless consumerism" (Beard 30). Instead, Beard views them as a commentary on the abandonment of the masses by postmodern capitalism (31), at a specific moment in US socio-economic history.

Indeed, the mindless zombie masses lend themselves to any number of readings. For Harper, the zombies function as "lumpenproletariat," and as symbols of an oppressed group, with a reference to the origins of the zombie myth in slavery (Harper). In a similar vein, Bishop describes the zombies as "pathetic metaphors for colonial native peoples" during the protagonists' conquest of the mall (*American* 146). According to Wood, the zombies metaphorically represent "the whole dead weight of patriarchal consumer capitalism" (Wood 118), and Shaviro finds that the "life-in-death of the zombie is a near perfect allegory for the inner logic of capitalism" and its regime of exploitation, regimentation, and stimulation (Shaviro 83). More examples abound, but it should be obvious at this point that *Dawn of the Dead's* (1978) zombies are absolutely crucial to any reading of the film. Therefore, a closer look at these monsters and their relationship with normality is required.

"They're us": Zombies and Humans

The zombies in *Dawn of the Dead* (1978) correspond to the monster type Romero had established in *Night of the Living Dead* (1968), which had significantly departed from previous cinematic zombie traditions. Their (diegetic) origins are never explained, but their modus operandi is quite simple, as explained in the film's opening scenes: "Every dead body that is not exterminated becomes one of them. It gets up and kills! The people it kills get up and kill!" The zombies are regular humans who return from the dead, no longer capable of reason or communication, but equipped with a voracious appetite for the flesh of the still living. Breaking the taboo of cannibalism is an unambiguous marker of monstrosity, as is the violation of the boundary between life and death. Apart from the fact that their bite is infectious (as the example of Roger proves), they seem to possess no special or supernatural capabilities. In fact, the zombies are fairly harmless, as far as horror film monsters go. Most are limited to slowly shuffling about, and have to rely on numbers or the gross incompetence of the living to catch their prey.

The zombies are numerous and colorful in more than one sense. Their dead skin sports an oddly blue-ish color, and while some of the zombies are dehumanized in appearance by severe wounds or signs of decay, the majority of the zombies found in the mall still resemble regular people (see fig. 6). For Shaviro, the zombies appear most human when performing their role as shoppers (91). In gender and appearance, they form a cross-section of society (cf. Williams, *Knight* 94), even including a zombie bride and a zombie Hare Krishna monk in their ranks. Despite these signs of difference, however, the zombies "all act in the same way" (Shaviro 85). Still, for a mindless mass, the depiction or rather evaluation of their monstrosity has a surprising range, and Muir asserts that "the zombies, simultaneously funny, sad and repugnant, never come off worse than the humans do" (*Horror 1970s*, 595).

The opening TV interview invokes a dichotomy between zombies and humans, between monsters and normality, which informs the authorities' policy of containment and extermination. The same opposition is later reiterated by Dr.

Rausch, who is adamant that the undead cannot be considered as human: "These creatures are nothing but pure, motorized instinct. We must not be lulled by the concept that these are our family members or our friends. They are not." These statements are delivered with the authority of scientific experts and clearly establish the zombies as an inhuman, monstrous Other, and the conflict between humans and zombies as existential. Indeed, no communication or appeasement is possible, and after being treated as harmless by the raiders, the mall zombies return to kill and consume humans in the film's most graphically violent scenes as a reminder of their monstrosity. In addition, the drastic depictions of damaged and destroyed bodies serve to "make us lose all faith in bodily integrity," an effect that is only increased by the comedy permeating the film (J. Russell 95). Ultimately, though the dread of zombies is more a fear of infection than of annihilation (Shaviro 97), as the loss of individuality and humanity is perceived as more terrifying by the characters.

Nevertheless, the distinction between the humans and zombies is progressively dismantled throughout the film. At the raid in Philadelphia, Peter is revolted at having to execute passive and defenseless zombies, and the later mass killing of zombies at the mall is presented like a massacre (Waller 311). When Fran asks about the zombies, Peter explicitly equates the two groups: "They're us, that's all." This statement neatly undercuts the Us vs. Them opposition that has been built up previously.[6] The monsters are identified not as an external force intruding normality, but as originating inside the same normality, or as Shaviro puts it, the zombies do not "stand for a threat to social order from without. Rather, they resonate with, and refigure, the very processes that produce and enforce social order" (86). The zombies are rendered monstrous only by the extreme amplification of their obsession with consumption, or, even less favorably, they are merely consumers taken to the logical conclusion, the "dead end or zero degree" of capitalist logic (Shaviro 92-93). In fact, their fondness for the mall can be seen as an attempt to restore normality (Waller 306).

The progression of unthinking obsession into zombiedom can also be observed in deaths and transformations of Roger and Stephen. Roger's loss of control over his power fantasies leads to his injury, and subsequent illness, death and rise. Likewise, Stephen's blind rage at the raiders leads him to open fire, and the ensuing battle leads to his death and return as a zombie. Notably, zombie Stephen then leads the charge to repossess the mall for the undead. His allegiance to

---

6 As another point of view, Harper views the scene as a dramatization of consumer becoming aware "of the social costs of consumerism" and concludes that "Romero's take on consumer society constitutes a humanist, radical, and one might say Adornian critique of racism, sexism and exploitation" (Harper).

the living may cease, but his drive to own the mall does not. In each case, the character's obsession may not be the direct cause of their zombiefication (that would be zombie bites), but the logical continuity is clear. A decline into irrationality and obsession finds its ultimate consequence in becoming a zombie. The film's disinterest in providing a scientific explanation for the zombie state (speculations about a possible virus, overheard on the radio, never lead anywhere) keeps the focus on the progression of human into zombie, as opposed to fixating causality on a biological process.[7]

Furthermore, the narrative turns in the last quarter of the film continue to erode the dichotomy of humans and zombies. With the arrival of the raiders, Wood observes the same triangular structure (zombies/besieged/gang) as in *Night of the Living Dead* (1968) or *The Crazies* (1973) (118). For some time, the zombies are sidelined as the (human) raiders turn out to be the greater, if equally implacable threat. Distinctions are undermined, and all groups are ultimately revealed as "consumer-predators" (118), who will kill for possessions without reservations.

The only exception, and thereby alternative to self-destructive obsession with obsolete concepts is represented by the only female character, Fran. From the very start of the film, where she realizes that TV ratings no longer matter, to her resistance to settling at the mall, Fran is the only survivor "living in the future" (Bishop, *American* 162) and the "sole voice of morality" (Waller 301). Consequently, she serves to summarize the film's social critique in pointed statements, refusing Stephen's marriage proposal on the grounds that "it wouldn't be real" to asking "What have we done to ourselves?" when the detrimental effects of the mall lifestyle become evident. Wood rates Fran as progressive, and while he admits that she acts stereotypically female on occasion, she also assumes "a genuine autonomy" (Wood 120), signaled by her refusal to play "den mother" for the men. Shaviro, likewise, finds Fran more active and involved as the film progresses (87). Harper, by contrast, views the film's employment of "classical images of female false consciousness" as "problematic from the perspective of postmodern feminism" (Harper). Unlike Wood and Shaviro, he finds that the "spiky feminist heroine" turns more stereotypically feminine as the film progresses. Not only does Fran indulge in dress-up fantasies, she also remains completely passive during the film's climactic battle, and afterwards defers decision making to Peter.

Despite these flaws, though, Fran shows the potential to move beyond an obsolete past and its habits. The fact that Romero casts the voice of reason and

---

7   The alternative suggestion that the "zombie apocalypse might be a divine punishment is left unresolved" (J. Russell 96).

progress as a woman reinforces the notion that the old order's (self-)destructive patterns are tied to patriarchal structures.[8] Patterson summarizes that attitude more concisely; with reference to Grant, she notes that Romero has empathy with women, but writes men as idiotic (110). A similar point can be made with regards to race, as Fran is joined by the African-American Peter. After all, Peter was introduced as a figure of resistance against the uncaring racist authorities he served during the raid early in the film. His final symbolic surrender of possessions and violence – leaving his rifle with a zombie – allows him to move on as well.

The ending, as Fran and Peter depart with little fuel and without a particular destination, is remarkable in its ambivalence. According to Wood, it broke new ground in the genre, since it represents neither a "restoration of the traditional order", nor an "expression of despair" (121). Instead, in Wood's estimation "Dawn is perhaps the first horror film to suggest – albeit very tentatively – the possibility of moving beyond apocalypse" and towards a new social order (121). The film's conclusion thus opens a "world of possibility" (Waller 322), yet it also marks the reactive, indecisive character of the film's critique of capitalist American society and everything it associates with it. The problem is clearly identified, but the film advances only the vaguest idea of alternatives. The question what a new society would look like remains unanswered (Williams, *Knight* 97).

As this chapter has shown, *Dawn of the Dead* (1978) is highly charged with a radical dissatisfaction with the social, political and economic structure of 1970s America. The sheer crudeness of the film's critique certainly helped to achieve its exceptional cult status among fans and academics alike, but the film is also remarkable its thorough dissolution of the boundaries between normality and monstrosity. The zombies are us, and they do not so much intrude normality as perform it to an extreme degree. The main source of horror is not foreign, alien or ancient, but the dehumanizing developments of consumer culture. Consequently, the protagonists face a much larger challenge than surviving the attack of a monster: they need to escape a monstrous culture.

---

8   Unlike *The Crazies* (1973), in which women do not play a significant role yet, and the potential for going beyond is only found in the (white, male, working class) protagonist who is immune to the insanity-inducing Trixie-virus. Viewed as a sequence, from *Night of the Living Dead* (1968) to *Day of the Dead* (1985), it becomes evident that Romero's views of women and ethnic minorities mark a clear progression, with minorities being cast increasingly as representing better alternatives to a white patriarchal establishment.

DAWN OF THE DEAD (2004)

Dawn of the Dead (1978), with its combination of grim humor, satirical edge and splatter effects, had served as the paradigmatic text for zombie films throughout the 1980s, yet the genre slowly petered out during the early 1990s. Romero's own remake of *Night of the Living Dead* (1990), with Tom Savini directing, failed commercially as well as critically, and would mark a temporary end to Romero's zombie cycle that had defined both the director's career and the genre. However, interest in zombies was slowly rekindled through other media, most significantly the *Resident Evil* series of video games, which again paved the way for a new wave of zombie films starting in the early 2000s (Verevis, "Redefining" 25; J. Russell 183). *Dawn of the Dead* (2004) marked an early high point in that wave, reaching the top spot at the US box office and surpassing any of its generic predecessors in purely commercial terms.[9] Its success would not only (directly or indirectly) encourage the production of more remakes of Romero films, such as *Day of the Dead* (2008), it would also allow Romero to return to the zombie genre and produce three more films in his *...of the Dead* cycle (cf. Verevis, "Redefining" 26). In this case, the remake not only confirms the canonic status of its predecessor, it arguably enables new cultural production.

These merits, however, were not on the minds of zombie film fans and critics when the 2004 remake was first announced. Remakes are usually greeted with skepticism by a vocal segment of the audience, but the idea of remaking *Dawn of the Dead* (1978) was met with exceptional fury. Reiterating the main points of criticism, Russell calls the film "An unnecessary rehash of a landmark genre film . . . forced into production without Romero's artistic blessing" (J. Russell 183), and accuses it of "cynically keeping only the zombies and the dollar spinning title" (184). In response to fan protests, the filmmakers found it necessary to distance themselves from the term "remake", and instead called the project a "re-envisioning" (quoted in J. Russell 184) to claim more creative freedom. The difference is entirely a matter of public relations, and under any definition featured in this study, *Dawn of the Dead* (2004) is of course a film remake. Still, the debate and the film makers' resort to different terminology demonstrate how entrenched resistance to the concept of remakes has become among the segments of the audience most invested in a canon of (genre) classics.

---

9 Notably, the remake was released at the same time as the more humorous, parodic Romero homage *Shaun of the Dead*. The two productions were not related, but suggest that *Dawn of the Dead* (1978) had achieved a moment of heightened significance.

Dawn of the Dead (2004) is a new take on the rough premise of the 1978 film with an entirely different cast of characters. After a regular day at work, Ana, a nurse at a Milwaukee hospital, wakes up to find her city disintegrating under a zombie epidemic. She barely manages to escape her zombified husband and joins a group of survivors, among them Kenneth, a police officer, and Michael, who tries to lead the group. As the way towards a designated shelter is blocked, they seek refuge in a shopping mall, where they submit to the authority of the mall security guards and their leader C.J. Together, they dispose of the few zombies inside the mall. When a truck of refugees arrives the next day, Ana, Michael and Kenneth stage a coup and lock up C.J. They let the refugees into the mall, but repeatedly have to deal with zombie bites turning humans into dangerous zombies.

Even though the mall is besieged by growing hordes of zombies, the group lives in relative safety for a while, until another series of deaths from an undisclosed infection convinces them to plan an escape to an island, which they assume will be safer. The plan unravels when an attempt to relieve an isolated survivor in an adjacent building goes wrong, and during the chaotic escape towards the harbor most members of the group perish, either from accidents or zombie attacks. Michael chooses to stay behind and commit suicide, as he, too, has been infected, and only Kenneth, Ana, and a young couple board a sailing boat and set off. However, as an epilogue in the style of found footage suggests, their destination is also overrun by zombies, leaving little chance of survival.

The remake, for the most part, does not bother with restaging specific scenes of its predecessor. It employs the same basic premise, a small group of survivors hiding in a shopping mall while the zombie apocalypse rages outside. The sequence of events is vaguely similar: civilization collapses, a group of survivors finds refuge in the mall and settles in, only to ultimately lose control over the mall and look for refuge somewhere else. Even taking differences in filmmaking styles between the 1970s and the 2000s into account, the pace of the remake is significantly faster, with events occurring in quicker succession, and despite elaborate chase and fight scenes, the 2004 film is more than 20 minutes shorter than its predecessor. The cast of characters, by contrast, is expanded. The mall houses 14 (living) people at the film's midpoint, most of which bear no resemblance to the characters of the first film. Only Kenneth, the capable but disillusioned cop, is similar enough to 1978's Peter to count as a new take on the same character, and arguably, Ana as the voice of reason among immature men echoes Fran.

Despite these departures, the film is also "reverential of its source material," as Russell puts it (J. Russell 184). Homage to the 1978 film is paid through small reappearances by several actors. Ken Foree (Peter), Scott Reiniger (Roger), and Tom Savini (the unnamed antagonist extratextually referred to as "Blade") all appear on TV broadcasts watched by the 2004 characters, with Foree repeating his signature line "When there is no more room in hell, the dead will walk the Earth." *Dawn of the Dead* (2004) not only alludes to its immediate predecessor, as Savini's scene (a Sheriff giving advice on how to kill zombies) almost directly quotes Romero's *Night of the Living Dead* (1968). A few of the other news broadcasts also draw from either *Night* or *Dawn of the Dead* (1978). The desire to pay respect to earlier films is quite pronounced in the 2004 film, even though the story is hardly concerned with fidelity to its cinematic source. Therefore, the remaking stance of *Dawn of the Dead* (2004) is difficult to grasp using Leitch's categories. The film is committed to homage, but delegates it to texts inside its main text, namely the TV broadcasts. At the same time, the 2004 film is determined to surpass the first film with a more exciting pace and more terrifying monsters, yet it does not match Leitch's "true remake" because it negotiates only one source (cf. Leitch 49). Arguably, the abundance of small references and in-jokes serves to counterbalance how far the main narrative, style and mood actually depart from the 1978 film.

Survivors, Consumers, Family

Given the liberties the 2004 film takes with its source, a detailed juxtaposition of individual scenes is not a promising approach for this chapter. Instead, I will focus on key themes, and on the mall as a site of normality and intrusion. The critique of consumer culture is notably weakened in the remake, and a longing for community becomes pronounced instead.

Despite the initial fan skepticism, *Dawn of the Dead* (2004) generally earned positive reviews citing its qualities as a tense and effective horror film,[10] but was also criticized for removing the social critique from its predecessor. For example, J. Russell complains that the film "shows little interest in the mall location as a comment on American consumerism" and adds that with "plenty of splatter yet little else, this is Romero-lite" (185). Indeed, the film is far more focused on evoking suspense and horror from the zombie scenario than on satirizing consumerism. Nevertheless, it would be inaccurate to assume that the shift in focus means an uncritical acceptance or even celebration of consumerism. The fundamental absurdity of the premise, that a shopping mall is turned into a bastion of normality even when the outside world has ended, is still intact. Simply setting

---

10 The film ranks at 75% positive reviews at *Rotten Tomatoes* ("DAWN OF THE DEAD (2004)").

the life and death struggle of its characters in perfectly clean and intact stores creates a disruption, and the soundtrack frequently generates ironic distance.

For a start, the montage of newscasts documenting the global collapse is accompanied by Johnny Cash's "The Man Comes Around," which quotes the Book of Revelations to an upbeat rhythm. This sequence is followed by the discovery of the mall, which appears empty and untouched by the disaster outside, with fountains working and an easy listening version of Bobby McFerrin's "Don't Worry, Be Happy" playing. The previous montage leaves little doubt that the world is coming to an end, yet the shopping mall denies these realities and invites its guests not to worry. As in the 1978 film, the culture of consumption is thus an illusionary refuge from reality and the various crises of the outside world. Still, the 2004 film spends much less time elaborating the fake and empty life inside the mall, and its characters offer only small realizations such as that the bathrooms in model apartments are not working. The lengthy descent into ennui in the 1978 film is replaced by a montage of life at the mall, showing the inhabitants watching TV, playing sports, making pornography, and shooting zombies for fun. The sequence is again ironized by the soundtrack, a lounge version of Disturbed's "Down with the Sickness." The cheerful rendition of a song rambling about infection, death and violence comments sarcastically on the futility of the survivors' attempts at distraction, asking them to "get down with the sickness" and "get ready to die."

The conclusion that might be drawn from the depiction of life at the mall is slightly different from the 1978 film. The safety of the mall is an illusion, and the characters would rather die trying to reach complete safety than wait for something to go wrong in the mall. Although the remnants of consumer culture are pointless, the film does not equate consumers with zombies or vice versa. The zombies of the 2004 film never resemble aimless shoppers, but remain threatening monsters at all times. The satirical edge thus is not removed, but rather reduced to an aside in a film more concerned with horror.

While *Dawn of the Dead* (2004) spends less time contemplating consumption, it puts significantly more emphasis on family (cf. Borrowman 78). In the 1978 film, David's attempts at forming a nuclear family were depicted as highly questionable. In the 2004 film, the main characters are all defined by their loss of relatives or romantic partners. Ana's relationship is disrupted when her partner dies and turns into a zombie, while Kenneth wants to reach his brother, but has to give him up. As the biggest failure in his life, Michael lists his failure as a husband, but not as a father. Most importantly, Andre, a stereotypical African American gangster, is convinced that that the birth of his child would redeem his crimes. Even after he learns that his wife Luda is suffering from the zombie infection, Andre insists on putting his family first, thereby transcending the human/zombie divide. He protects the newborn zombie ("You wanna kill my family?"), resisting attempts to kill it with violence and at the cost of his own life. The birth sequence easily rates as the most grotesque scene of the entire film, as the unborn child practically claws its way out of its undead mother. Matching the apocalyptic tone of *Dawn of the Dead* (2004), the pregnancy turns into a source of horror, one that Borrowman terms the "ultimate inversion of family values" (78). Nevertheless, the film advances family as the institution that outlasts any other, playing a central role in the lives of the characters even when the rest of civilization has dissolved. As Borrowman remarks, the group of survivors at the end of the film represents a "perfect family structure . . . mom, dad, and two kids. There's even a dog" (78).

By contrast, the authorities disappear so quickly that they have practically no impact on the narrative. During Ana's escape from her suburb, an ambulance and a police car do not offer relief, but are additional threats in the general chaos. Kenneth may still wear his uniform, but renounces all allegiance to the police. Apart from a military helicopter passing by without any response, only TV broadcasts serve as reminders of state authorities. The president is seen to be evacuated and never heard from again, and a Sheriff and a military officer give questionable advice. The only show of confidence comes from C.J., who asserts that "America always sorts its shit out." The line is not commented upon, but given C.J.'s general lack of judgment and almost delusional beliefs, it can only be taken as hollow. Evidence clearly points to America not being able to handle its problems.

Since federal and local governments fold overnight, it is up to the group of survivors to organize their lives and reestablish normality, or replace it with a more promising alternative. The ensemble is the last remnant of American society, but does not represent a perfect cross section of the population. Instead, the 2004 film is slanted towards "blue collar" characters (Paffenroth 102, Wetmore 161). Its cast of lower-to-middle class professionals includes a police officer, a nurse, a sales clerk, several mall security guards, a trucker, and a church organist, with the outliers being a repentant gangster (Andre) and a smug, rather wealthy man of unknown profession (Steve) (see fig. 7). Notably, both of the latter endanger the rest of the group at some point, and Andre's deranged attachment to family has already been mentioned. Steve, by contrast, appears only interested in himself and abandons the group on two occasions. The deaths in *Dawn of the Dead* (2004) do not follow a logic of sin and punishment that is prevalent in some horror subgenres, but Steve's demise marks an exception. When he refuses to help and sets off on his own, only to be killed by zombies, his death is "treated as justice instead of a tragedy" (Wetmore 161). Paffenroth reads the character of Steve and his fate as a critique of class and wealth, as Steve is the only rich man among the blue collar group (102). That critique is reiterated in the film's macabre celebrity shooting game, in which the participants shoot individual zombies based on their resemblance to media celebrities. Paffenroth views the game as a "violent parody of class envy and warfare" (102), where the "rich and famous" are shot by the "lower classes" (102).

When it comes to class, then, the group is mostly homogenous, and it has no experts to speak of, even though Ana as a nurse comes closest and manages to deduce the zombie infection process. Authority is fought over, and leadership in the group is initially negotiated between Kenneth, who refuses to follow anyone, Michael, who seeks cooperation, and C.J., who seeks sole power. The authoritarian stance is discredited soundly, as C.J. plays the antagonist for much of the time, being irrational, power hungry, and ignorant.[11] Once C.J. has been deposed, the group organizes in a roughly democratic manner, and develops what might best be described as a communitarian fighting spirit. Characters prove their worth by working together, ensuring each other's safety, and being competent at shooting zombies. C.J. rehabilitates himself from "jail" by being capable under pressure, and grows to accept the group's decisions. The plan to escape the mall in favor of a small island is developed and decided on communally and unilaterally. It may be a stretch, but in the face of complete global breakdown, *Dawn of the Dead* (2004) still puts its faith in somewhat democratic organization guided by group interests and practical common sense.

Once the epilogue is taken into account, all of the survivors' struggles result in failure, but evaluating that failure is more difficult than for *Dawn of the Dead* (1978). In the 1978 film, the blame for the collapse of society lies with inept authorities, and the blame for the later collapse of the mall society lies with the greed of the humans outside, and the obsessions the men within. These points are made by Fran and the televised Dr. Rausch, who serve as the narrative's voices of reason and point out the flaws in, respectively, individual and cultural attitudes. The zombies certainly are a threat, but do not appear impossible to handle, and therefore, humanity's apparent extinction is at least partly its own fault. The 2004 film refrains from such a blanket condemnation of human nature. The authorities' rapid collapse is put into perspective by the raised aggression of both the zombies and the infection that creates them. Where the 1978 zombies stum-

---

11 C.J. also holds a xenophobic or isolationist position by arguing that if they start letting people in, they will let "the wrong ones" in. The fact that two of the refugees really are infected, and that one attacks Ana is however not taken as confirmation that C.J. is right.

ble forward in a slow and often aimless manner, their 2004 counterparts quickly charge towards their targets, and the dead rise almost instantly to attack the living. They are depicted as a far more dangerous threat, which in turn excuses part of the authorities' failure to form an effective response. The same applies to the characters of the 2004 film. As outlined above, most of the survivors in the mall are fairly effective, and the central characters – Ana, Kenneth, and Michael – display none of the character flaws and obsessions that lead 1978's Roger and Stephen to self-destruction. The group is instead endangered by the self-obsessed at its fringes (becoming father Andre and egotist Steve), along with simple accidents.

Paffenroth views the human community as more effective and resilient than its 1978 counterpart (92), and concludes that it is happy as it can be under the circumstances (99). He adds that unlike in Romero's films, genuine loving relationships between the characters develop (106). Reading the film as a religious scholar, Paffenroth also notes a lack of faith and hope (113), and finds that "organized religion in this movie is implicitly on the same level of ineffectiveness and corruption as the government, military, and the media – a mixture of lies and platitudes to cover up inequities, power struggles, and ignorance" (109-10). That assessment hinges on only a few scenes and asides, but Paffenroth's more general conclusion, that the 2004 film has more faith in humanity than its predecessor, is harder to deny.

Russell's more critical analysis of the film takes a different route, but comes to a vaguely similar conclusion. The film has little concern with the philosophical and religious themes it brings up, Russell argues, and ultimately "lacks the dark nihilism of Romero's trilogy" (185). The reason is not just the lack of social critique, but the fact that the film's zombies are merely the victims of a virulent plague. Therefore, it is not really "Judgment Day," but "just another common or garden viral outbreak" (J. Russell 185). However, Russell's distinction is based on a technicality at best, as neither film leaves much doubt that humanity is coming to an end. The scenario of the 2004 film is apocalyptic, and it is perceived by the characters as such. During the opening news montage, a reporter is heard asking whether it is a virus, whether it is airborne, and whether these people are alive or dead, and each time the answer is "We don't know." Just like the 1978 film, which also played with viral explanations, the remake never resolves these questions, nor is the possibility of a cure even considered by the survivors. In both films, the zombie condition certainly acts like a contagion, but it is never explained in definite scientific terms. Russell is still correct in that *Dawn of the Dead* (1978) displays a darker sense of nihilism, but that is derived from its despair with human nature, not from its supposed pronouncement of Judgment Day.

Faster Zombies, Shifting Ideologies

If humans are more capable of cooperating and solving their problems in *Dawn of the Dead* (2004), then the monsters bear more responsibility for the apocalyptic breakdown. In short, if humans do better, then the zombies must be worse, more monstrous, more threatening, for things to turn out just as dire. As mentioned earlier, the 2004 film's zombies are faster and more aggressive. There are no scenes of 2004's zombies being passive or helpless; instead, they are always attacking. Where the 1978 film showed zombies peacefully wandering the mall, or being subjected to a slapstick pie fight, their 2004 counterparts are always attacking. Likewise, the transformation process is quick and instantly removes humanity, which is signaled by the zombies' eyes taking on a cold shine. No trace of human behavior remains, and the appearance and sound of the zombies are also more thoroughly dehumanized. The makeup, reportedly modeled after photos of accident victims, more credibly models injury and death than the cartoonish blue skin of the 1978 film, and the zombies utter a variety of hisses and growls reminiscent of rabid animals.

Significantly, the dialogue no longer features the line "They're us," further underlining their status as a monstrous, inhuman Other.[12] Another key dialogue explaining the zombies' interest in the mall ("Why do they come here?" – "Some kind of instinct. Memory, of what they used to do. This was an important place in their lives.") is shortened to "Why are they coming here?" – "Memory? Instinct? Maybe they're coming for us." The alteration neatly encapsulates the 2004 film's thematic shifts. It removes the reference to the mall and its uncanny power over consumers, and ends the exchange on the zombies' intent to kill, which again underlines the threat they represent. The 2004 film leaves no doubt that the zombies are no longer us, and hints of memories, such as with 1978's Stephen, are not found. According to Wood's criteria (cf. Wood 192), the dehumanization of the monsters would move the 2004 film in a more conservative direction, in line with the increased focus on family and religion.[13] Since the zombies are no longer presented as consumers, the 1978 film's core metaphor (that

---

12 The rest of the dialogue (Peter quoting his grandfather that "When there's no more room in hell, the dead will walk the earth.") is transferred to a rambling Televangelist, who uses it in a screed blaming the end of the world on homosexuality and other perceived instances of moral decay. In the changed context, the line changes meaning, from an introspective moment to an expression of irrational hatred.

13 A more drastic conclusion could be drawn with Canavan, who argues that the "racial binary" (433) constructed in the zombie genre serves to act out racial violence that still forms the foundation for "technological civilization" (439-440).

consumers are the real zombies, cf. Bishop, *American* 130) no longer applies, and by extension, contemporary capitalist America is in no way responsible for the horror of the zombies.

The 2004 film also removes the characters that acted as voices of reason and pointed out alternatives in the 1978 film. Where the first film featured a priest who advised that the killing must stop, the remake only offers a hateful televangelist that blends into the cacophony of collapse on television. There is no voice of cold reason comparable to Dr. Rausch, who suggests that the zombies might have to be fed. The 2004 film never grows beyond the "shoot them in the head" attitude that symbolized the authorities' wrongheadedness in the first film (cf. J. Russell 93). In this scenario, killing is absolutely necessary, even celebrated. There is no alternative to terror and having to do terrible things, as summarized by a Sheriff on TV, who shrugs off the prospect of having to shoot familiar people: "What can you do? It's got to be done."

As *Dawn of the Dead* (2004) maintains its absolute distinction between humans and monsters, it also maintains normality as a (relatively) pure space invaded by external monsters. The loss of normality occurs twice. First, Ana's regular life is disrupted by a zombie home invasion and the subsequent death and zombification of her partner. Normality, here, is getting home to the suburbs from a day of work, a modest but otherwise flawless existence. Next, normality is reestablished at the mall, albeit as a façade of immaculate stores and shallow entertainments. A failed rescue plan leads to another zombie invasion, which instantly collapses the barely established security. Picking up Borrowman's reading of the last survivors as a nuclear family (78), one might argue that normality is restored a third time, even though it does not last past the epilogue during the closing credits. In all cases, once a zombie pierces the borders of the safe zone, normality is irrevocably destroyed, so it would appear essential that the Other must be kept locked out, while a community can only exist under lockdown. Safety is prized but unattainable in *Dawn of the Dead* (2004), which may be read as a statement on a particular socio-historic moment.

Michel makes a rather broad statement on this type of ending, which she observes in several zombie films of the 2000s, concluding that "it is not possible to seal oneself off from the immense social problems of our world. The repressed awareness of class antagonisms, family conflicts, and the deadening effects of modern life return with a vengeance" (Michel 396). Speaking specifically about *Dawn of the Dead* (2004), however, Russell laments that ominous images like the news montages and lines like "America always sorts its shit out" never build towards anything but a "vague sense of apocalyptic chaos and social breakdown" (J. Russell 185). Still, that indeterminacy may be the most accurate representation of a cultural anxiety that is not directed toward one particular source, but instead consists of a blur of insecurities, one that neither the film nor its characters are capable of grasping and expressing clearly.

Still, some authors read *Dawn of the Dead* (2004) and its generation of zombie films as more specific expressions of contemporary fears. For example, Bishop argues that the end of the world resonates more strongly with American audiences because of the experiences of 9/11, the Iraq War, Hurricane Katrina and so forth ("Dead Man" 22). For Bishop, *Dawn of the Dead's* (2004) montage of news broadcasts evokes news footage of 9/11 (22), and he tends towards explaining the zombie film resurgence of the 2000s with post 9/11 terror fears (24). At the same time, he is uncertain whether that connection is made purely in the perception of the audience and whether the films have not changed after all (24). That question may have to be decided on a case-by-case basis, with earlier films serving as references.

Dawn of the Dead (2004) makes no recognizable quotation from historical events, but scenes like the characters trying to come to grips with the shock of the disaster by watching a confusing barrage of breaking news snippets have significant parallels to the media perception of 9/11. The zombie apocalypse is also framed as "civil unrest," and news footage of military and riot police suppressing what is supposed to be zombie hordes is indistinguishable from regular news footage. More likely, actual archive footage of riots around the world is used, which arguably equates violent protestors, regardless of cause, and the disruptive force of the zombies. For Wetmore, the case is more specific: the Middle Eastern-looking elements of the sequence visually link "zombies with praying Muslims and Middle Eastern mobs," underlining his argument that *Dawn of the Dead* (2004) is a "post-9/11 zombie film" (160). The post-9/11 world may well inform the film's political unconscious, yet when Borrowman is disconcerted by the fact that his mind combines a shot of Muslims from the opening news montage with the final zombie assault, resulting in his impression of watching "Islamist extremist hoards [sic]" (79), that may not say much about the text itself. In a similar vein, Neumann claims that many contemporary zombie films have moved from critical reflection towards a paranoid and reactionary worldview, and that the primitive, but effective undead horde parallels enemy images in the War on Terror (82). The dehumanization of the zombies in *Dawn of the Dead* (2004) offers support for the first point, but the second is harder to prove conclusively, especially considering that the same argument has been made much earlier about zombies and the Viet Cong (cf. Jones 162).

It is worth pointing out that while the zombies' status as Others is reinforced in *Dawn of the Dead* (2004), some of the *other* Others that had previously been marginalized or invisible in genre films are subsumed into normality. For example, Paffenroth notes that sexism and homophobia are delegated to antagonist characters designated as unlikable (C.J. and his idiotic subordinate Bart), and that C.J.'s rehabilitation is initiated by his lecture and appreciation of women's magazines (104-05). Gender roles also change to some degree. Despite the fact that 1978's Fran had refused to play "den mother" for the men and claimed a gun for her own use, her role was still mostly limited to delivering criticism from the sidelines. 2004's Ana is somewhat more independent, acts as the ethical center of the group in actively stopping a premature execution, and displays bravado during the final escape scene, where she delivers on the promise of shooting the zombified Steve in a dramatic turn more apt to action films. The rest of the characters driving the narrative are still male (Kenneth, Michael, C.J.), but Ana nevertheless possesses more agency than the outspoken, but largely irrelevant Fran.

In conclusion, *Dawn of the Dead* (2004) may pay respect to its famous predecessor, but completely rearranges the thematic focus and the ideological underpinnings of the mall siege scenario. It has more faith in humanity's capacity to cooperate even against impossible odds, and is more likely to attribute failure to outside factors than internal flaws. Consumerism is an exercise in shallow distraction, but it is not the core problem of either the survivors or society at large. In the face of complete social collapse, the survivors seek safety and community – normality – above all else, and appear justified in doing so. Significantly, the 2004 film does not dissolve categories and dichotomies like human/monster, but reinforces them. Compared to the 1978 film, this represents a clear ideological shift towards what Wood identified as the reactionary horror film (192; see ch. 1), as the sharp division between human and monster, between good and evil, affirms the status quo. The two films still share a strong underlying fear of infection and loss of humanity, but where the 1978 film ties the zombie state to a numbing consumer society, the 2004 remake fails to reflect on its fears. While the first film offered the slim hope of moving beyond the apocalypse, the remake cannot conceive of a new social order, or a world in which violence is not ubiquitous, necessary and justified. The remake's ultimate turn to pessimism stands in sharp contrast to its image of humanity: humans are basically decent, but have no chance to survive, whereas the 1978 perceived humans as deeply flawed and incapable of survival, but with the capacity to change and move on. As a film/remake pairing, the two versions of *Dawn of the Dead* stand out as effective films with very different objectives, deriving wildly divergent results from the same basic premise.

Fig. 5. The Crazies *(1973) and the self-immolation of Thich Quang Duc, Saigon 1963, photograph by Malcolm Browne (image from "Thich Quang Duc," Wikipedia)*

Fig. 6. Mall zombies in Dawn of the Dead *(1978)*

Fig. 7. The diverse survivors of Dawn of the Dead *(2004)*

7. Cannibal Hillbillies and Backwoods Horror

When other horror films used aliens, demons or the undead to inspire terror in their audiences, *The Texas Chain Saw Massacre* (1974) looked inward and found its monsters in the American backwoods, paving the way for a wave of horror films featuring deranged and often cannibalistic country folk that have since become a staple of the genre. The film also stands out as one of the key texts of the genre canon, whether among fans or critics, who view it as a high point of the wave of independent horror films in the 1970s. Its iconic status among aficionados and, perhaps more importantly, brand name recognition far beyond those circles made *The Texas Chain Saw Massacre* (1974) ripe for remaking.[1] Even though the 2003 remake enjoyed tremendous success at the box office, it predictably failed to endear the critics that had celebrated its predecessor. And while the remake amplifies the depiction of violence compared to the first film, it also makes significant changes regarding the agency of its protagonist and, arguably, the underlying ideology, transforming a disturbing and inconclusive film into a something more in tune with both conventional film narrative and family values.

THE TEXAS CHAIN SAW MASSACRE (1974)

Upon its release in 1974, *The Texas Chain Saw Massacre* set a new genre standard in terms of relentless terror and nihilistic absurdity, though not, as might be expected, in its depiction of blood and gore. The intensity of the murders and psychological torture depicted on screen led to the film's banning in several countries around the world, which only served to increase its cult status. The

---

1 A note on titles and power tools: the 1974 film title is spelled *Chain Saw Massacre*, while its sequels and the remake went with the more modern spelling, "chainsaw."

film was simultaneously reviled by the mainstream (Phillips 102) and a critical favorite (Dika 9), though its often quoted addition to the collection of the New York Museum of Modern Art was less due to its perceived artistic merit, but the result of a PR stunt by its distributor (Jaworzyn 99). Like its peers from the 1970s independent horror film canon, *The Texas Chain Saw Massacre* (1974) was produced on a low budget, struggled to find distribution and only saw limited release, but went on to enjoy respectable commercial success over the course of later rereleases. With some delay, it also spawned a franchise, with three sequels between 1986 and 1994, and yet another sequel in 2013, none of which earned the acclaim or the success of the first film.[2]

The film follows a group of five young people travelling across rural Texas in a van. Two of them, Sally and her brother Franklin, intend to take care of their father's grave, following reports of vandalism, and plan to visit the deserted family house afterwards. On the way, they encounter a psychotic hitchhiker, who first cuts himself with a knife and then attacks the group before they can throw him out. Once they have arrived at the family house, the travelers disregard earlier warnings and wander off to the neighbors' house, one after the other, where they are killed by Leatherface, a heavyset man wearing a mask made of human skin. After Leatherface ambushes and kills Franklin with a chainsaw, the sole survivor Sally escapes to a gas station, only to learn that the attendant is part of the same murderous family of cannibalistic former slaughterhouse workers. She is taken back to the house and forced to attend dinner with the rest of the family, including the hitchhiker and Leatherface. When the barely animate grandfather fails to kill her despite repeated attempts, Sally escapes yet again, this time reaching the road. There, the hitchhiker is run over by a truck, and Sally makes it on board of another truck, leaving the furious Leatherface behind.

The Texas Chain Saw Massacre (1974) is frequently named as the forerunner of two somewhat related (sub)genres of horror films. First, the slasher film, which focuses on a psychotic, usually masked killer who stalks and murders an ensemble of careless teenagers over the course of the narrative. The second is

---

2   The continuity between the seven *Texas Chainsaw* films (as of this writing) is again convoluted. The 1974 film and the first three sequels (1986, 1990, 1994) supposedly occur in the same continuity. The 2003 remake and the 2006 prequel set up their own continuity, which is however discarded by the next film in the franchise. *Texas Chainsaw 3D* (2013) serves as a sequel to the 1974 film, and its narrative developments most likely invalidate the 1986-1994 sequels. Given that the films mostly repeat the same scenario with variations in murder and torture sequences, their intertextual relationships would seem less important, but it is worth pointing out that the most recent iteration returns (and pays homage) to the canonical 1974 film.

variously labeled as hillbilly, redneck, or backwoods horror by fans, and deals with modern, urban Americans who find themselves trapped in remote, rural parts of the country and are subsequently abused, murdered and possibly eaten by the savage locals. Basic elements of both types can be found in the film, and Clover, for example, positions it as an evolutionary step in the slasher genre between *Psycho* (1960) and *Halloween* (1978). Phillips makes the same point (106); Sharrett, however, firmly denies that *The Texas Chain Saw Massacre* (1974) is a forerunner to the slasher film ("Idea" 256). Likewise, Nowell insists that the film does not work as an ancestor to slashers (nor does *Psycho*). According to Nowell, the inclusion of *The Texas Chain Saw Massacre* (1974) in the slasher canon was a calculated move, with the purpose of adding prestige, and to set a compelling high point in a rise-and-fall-narrative of the genre that posited the slasher wave of the early 1980s as a low point (58-61).

Regardless of debates over broad and narrow definitions of subgenres and canonization, *The Texas Chain Saw Massacre* (1974) remains a highly influential film. The structure of its narrative is extremely simple and circular: one young traveler walks into the house, is killed, and the next one follows. Then, Sally escapes from the house, is brought back, and escapes from the house again. The characters are barely developed, and the film is narrowly focused on evoking terror with the slaughter of the victims, Sally's intense suffering, and the displays of sheer insanity by the killers. The ending is hardly conclusive; Sally may escape, but Leatherface, the old man and their house are still around. The film's lack of closure and general denial of narrative conventions play a significant part in its disturbing effect. Yet despite all challenges to making meaning (cf. Bould), the film has yielded no shortage of critical interpretations revolving around regional and historical oppositions, a subversive family discourse, and gender dynamics.

The Collapse of Reason and a Brutal American Past

Even though some aspects of the narrative may be underdeveloped or incoherent, the film clearly establishes its contexts, both in terms of geography and history. The title already locates the narrative not in any rural area, but specifically in Texas. Furthermore, an introductory text claims that the film recounts a real story and gives a date, August 3rd 1973. It also stresses the age of the victims:

The film which you are about to see is an account of the tragedy which befell a group of five youths, in particular Sally Hardesty and her invalid brother, Franklin. It is all the more tragic in that they were young. But, had they lived very, very long lives, they could not have expected nor would they have wished to see as much of the mad and macabre as they were to see that day. For them an idyllic summer afternoon drive became a nightmare. The events of that day were to lead to the discovery of one of the most bizarre crimes in the annals of American history, The Texas Chain Saw Massacre.

As might be expected, the introduction's claim is a fabrication designed to increase the film's impact (Jaworzyn 90-91). Even though the film was partly inspired by the murders of Ed Gein, the Wisconsin man who murdered at least two women, exhumed graves and made artifacts from the dismembered bodies in the 1950s, there was no historical chainsaw massacre (38-39). The sensational claims about "the mad and macabre" set the mood for the film, which is enhanced by the subsequent montage of news footage. Reports of grave robbery, attributed to elements from outside the state of Texas, are followed by reports of a catastrophic oil leak, suicides during a TV blackout, the unexplained collapse of a building in Atlanta, and deaths in Indiana. Only the first item is related to the plot: the hitchhiker went looking for bodies for his craft, and the reports are the reason for Sally and Franklin's journey. The rest of the report places the events in a context of a senselessly violent America; unexplained death and destruction are everywhere. The universe in which the narrative is about to unfold is established as random and uncaring (Muir, *Horror 1970s* 336-37). Pinedo makes a similar point and considers this unstable state as a postmodern condition (48).

Sharett reads the scenario as apocalyptic, and considers it as part of a lengthy tradition in American art ("Idea" 255). Accordingly, director Tobe Hooper "establishes the idea of an Evil Age and the collapse of causality. From the media reports to the events of the movie, there's no clear reason or explanation for anything" (261). There is no sense of revelation or reconstitution associated with apocalypse, Sharett continues, only the destruction of "what cannot be changed", the disappearance of shared cultural beliefs, and no possibility of change or control over one's role in history (263). The belief of one of the characters, Pam, that everything has meaning is disproven: Nothing has meaning, because "reason has collapsed into a condition of hysteria" (267). Similarly, Wood locates *The Texas Chain Saw Massacre* (1974) in a group of contemporary horror films in which humanity is powerless to stop an inevitable annihilation (88), and points out its emphasis on "uncontrol," meaning that neither victims nor killers have full control over the situation (90). Conceptions of order, and any attempts to impose order, are thoroughly dismantled.

This challenge to conventional categories does not extend into an explicit rejection of scientific rationality through supernatural monstrosities, as in other types of horror. The monstrous family violates morality and sanity, but remains only human, albeit grotesquely distorted. Yet, even though the film is generally perceived as devoid of fantastic elements, Bould finds that supernatural explanations are hinted at with the mention of solar flares, astrology, and "ritual" burning of Franklin's photo (97). A supernatural explanation thus could be seen as "the root of the economic and social causes of the horror rather than its proximate cause" (98). As an alternative, Bould offers a "secular apocalypse" expressed in the dependence on superstition found among both victims and killers; either way, he argues, the film undermines the coherence of its rationales (98).

The young travelers' journey into the remote parts of Texas is also one into the past, in this case, a very recent, ugly and violent America. During his first appearance, the hitchhiker explains that his family had always been "in meat," and discusses the changes in the methods of cattle slaughter. He expresses disappointment in the introduction of air-powered tools for killing instead of sledgehammers: "The old way, with a sledge! See, that was better; they died better that way." The more brutal, personal way of killing appeals to the hitchhiker and, as we learn later, is still held up by his family. Leatherface uses a sledgehammer for two of the murders, and applies his slaughterhouse training to the others as well. He hangs Pam, his first female victim, on a meat hook while she is still alive, and later stows her in the freezer. The old ways stand for brutality and dehumanization in *The Texas Chain Saw Massacre* (1974), and the family's treatment of their victims as cattle for the slaughter is one of the film's key strategies for evoking horror.

The replacement of these old ways by a modernized, depersonalized meat industry sets the stage for the family's deeds. As the hitchhiker mentions, the new way "put people out of jobs," so the family who had made a living of killing simply continues their work on human beings instead. The family members are victims of modernization, as the changing industry left them stranded without an outlet for the murderous energy it had previously fostered. In his assessment of the situation, Wood further emphasizes the class aspect and casts the family as representatives of an "exploited and degraded proletariat," themselves victims of both the slaughterhouse environment and capitalism (91-92). In this context, he interprets their cannibalism as ultimate possessiveness and thus the logical end of capitalism (91).[3] This reading leads into another issue, that of class anxieties, which will be discussed in a later section. At this point, it is worth mentioning that industrial or social progress plays a role in the family's turn to cannibalism, but considering the film's general dismantling of rationality and causality, it may

---

3   The link between cannibalism, consumption and capitalism is also invoked for *Dawn of the Dead* (1978), whose mall shopper zombies more obviously invite such readings.

be a leap to blame their habits on any one reason. The family may be deranged because they are remnants of a more cruel past age, or because of their abuse and abandonment by industry or society; at any rate, they are mired in the past. One of the most striking pieces of decoration around the house is a watch with a nail driven through it, which may be read as a symbolic attempt to stop the passage of time, or as a more general rejection of order and structure.

The clash of past and present in *The Texas Chain Saw Massacre* (1974) is also expressed in the locations. Both the Hardesty family home and the cannibal family's house are wooden farm houses built by earlier generations and now derelict to varying degrees. The Hardesty home is tied to vague childhood memories for Sally and Franklin, but its ruinous state and a dried out swimming hole in the back mark the passage of time and the force of entropy. Both houses now function as Gothic structures, and Jerry, one of the young travelers, remarks that the Hardesty home looks like Bela Lugosi's birthplace, invoking the horror cinema of the 1930s and 40s as a reference. Of course, the cannibal family's home with its macabre decoration and secret sliding door is a much stronger example of a Gothic structure, and Wood places it in the long history of the "Terrible House" (90). Again, the house is a site of a menacing past, as it "signifies the dead weight of the past crushing the life of the younger generation" (91). The acts of cannibalism that take place inside also figure into this historical clash, as they enact "present and future (the younger generation) being devoured by the past" (91). In short, and in the simplest of terms, the remnants of the past threaten the present throughout the film.

A number of critics try to trace the defining features of *The Texas Chain Saw Massacre* (1974), its intense depiction of physical and psychological suffering and its general assault on reason and conventions, to a specific historical moment. In a fairly broad attempt at contextualization, Phillips relates the film, along with 1973's *The Exorcist*, to a general gloom and pessimism of the 1970s. Phillips's sweeping picture of the decade's anxieties include a "paranoid fragmentation" following Nixon's fall over Watergate and the loss in Vietnam, an upswing in conspiracy theories, a decline of the family and rising divorce rates, and also fears of overpopulation and energy crisis (107-10). The apocalyptic tone in cinema, Phillips suggests, was only reflective of an apocalyptic tone in (American) culture (112).

Becker, by contrast, is a little more specific in tracing the root anxieties behind *The Texas Chain Saw Massacre* (1974) and other horror films of its period, and chooses the filmmakers' attitudes as points of reference. Becker considers director Hooper, along with fellow horror directors George A. Romero and Wes Craven, as part of a "predominantly white, middle class, and politically leftist hippie counterculture of the late 1960s and early 1970s" (42). While Becker is fairly loose with the term "hippie," there is no doubt that Hooper was involved with or sympathetic to at least some countercultural movements of the period.[4] With that in mind, Becker counters Wood's reading of the 1970s horror film canon. Instead of a "collective nightmare," he sees a nightmare specific to the "hippie counterculture" (44). The "total negativity" particular to these films can not only be read as radical or progressive, but also as reactionary, and it conveys a sense of hopelessness that suggests political disengagement in the wake of the counterculture's decline (58). The conclusion of *The Texas Chain Saw Massacre* (1974), with Sally driven insane and Leatherface triumphantly waving his chain-saw, could thus be read as expressing a sense of failure and anxiety of the return of a violent and reactionary America.

In a similar vein, Bould also links the film to the counterculture of the period, but offers a more differentiated picture of 1960s and early 1970s political protest and counterculture movements. Bould reads *The Texas Chain Saw Massacre* (1974) in relation to the road movie, which as a genre holds particular significance for the counterculture, but figures it as the counterculture's "end-of-the-road movie" (101; 103). As the young travelers' road trip across Texas is interrupted by senseless murder, the film puts a halt to the sense of energy and freedom encapsulated in the road movie (102-03). In order to establish interpretive context, Bould describes the decline of political protest movements (the capital-M Movement), which he keeps distinct from a broader counterculture, between a bleed into sex, drugs, and rock'n'roll, the mainstream, and the suppression and infiltration of various movements (105). He stresses the importance of the historical moment in the discussion of *The Texas Chainsaw Massacre* (1974), "to treat the US invasion of Vietnam, domestic repression, economic recession and the kind of brutality depicted in the movie as specific manifestations of a more deeply rooted, more general phenomenon" (106). The film, argues Bould, fits "somewhere" into a group of artworks and texts dealing with the brutality of the war in that "it brings the atrocities home, indicating how deeply entangled they are in US culture and society; through its references to unemployment, the oil crisis and the cost of living, it establishes . . . a broader context, linked to industrial capitalism, within which its everyday atrocities occur"

---

4   To substantiate his claims, Becker collects a number of quotes where filmmakers call themselves "hippies" and takes them at face value. Furthermore, Becker also takes appearances (hair and beards) and purported drug use into account, along with the directors' early films (44-45).

(107).[5] The film is not about Vietnam, Bould concludes, but it is "about a general condition, of which the invasion [of Vietnam] is symptomatic and constitutive" (109). While that condition remains vague, it is evident that socioeconomic conditions breed brutality and dehumanization in *The Texas Chain Saw Massacre* (1974).

Monstrous Family

The Texas Chain Saw Massacre (1974) maps the basic horror conflict between normality and monster onto two groups of human beings, but the relationship between the two is not exactly straightforward. In a partial reversal of the respective definitions, normality is represented by the "quasi-liberated, permissive young," while "the monster is the family" (Wood 90). The more typical constellation of the genre would define the family as the purest site of safety and normality, and therefore the target of external monsters. Notably, the members of the cannibal family do not act as intruders. Instead, it is the young travelers, at least the first three, who transgress the boundaries of the family's house without provocation. With Sally's escape at the end of the film, the outsiders have been expelled and the family can carry on with its business. Their patch of Texas retains its state of monstrosity, and the normality represented by the now physically and mentally damaged Sally cannot be restored. This outcome is underlined by the film's final shot, which is not of Sally, but instead shows Leatherface swinging his chainsaw in the middle of the road, in broad daylight, leaving no doubts regarding the monster's supremacy.

Throughout the film, normality is completely defenseless against the monstrous family. The first victims unwittingly walk into their deaths, with little chance to resist, and even the survivor Sally can only fight back ineffectively. The boldest act of resistance is a truck driver throwing a wrench at Leatherface, with moderate success. Remarkably, local or state authorities are completely absent from the narrative. In the early graveyard scene, there is mention of a sheriff, but he is never seen, and the possibility of involving law enforcement is not raised at any point in the narrative. The Texas countryside, then, appears to be a lawless, uncivilized space, the uncontested territory of the monstrous family.

The three active members of the family are never named, and only listed as "Leatherface," "Hitchhiker," and "Old Man" in the credits. Likewise, their exact relationship is unclear and can only be inferred from age differences and social

---

5 Bould refers to Martha Rosler's photo collages *Bringing the War Home (House Beautiful)*, Norman Mailer's novel *Why Are We in Vietnam?* and Joe Lansdale's short story "Night They Missed the Horror Show" (106-107).

roles, as the old man acts as the head of the family.[6] Their deviance from normality is fairly visible, except in the case of the old man, who is able to blend in as a gas station attendant. The hitchhiker, the youngest family member, has a large red mark on his face, presumably a birthmark that appears like smeared blood, and his expressions and speech patterns suggest some form of intellectual disability. Leatherface is more obviously monstrous, with a huge, hulking body and various masks of human skin obscuring his face. He never speaks, but makes inhuman grunting or squealing noises. Finally, the grandfather appears pale, old and wrinkled enough to pass for a dead body; in fact, only sucking blood from Sally's finger seems to revive him.[7] His feeble body and utter physical failure are used both for horror and comedy, as he is all but inanimate despite the insistence of his offspring. The family members have grotesque bodies to varying degrees, marked either subtly or obviously, and their physical and mental disabilities are basically cast as monstrous.

Throughout the first two thirds of the film, the family members seem to be unconnected individuals, and only the old man's capture of Sally and the ensuing dinner scene reveal their family relation. The scene stands out as one of the most iconic of the film, and plays out as a shrill, deranged parody of "normal" family life (see fig. 8). Leatherface takes over the role of the wife and mother, signaled by his outfit: he wears a feminine mask including make-up, along with a wig and an apron. The old man acts as the father, leads the proceedings, beats the disobedient younger family members and at one point orders the motherly Leatherface to "get back in the kitchen." His authority is not uncontested, though, as the hitchhiker reminds him that he is "only the cook." The hitchhiker, then, acts like an excited child, while Sally, restrained in her chair, acts as both guest and main dish. As the eldest, the grandfather gets the honor of killing her, or at least to try.

Each of the members plays a recognizable role in the family unit and in the familiar dinner ritual, only distorted into grotesque. Between the table decoration made of a chicken carcass, Leatherface's costume, the barely living grandfather,

---

6   The script intended the three to be brothers, but that is never made clear in the film (Jaworzyn 41). The closest hint is that the old man refers to the grandfather as "my old grandpa," but that line is easily lost in the general confusion of the dinner scene. The 25 year age difference between the actors of the old man and the hitchhiker would seem to suggest that the two characters are father and son instead, and they are commonly read as such (e.g. Wood 90).

7   The grandfather's bloodsucking and appearance of near death are also reminiscent of cinematic vampires, proving Franklin's earlier speculation about a "whole family of Draculas." Despite its radical shock tactics, the film still draws on at least some traditional horror characters to construct its monsters.

the mockery of Sally's terrified pleas, and most of all, the clear threat of death and cannibalism, the scene firmly establishes that the family is monstrous. The old man's demands to kill Sally quickly and without further torture hardly ameliorate this impression; after all, he has no objections to killing and eating Sally in the first place and even stresses the necessity of the act. Any human traits would be outweighed by the sadistic glee of the family, their transgression of the distinction between human and animal in the treatment of their victims, and the old standby of cannibalism.

However, for Wood, the mere fact that these human monsters live together and care for each other causes ambivalence (92). The family ties that keep them together are familiar to the audience, and therefore, "We cannot cleanly disassociate ourselves from them" (92). If they are capable of affection, they cannot be that bad, it would seem, and that Leatherface sets dinner for his relatives and suffers abuse contradicts his previous image as a single-minded killer, thus humanizing him. If monsters are still capable of organizing according to the established structures of normality, they are not totally opposed to it, and not an absolute Other. Yet, the reverse reading is also possible; instead of the monsters being elevated by their family ties, it may be the institution of family that is rendered monstrous by association.

Expanding on Wood's interpretation of the film, Bould places the family in the "comic-horror tradition of the family of monsters", such as *The Addams Family* (99-100). The interactions between Leatherface and the old man recall American sitcoms, he continues, and since the family is a family, "Wood's formula is not reversed at all," but instead "subjected to a significant shift in values" (100). Normality is thus the family "and the bourgeois capitalist order they represent," while the youths are the sympathetic monster (100). Like Wood, Bould views the cultural functions of horror in relation to repression and surplus-repression, as defined by Marcuse. In this reading, the extent of Sally's torture expresses the "tyranny of the family as an institution" (100). Her suffering in the roles of wife and mother assigned to her at the dinner table forms the film's "indictment of the surplus-repression necessary for the perpetuation of the bourgeois capitalist order and embodied in institutions like the family" (100). The monstrous excesses of the cannibal family, then, only dramatize the oppressive nature already inherent in the family.

The portrayal of the monstrous family also draws on a number of other discourses, including social class and regional attitudes and prejudices. The hitch-hiker, the old man and Leatherface are positioned as rednecks or hillbillies, members of an uneducated rural underclass, and *The Texas Chain Saw Massacre* (1974) plays a key role in establishing what might be summarized as "psychotic redneck cannibals" as a monster type, now a fixture in the genre canon among such standards as zombies, vampires and so forth.[8] The basic motif of this subgenre is the fear of modern, urban, middle-class Americans that the rural population is primitive and violent, and possessed by an insane hatred of said urban Americans. Consequently, Clover terms this underlying sentiment "urbanoia" (124), contracted from urban paranoia, and finds traces not only in *The Texas Chain Saw Massacre* (1974), but also in films not typically associated with the horror genre, such as the male rape-revenge thriller *Deliverance* (1972) (126).

Urbanoia involves the construction of country people as a "threatening rural Other" (Clover 124), based on notions that "country parents produce psychosexually deformed children" and live beyond social law (124-25). Leatherface, for instance, can be read as channeling his stunted sexuality into violence, even though that reading is better supported by his portrayal in the 1988 sequel. More importantly, urbanoia revolves around class difference (130), and Clover identifies "economic guilt" as its core motive (134). The wealth of the urban middle class, relative to a rural underclass, would thus invite fears of retribution. Furthermore, Clover draws some striking parallels to the most American of genres, the western. Like the western, she argues, urbanoia films admit "urban crimes" against the "economically dispossessed" (134), and then go on to demonize the latter, only rewriting redskin as redneck, as the redneck offers a safer target for anxieties no longer expressed in ethnic or racial terms (135). Nevertheless, the rednecks of urbanoia films bear a certain resemblance to movie Indians (136). *The Texas Chain Saw Massacre* (1974) provides plenty of examples for this reassignment of markers, such as the animal totems spread throughout the house, and even the cannibalism recalls early colonial imaginations of savage natives. The potential for economic guilt is likewise implied by the hitchhiker's mention of layoffs in the meat industry. Admittedly, the film does not really offer enough information about the young travelers to conclusively identify them as urban middle class, but it is obvious that they are strangers to this part of the country and its concerns.

In short, the cannibal redneck family is a distinctly American monster, which is hybridized from multiple historical discourses. It is rooted in both colonial fears of primitive savages and sentiments of class division, and then amplified by the experience of cultural division during the 1960s and 70s. If we assume that

---

8   Wes Craven's *The Hills Have Eyes* (1978) marks another key entry in the subgenre, and as a more recent example, *Wrong Turn* (2003) still managed to squeeze four sequels from the cannibal redneck formula (as of this writing). Perhaps most tellingly, the subgenre and its tropes are established enough to yield parodies such as *Tucker & Dale vs. Evil* (2010).

era's counterculture and its decline as the crucial historical moment for the anxieties that inform *The Texas Chain Saw Massacre* (1974), like Bould and Becker, it seems to be the obvious choice that the film positions rednecks as its reactionary opposition, distorted into the monstrous.[9] The construction of monsters still follows the same process, as political and socioeconomic Others, in this case, a politically reactionary lower class, are depicted as inhuman and threatening. These redneck monsters are located on the margins of civilization, in a space where social progress has stopped or regressed for unclear reasons.

Youthful Victims and a Single Survivor

Clearly distinguished from the monstrous family, the group of young travelers around Sally represents a contemporary, post-counterculture America. Except for Franklin, all members of the group are optimistic, "quasi-liberated, permissive young," to repeat Wood's characterization (90). The girls wear revealing clothes, Sally is opposed to killing animals for food, and Pam believes in New Age astrology, which, in combination with her appearance, implies some kind of affinity to hippie culture. For Becker, the group simply consists of hippies (53), and Phillips likewise considers the young travelers "remnants . . . of flower children" (117). Unlike the monstrous family, the young travelers have only the barest family connections. Sally and Franklin are siblings, but their relationship is uneasy and she frequently neglects her needy brother. The occasion for their trip is also rooted in neglected family matters, as their father's grave is the only connection Sally and Franklin still have to the area. No other caretakers are left in the area, and symbolically for the state of the Hardesty family, the family house has fallen into ruin.

In most regards, the young travelers and the monstrous family function as polar opposites, divided by age, family ties, regional and class background, and of course their respective attitudes on violence and cannibalism. There are, however, a few tenuous links between the two groups that slightly undermine the absolute distinction between monsters and normality. Franklin is morbidly fascinated by violence and recounts the details of slaughterhouse operations, much to the dismay of his fellow travelers. He engages the clearly disturbed hitchhiker and quickly finds common ground (Franklin's uncle, too, works in a slaughter-

---

9   The sentiment regarding "rednecks" is similar to that found in Romero's films, many of which feature simplistic and well-armed rural Pennsylvanians as antagonists or background presence, as in *The Crazies* (1973) and *Dawn of the Dead* (1978). Romero's image of rednecks is likely shaped by the same sense of cultural and political divide that informed Clover's urbanoia.

house). Franklin even fantasizes about following the hitchhiker's example and cutting himself. Arguably, his physical disability also links him with the grotesque bodies of the family, in that it marks a physical difference from the "normal" bodies of his fellow travelers. Therefore, Franklin can be viewed as a double of the monstrous family, and Wood even calls him "as grotesque, and almost as psychotic, as his nemesis Leatherface" (92). Among his group, Franklin also has the most noticeable Texan accent, which underlines his connection with the area and the way in which the film suggests insanity as a regional condition. However, Franklin's potential affinity to the monstrous family does little to spare him the fate of his companions.

Franklin is not the only character who can be read as a double, as Williams sees further parallels between the travelers and the family. Most importantly, Sally's relationship with Franklin caretaker mirrors the hitchhiker and Leatherface (Williams, *Hearths* 189-91). Both Sally and the hitchhiker are appointed as caretakers for their dependent brothers, and both neglect their wards at some point to pursue their own interests. The travelers may not form a full family, but their social unit still shares the same sibling dynamic. Furthermore, the hitchhiker represents the "dark aspect of hippie youth culture" for Williams (190), and thus may be read as a reflection of the travelers' own hippie leanings. Overall, Williams concludes, the cannibal rednecks function as the young travelers' "dark proletarian family counterparts" (192).

Previously quoted approaches have stressed the senseless nature of the murders and the film's disregard of convention and causality. This observation is generally correct when it comes to the killers' motivations and the seemingly arbitrary death and survival of characters, but the core narrative nevertheless adheres to a certain logic. The fate of the group of victims in *The Texas Chain Saw Massacre* (1974) follows a didactic pattern common to horror stories, as a disregarded warning and a transgression lead to horrible punishment. At a stop early in the film, the group is warned not to "mess around with others' property" because "some people don't like it," and they are told specifically to stay away from the old house. Of course, they disregard these warnings, and even the encounter with the dangerous hitchhiker fails to distract them from their plans. Running across the fields with Pam, Kirk mocks the possible dangers around them, which of course invites terrible things to happen. In addition, the first three victims are all intruders into the family's house, which means that Leatherface might have acted, albeit excessively, in self-defense. This argument does not quite hold up, however, as it does not explain the attack on Franklin, and the evidence of further murders around the house suggests that the family takes a more proactive stance.

The transgressions of the young travelers are compounded by various minor character flaws. They are described as "selfish and bickering youngsters" (Williams, *Hearths* 187), and characterized by "petty malice," expressed through malicious teasing (Wood 92). Despite their status as victims, they possess unsympathetic qualities (Becker 49). In addition, Williams points out that the Hardesty family had been involved in the cattle industry as well, and therefore qualify as exploiters against whose descendants the monstrous family might symbolically take revenge (*Hearths* 187, 190). If the film's underlying logic of disproportionate punishment is taken to its extreme, the victims would provoke their own deaths and suffering through their thoughtless transgressions, or suffer the punishment for their parents' misdeeds.

Of the group of five travelers, only one survivor – Sally – is left at the film's conclusion. Her characterization is hardly more complex than that of the other characters, and she mostly qualifies as the main character by virtue of being around for the whole film. From her first encounter with Leatherface onward, she spends the rest of the film alternately running away and in captivity. Sally's final escape owes more to her captors' negligence than her own actions, as the hitchhiker lets go of her to pick up the hammer. Even though she survives, the last shot shows her reduced to hysterical laughter. Nevertheless, Clover considers her as an early example of a new type of female horror character that arises in the mid-1970s (16), for which she coins the term "Final Girl" (35), referring to a self-sufficient sole survivor who manages to confront and defeat the monster on her own. The description does not wholly apply to Sally, who never really fights back against Leatherface and his kin, but she escapes under her own power, and even though she is aided by two truck drivers, no male hero defeats Leatherface for her. Considering Sally's lengthy ordeal, which takes up the last third of the film, Clover calls her will to survive "astonishing" (36).

The extent of Sally's suffering is also an enduring point of criticism for *The Texas Chain Saw Massacre* (1974). Over the course of the film, Leatherface may kill more men than women (three to one), but the two female characters suffer far more prolonged torture. For comparison, Jerry and Kirk are each hit over the head with a hammer, and Franklin is killed with a chainsaw to the chest. Each of the scenes takes only a few seconds, whereas Pam is hung on a meat hook while still alive, forced to watch the dismemberment of a friend, and later found in a freezer, still alive and panicked throughout. Sally witnesses the death of Franklin, is forced to attend dinner, where she is repeatedly mocked and teased with her coming death and consumption, and suffers a multitude of cuts and bruises during her escape.

This apparent discrepancy between male and female suffering has been read as evidence of misogyny, and in light of Sally's excessive torture, Wood suspects that "Woman" is not only the object of the characters' "animus," but also the film's (91). Lizardi, as a more recent sample, calls the 1974 film an "exemplary example of a misogynistic, allegorical text" (119). The basic argument rests on the assumption that the horror genre's tendency towards female victims at least partly originates in a sadistic impulse on behalf of male filmmakers and audiences, that is, on the idea that male horror viewers enjoy the suffering of female victims. While Clover confirms the gender discrepancy between monsters, heroes and victims (12), she does not believe that sadistic voyeurism is the main pleasure and function of horror and states that the "standard critique of horror as straightforward sadistic misogyny" needs critical and political interrogation (19). Clover suggests that the function of horror is instead geared towards providing a masochistic experience (229), and that the displacement onto female characters makes it easier for males to experience "forbidden desires" (18).[10] Notably, Clover's theory does not preclude the presence of misogynistic ideas in horror films, nor can it, or the approaches it responds to, account for every possible way in which individual viewers may derive pleasure or discomfort or both from watching horror films.

Despite the abundance of psychological torture, *The Texas Chain Saw Massacre* (1974) features no sexual violence, nor the threat thereof. That matches the Clover's impression of the slasher film in general, in which rape practically does not occur, and "violence and sex are not concomitants but alternatives," the former acting as a substitute for the latter (29). The distinction is made clear during the dinner scene, when Sally misreads the family's interest in her and offers to "do anything you want," only to earn incomprehension and mockery (Clover 29). Wood finds that among the all-male family of monsters, "sexuality is totally perverted from its functions, into sadism, violence, and cannibalism" (91). These "repressed energies" then find expression in Leatherface's "phallic chainsaw," a reading again more obvious in regard to the film's 1986 sequel (cf. Clover 25-26). In short, if Leatherface and his kin represent a monstrous distortion of the family, the same applies to their masculinity and sexuality.

There are a number of possible conclusions to draw from *The Texas Chain Saw Massacre* (1974) and its conflict between monstrous family and careless youths. It suggests that modernization processes are not all-encompassing, but leave behind backwards patches, areas off the map that are lethal to those who venture there. The monstrous family that dwells there focuses a number of con-

---

10 Clover's theses on the Final Girl, gender and the horror film, especially the slasher subgenre, are discussed in more detail in chapter 8.

temporary anxieties, including fears of a brutal rural underclass, and of family repression, fueled by the experience of post-1960s social divisions. As depicted by the opening montage, the state of the world is dire to begin with, and considering the survival of the monstrous Leatherface, it is only bound to get worse.

THE TEXAS CHAINSAW MASSACRE (2003)

With blockbuster producer Michael Bay attached and invoked in advertising, the 2003 remake of *The Texas Chain Saw Massacre* (1974) aimed for mass appeal instead of drive-in theaters or disreputable grindhouses. It appeared highly polished, had invested in a few recognizable actors, and was backed by a full-fledged advertising campaign, a far cry from the low budget origins of the 1974 film. Despite a fairly negative critical reception, the remake drew large audiences and reached the number one spot at the US box office.[11] Considering the reputation of the 1974 film as a controversial underground cult picture, the mainstream success of its remake may be taken either as a sign of horror film's increased acceptance, or as a testament to the decades-long myth-making surrounding the first film and its highly recognizable title. Among horror film remakes, *The Texas Chainsaw Massacre* (2003) rates as one of the most commercially successful examples.[12] Consequently, it was followed by yet another entry in the franchise, the prequel *The Texas Chainsaw Massacre: The Beginning* (2006), which fills in the back story of the 2003 film. More recently, the *Texas Chainsaw* brand has moved to 3D, with no signs of slowing down.

The story of the 2003 remake loosely follows the 1974 film. Five young people, including protagonist Erin, her boyfriend Kemper and their friends Andy, Morgan and Pepper, pass through Texas on the way from their Mexico vacation to a rock concert. They pick up a hitchhiker, a traumatized young woman, who kills herself in a panic. The group stops at a gas station to report the death and get directions, but get lost on the way to the Sheriff. Erin and Kemper go to a nearby farmhouse to ask for a phone, where the two are separated and

---

11 *Rotten Tomatoes* records 36% positive reviews ("THE TEXAS CHAINSAW MASSACRE (2003").

12 In terms of US domestic box office returns, it is only topped by two remakes of Japanese horror films, *The Ring* (2002) and *The Grudge* (2004), and by another ghost story, *The Haunting* (1999) ("Horror Remake"). To put this in perspective, though, all of these films did so on a PG-13 rating, which allows for a larger potential audience than *The Texas Chainsaw Massacre*'s (2003) more restrictive R.

Kemper is killed. While the rest of the group deal with the dubious Sheriff Hoyt, Erin returns to investigate the house with Andy. They are assaulted by Leatherface and only Erin escapes. The Sheriff is not interested in her story, and soon thereafter, Leatherface attacks the group's van, killing Pepper. Erin escapes again, is betrayed by two women who turn out to be in cahoots with both the Sheriff and Leatherface, and ends up in the cellar of the farmhouse. There, she finds the mutilated Andy, kills him (at his own request), and rejoins with Morgan. With the aid of a young child, they flee the house, again chased by Leatherface, and arrive at a slaughterhouse, where Morgan is killed and Erin tricks and injures Leatherface. She is picked up by a truck but inadvertently returned to the base of the Sheriff and his family. Undetected, Erin rescues a small child she identifies as stolen and takes off with the Sheriff's car, running him over and killing him in the process. Leatherface is still alive, but fails to stop Erin's escape.

The main story of the film is also framed by an opening voiceover narration that closely replicates the one from the 1974 film, including the claims of being a true story, and by a prologue styled as a police documentary that is said to have been "gathering dust" for 30 years. The documentary radically differs from the main film in style, as it is shot in grainy, hand-held black and white, and shows the local Sheriffs inspecting the crime scenes of the main story, thus foreshadowing the horrors to come. After the main story's conclusion, the framing documentary resumes to show Leatherface murder the Sheriffs and disappear. Like the 1974 film, the remake attempts to raise tensions by pretending to be based on a true story, a claim repeated by the paratexts of advertising and DVD packaging. The framing narrative expands on this technique by employing a style associated with authenticity, and also picks up on contemporary trends in the horror genre by emulating the found footage-style made popular by 1999's *The Blair Witch Project*.

Each of the elements of the 1974 film is significantly reworked in the 2003 version. Although the remake is set in 1973, the date is largely inconsequential. Both the appearance of the actors and the visual style confirm the film as a product of the 2000s, and the few period-specific elements (some of the fashion, cars, youths travelling to a Lynyrd Skynyrd concert) are purely decorative. As in most horror remakes, the depiction of violence is more drastic and more credible, even though the effects of chainsaw wounds are still left to the viewers' imagination, and the element of cannibalism is severely downplayed. More significant are the alterations made to the monstrous family, the group of victims and the logic of punishment, and to the Final Girl Erin, who is elevated to the status of a more active protagonist as well as moral authority. The much-criticized gender dy-

namic of the previous film is significantly changed, yet so are many of its underlying radical notions.

Normality, Deviance and Punishment

As in the first film, the group of young people works as the representative of
normality that comes under assault from the family of monstrous rednecks.
However, while the group in the first film is mostly careless and ignorant, or
mildly malicious at worst, the characters in the remake are downright criminal.
As is revealed early on, they have undertaken their trip to Mexico in order to
smuggle large quantities of Marihuana back to the US. The men (Kemper, Andy
and Morgan) are continually rude to the locals, and when stuck with the hitchhiker who committed suicide in their van, they vote to dump the body because it
is inconvenient and keeps them from reaching the concert. When Kemper does
not return from the farmhouse, the others favor leaving him behind. The subtext
of hippie permissiveness from the 1974 film becomes more blatant, with two
characters indulging in "free love," a joint being passed around and mention of
LSD; at one point Morgan declares to be "way too stoned for this."[13] At the time
of the film's release, the generic rules of slasher films had already been codified
throughout endless sequels and parodies, and following these tropes, sex and
drug use invite punishment by the film's monstrous killers.

Consequently, the transgressions of the young victims set up their excessive
punishment by Leatherface. Only Erin escapes death, because she stands out as
the sole moral authority. She not only refuses to smoke marihuana, but she is
outraged by the drug smuggling, insists on getting the suicide victim proper
treatment and asks to involve the authorities. At the farmhouse, she eagerly helps
a man in a wheelchair, and most importantly, she is also expecting a marriage
proposal from her boyfriend, urging a more traditional relationship instead of a
loose arrangement. Since Erin blatantly stands out from her friends, it might be
appropriate to view her as the only representative of normality, who not only has
to survive the threat of monstrosity, but also has to transcend the immoral transgressions of her peers. Therefore, the remake features not a clear dichotomy between victims and monsters, but a sliding scale from normality (Erin) to transgression (the rest of the group) to monstrous transgression (the murderous redneck family).

---

13 The depiction of the young travelers and their ostensible hippie affiliations is somewhat contradictory: their van sports a sticker declaring that "hippie chicks rule," and
their behavior is supposed to evoke lax hippie attitudes, yet they are traveling to see
Lynyrd Skynyrd, decidedly not a hippie band.

The previous film already insinuated that the young travelers partially invited their suffering through careless trespassing, but this logic is far more pronounced in the remake. Thus, it reinforces a sense of order and causality that was largely missing from the 1974 film, and that played part in its sense of cosmic horror. This is no longer an entirely random, pointlessly violent universe, it is ordered by a logic that sees the immoral and self-absorbed punished (all of the men, Pepper) and the upstanding survive (Erin). Without the context established by the opening montage of newscasts in the 1974 film, the remake turns the events of the narrative into a unique exception, as opposed to the rule, and loses the sense of apocalypse. Where the 1974 film was set in an America filled by inexplicable death, the opening of the remake's main story emphasizes a carefree, romanticized normality with "Sweet Home Alabama" on the soundtrack. Furthermore, the narrative is more conventionally structured, introduces character motivations and conflicts and resolves those, whereas the youths of the 1974 film randomly stumbled into their deaths without narrative progress (Muir, *Horror 1970s* 337).

Finally, while reading the events of the 1974 film as punishment for the young travelers is certainly valid, that explanation does not account for Sally's survival. A morality tale would punish the bad and reward the good, yet Sally is not distinguished from her group, and she is hardly morally superior. There is no particular reason for her survival; it is, in an almost naturalist turn, a random event in an uncaring universe. The case for Erin is different, and supports a far more didactic narrative.

The character of Erin marks a departure from her predecessor in numerous ways. As mentioned, 1974's Sally is considered the main character of her film mostly by virtue of surviving until the end. She displays little depth or character development, and is reduced to screaming and running during last third of the film. Her 2003 counterpart Erin, however, stands out from the start as a heroic character, and the casting of then up-and-coming star Jessica Biel among mostly unknowns underlines the character's importance. Erin is morally superior to her friends, and frequently initiates actions and decisions, from taking charge of finding a phone to launching an effort to find the missing Kemper. While her friends are still alive, she drives the group, and once they are dead, she not only survives on her own, but takes further risks to retrieve a stolen child and earn revenge. In short, Erin possesses agency far in excess of Sally.

The difference becomes particularly evident towards the climax of the film. While Sally escapes thanks to the sheer negligence of her deranged captors, who are so busy cheering their barely animate grandfather that they forget to subdue their victim, Erin eventually outsmarts and outfights her opposition. In the slaughterhouse, she sets a trap for Leatherface (using a piglet as a decoy) and chops his arm off with a meat cleaver. Shortly thereafter, she recovers from the same traumatic situation that had driven the hitchhiker to suicide. Having mastered the panic attack, Erin goes on to take the baby from under the noses of the family and runs Sheriff Hoyt over with his own car. To top off her arc of empowerment, she even takes the time to reverse the car over Hoyt's body to ensure his death.

Over the course of the film, Erin learns from the monster. She successfully stalks her opposition, leads them into traps, and turns their own methods against them. After Leatherface, she is actually the most violent character of the film, killing Hoyt (for revenge) and Andy (out of mercy) and mutilating the otherwise unstoppable Leatherface. This evolution seems like a radical departure from the 1974 film, but it follows the pattern of the Final Girl point for point, thereby bringing the remake's protagonist to a more recent genre standard. Erin encompasses the key aspects of the Final Girl, combining "the functions of suffering victim and avenging hero" (Clover 17), whereas Sally barely transcends the first function. Erin, then, is almost a textbook case of the Final Girl, and even though she does not strictly fulfill the criterion of sexual inactivity (Clover 39), her insistence on marriage marks her as more restrained and conservative than her peers.

Along with the empowerment of the last survivor, the remake reshuffles gender roles quite thoroughly. While the 1974 film focused much of its more explicit violence and torture on females, suffering is more evenly distributed in the 2003 version (Lizardi 119). Of the three male victims in the 1974 film, two are hit over the head with a hammer, and the third (Franklin) is killed by chainsaw, relatively quick deaths, whereas the females are captured and tortured for longer, with Pam being suspended on a meat hook and later found (still alive) in a freezer. The remake swaps these tortures around: now one of the men (Andy) is first mutilated, and then hung on a meat hook, while a woman (Pepper) is quickly killed by chainsaw. Another one of the males, Morgan, also suffers sexually charged torture. First, he is forced to put a gun into his mouth in a scene evocative of oral sex, and later he is killed by having a chainsaw driven up through his crotch.

Moreover, the monstrous family is no longer exclusively male. First, two women (Henrietta and another woman only credited as "Tea Lady in Trailer") actively take part in their murderous activities by capturing Erin and returning her to the house. Second, the family is headed by the elderly matriarch Luda May, who orders her sons Leatherface and Hoyt, referred to as "Junior," around. Luda May's authority is unquestioned, and she delivers the only hint at an explanation for the family's murders, namely that they are retribution for the cruelty of normal people towards her disabled son Leatherface. The activities of the family can thus no longer be explained with the lack of a tempering feminine presence (cf. Wood 91), as 2003's female family members support and enable murder and torture. Gender divisions between victims and monsters are eroded in the remake, yet the core characters and conflict still match the typical setup of the slasher genre: during the climax, a Final Girl (Erin) faces a male monster (Leatherface, and a case can be made for Sheriff Hoyt as well).

Nevertheless, *The Texas Chainsaw Massacre* (2003) raises some interesting questions regarding Clover's theories on gender in horror. Clover suggests that victims in horror films are predominantly female because displacement makes it easier for male audiences to engage in a masochistic watching experience (18), and one of the functions of the Final Girl is to serve as a double for adolescent males (51). However, if victimhood is usually displaced onto female characters to be acceptable, would the increased male suffering in the 2003 film undermine its functioning as a horror film? Either the film would lose effectiveness with male audiences, who would reject identification with the helpless males on screen, or, perhaps more likely, changes in gender roles since the time of Clover's writing have resulted in slightly more flexible audiences. Either way, the 2003 film is more capable of conceiving of men as victims, not only as monsters, even though Clover's point about the Final Girl still stands.

The substitution of violence for sex, stated as another key feature of the slasher genre by Clover (29) and very much in evidence in the 1974 film, is also challenged in the remake. Sheriff Hoyt gropes the female hitchhiker's corpse while wrapping her up for transport, and claims that he frequently engaged in acts of necrophilia in similar situations. He also accuses the males of doing the same. Combined with his sexualized torture of Morgan, Hoyt is clearly depicted as a threatening sexual deviant. Unlike the monsters of the 1974 film, he not only channels his distorted sexuality into violence, but seems to combine the two. Where Sally's expectations of rape were laughed off in the 1974 film, the interests of the monsters have shifted in the 2003 film, especially considering the encounter with the hitchhiker early in the film. In a scene that is as puzzling as it is disturbing, the traumatized woman appears to pull a gun from her crotch and shoots herself with it. The scene is frankly difficult to rationalize; the likely explanation is that the gun has been left behind after being used as a tool in an act of rape. The fact that Hoyt is later confirmed as the gun's owner and uses it as a penis-substitute in the abuse of Morgan would seem to confirm that theory and amplifies the film's subtext of sexual violence.[14] Where the chainsaw could (and still can) be read as a phallic symbol for the sexually repressed Leatherface, the gun may perform a similar, even more crass function for Hoyt.

Finally, the suffering and death of Andy also introduces an unprecedented Christian subtext to the 2003 film. After Andy is dragged into the cellar by Leatherface, he is not only hung on a meat hook like Pam in the 1974 film, but suspends himself on a ceiling beam in a manner that strongly resembles crucifixion. When Erin's attempts to free Andy fail, he begs her to kill him, which she does after some wavering. The scene puts a heavy emphasis on Erin's emotional anguish, and its framing, alternating between low angle shots of Andy's head and high angle shots of Erin at his feet, again evokes Christian imagery. It is worth pointing out that this scene, the act of mercy killing, and the crucifixion imagery have no equivalent in the 1974 film and represent an entirely new addition to the remake. That Andy is crucified and dies for his sins lends another dimension to the narrative's strongly implied logic of transgression and punishment; not only does the 2003 film supplant the random, uncaring universe of its predecessor, it alludes to a higher power behind its more ordered worldview.

Family and Ideology

Inevitably, the monstrous redneck family again plays a central role in *The Texas Chainsaw Massacre* (2003), and even though the mechanics of chainsaw murder remain superficially the same, the underlying contexts and motivations have shifted significantly. The remake not only dramatizes the divide between a younger urban generation and a rural underclass perceived as backwards, it also battles over conceptions of family. Compared to the "hippie nightmare" of the 1974 film (cf. Becker), an ideological shift towards more conservative positions is evident.

The monstrous family is almost entirely recast and expanded in the remake. Sheriff Hoyt roughly resembles 1974's old man as the family's respectable link to the outside world. There is no clear equivalent to the first film's hitchhiker; only Leatherface remains mostly unchanged as the signature character of the film franchise. He is still a hulking brute who wields a chainsaw and commits most of the murders, and his habit of wearing his victims' faces as masks is explained with his own facial disfiguration. Furthermore, the family is now headed by Luda May, a very forceful replacement for the mostly dead grandfather. Mi-

---

14 Despite the unpleasant implications, the film puts rather little emphasis on the role of the gun in the hitchhiker's ordeal, and Lizardi's indictment of misogyny in the 2003 remake oddly makes no mention of it either.

nor characters also include Old Monty, a legless man in a wheelchair who also approximates the grandfather role, Henrietta and the "Tea Lady" who, in keeping with redneck stereotypes, live in a trailer, and Jedediah, an unkempt young boy with split loyalties. All of the family members are presented as physically unattractive or downright disfigured, obviously marking the difference between the grotesque monsters and the young, attractive victims. Notably, the physical disability of Franklin is transferred to the monstrous family, which removes an ambiguous element and neatly aligns the flawless bodies of the young travelers with normality and any kind of deviation from the physical ideal with monstrosity. While the bodies of the family members act as clear markers of difference, their behavior is more sedate than the hysterical insanity of their 1974 counterparts, though not lacking in monstrous sadism. Instead of the deranged dinner scene, the remake encapsulates family life with Luda May ironing Hoyt's pants (also symbolizing who wears the pants in the household) while Old Monty makes cranky remarks from his rocking chair.

The 2003 film does not feature a family that could serve as a counterexample, and it even does away with the withered family ties that linked Sally, Franklin, and their dead grandfather in the 1974 film. Nevertheless, it affirms the concept of a traditional, or normal, family, expressed mainly through Erin. Erin not only urges her boyfriend to get married, which is an issue that never came up in the 1974 film, but also insists on respectful treatment for the dead hitchhiker because she (the hitchhiker) has family, too. The death of Kemper (who, despite his other failings, actually carried an engagement ring) puts her marriage plans on hold, but Erin's commitment to family does not end there. In the film's conclusion, she risks her own life to take a small child that had been abducted by the murderous family, thereby forming her own nuclear family and taking responsibility as a (surrogate) mother. The conclusion, then, sees Erin's normal family model succeed over the monstrous family of the Sheriff and Leatherface. Where the normal family had declined and dissolved in the 1974 film, as symbolized by the Hardesty family, it is reaffirmed by Erin's actions in the 2003 version. Consequently, with the band of monstrous rednecks no longer the sole family model, it becomes difficult to interpret them as a critique of the repression shared by all families, as for example Bould did for the 1974 film. In addition, Erin's dedication to traditional family may be read as a regression towards reactionary gender roles, thus offsetting her increased agency (Lizardi 121).

Family is not the only institution of American life to receive more appreciation in the remake. The Texas of the original is a lawless wilderness, with practically no trace of any authority. The remake, by contrast, features two examples of law enforcement: the Sheriff from the framing video, who appears to be a concerned professional, and of course the monstrous Sheriff Hoyt. While there is a strong possibility of Hoyt being a pretender, the film does not present evidence in that regard, and the presence of corrupt local Sheriffs also matches urbanoia-induced backwoods stereotypes.[15] Either way, the remake presents a law enforcement officer as the chief opposition, the articulate counterpart to the more animalistic Leatherface. The fusion of cannibal family and morally corrupt institutions into one monstrous entity holds a certain radical potential; after all, the fundamental institutions of American life are depicted as monstrous. Yet as with the family and Erin, the film counterbalances that potential with the framing police documentary and Erin's unshakeable belief in law and morality. While Erin receives no help during the main story, the framing documentary proves that the police are on the case and have shut down the house. Even though Leatherface cannot be contained, the conclusion does not achieve the apocalyptic quality of the 1974 film.

The socio-historical context for the monstrous family is somewhat reduced in the 2003 film. While the aspect of class difference is still present, along with the sentiment of urbanoia regarding the rural white underclass, the role of the Texan meat industry is mostly cut from the family's background.[16] While the 1974 family could be interpreted as the victim of modernization and economic hardship, their 2003 counterparts only point towards exclusion and lack of sympathy towards their disabled children. Therefore, reading cannibalism as a result or symptom of capitalism (cf. Wood 91-92) is somewhat less feasible for the remake, as economic factors are entirely absent from the text. Luda May's claim "I know your [Erin's] kind" may be interpreted as an expression of class resentment, easily folded into urbanoia, but the lack of information makes it difficult to draw further conclusions. Thin as it may sound, the 2003 film offers an explanation why the family would do what they do; they are thus a monstrous, if not entirely inscrutable Other.

As should be well established at this point, this study investigates cultural contexts for each film as a basis for interpretation, and one of the underlying assumptions for this approach is that each work will, consciously or unconsciously, deal with the cultural discourses and anxieties of its period. *The Texas Chainsaw Massacre* (2003) marks an exception from most of the texts in this study in that it is technically a period piece. The 1970s setting, however, is of little consequence to the film; it is safe to assume that accurately capturing the year 1973

---

15 The prequel *The Texas Chainsaw Massacre: The Beginning* (2006) confirms that Sheriff Hoyt is in fact an impostor, but no hints are found in the 2003 text.

16 The 2006 prequel provides an origin story to Leatherface, linking him to the meat industry, but again, none of that is insinuated in the 2003 film.

was not one of the filmmakers' top priorities. In any case, the film exhibits a 2000s conception of the 1970s, more attuned to its own period than the one it supposedly emulates. Consequently, the revaluation of family in the remake might be attributed to more conservative "family values" in the 2000s, and the pattern of transgression and punishment of the young travelers may be read as a retrospective critique of the perceived permissiveness of the 1970s, with Erin as a counterexample and role model for a different time and ideology. The crudely drawn hippie characters have no future, but the virtuous Erin does.

These shifts may also be traced to the vastly different backgrounds of the filmmakers and circumstances of production. As mentioned in the previous section, Tobe Hooper was somewhat aligned with the 1960s and 70s counterculture when he worked on *The Texas Chain Saw Massacre* (1974) as director, co-writer and producer (cf. Becker). By contrast, Marcus Nispel had been an accomplished director of commercials and music videos in the 1990s, and was hired to direct the 2003 remake as his first feature film (Southern).[17] Nispel's employer, the production company Platinum Dunes, specializes in horror film remakes, and also turned out new versions of *The Amityville Horror* (2005), *Friday the 13th* (2009, also directed by Nispel), and *A Nightmare on Elm Street* (2010). In the introduction to this study, I suggested that the generic properties of horror films are well-suited for remaking, and therefore enable a horror remaking industry. Platinum Dunes is a prime example of that industry, a business venture dedicated to the reproduction of horror, and the fact that its output remained mostly profitable while earning invariably negative reviews would seem to both vindicate the concept from a commercial point of view and confirm the misgivings of fans and critics.[18]

It is tempting to further draw a connection between the ideological shifts of the 2003 film and Platinum Dunes co-founder Michael Bay, whose excessive blockbuster movies frequently exhibit a conservative slant. However, this type of speculation leads further away from the text and into progressively weaker arguments mired in suspected authorial intent. It seems obvious that different patterns of production will imprint different ideologies onto the resulting films, and if remaking reflects changing times, it is bound to reflect a changing film indus-

---

17 A similar trajectory can be observed for several of the canonical horror films of the 1970s, first made by counterculture-attuned independent directors, then remade by well-funded Hollywood production companies, with music video and commercial directors as hired hands. The same applies to *Dawn of the Dead* (2004), for instance.

18 The films of Platinum Dunes offer great potential for a case study in horror film remaking in the 2000s, but due to constraints in time and space, *The Texas Chainsaw Massacre* (2003) will have to suffice as representative of the method.

try as well. In academic as well as fan criticism, this realization frequently over-laps with a tendency to revere the director as an individual artist, an *auteur*, as opposed to faceless and efficient systems of production. The fact that celebrated auteurs are still subject to many of the same pressures and incentives, and fully intend their films to make a profit, is often ignored in these debates. At any rate, concerns about perceived quality, originality and artistic integrity are not rele-vant for this study, and the systems of production are not visible to the viewer without further effort.

The various iterations of a horror film may have undergone vastly different production processes, but they are still vehicles for historically specific cultural fears and therefore still valid as objects for study. So far, the case of *The Texas Chainsaw Massacre* (2003) has yielded some intriguing results in comparison to the 1974 film: a reinforced sense of normality and morality, a revaluation of family, but also a noticeable reassessment of gender roles, with more even-handed victimization and a strengthened female protagonist. Evaluating these al-terations illustrates the problems inherent in assigning ideological positions to entire films on a simple left/liberal to right/conservative axis, based on a handful of criteria. The 2003 remake's move towards conservative family ideology, then, would be contradicted by its slightly more balanced stance on gender.

The case is much clearer for Lizardi, who finds "remarkable ideological con-tinuity" in *The Texas Chainsaw Massacre* (2003) as well as other slasher film remakes when it comes to misogyny (114). Although he admits the addition of hopeful elements, Lizardi considers Erin's ordeal not only a more "emphasized version" of the 1974 film's misogyny, he also accuses the remake of promoting "socially destructive themes" and subverting "progressive social power struc-tures" (121). Lizardi's argument is problematic in several ways. For one, his concern with the potential damage of intensified depictions of violence fails to take into account that audience expectations and sensitivities have changed in the 30 years between the two films, which means that more drastic means may be needed to achieve the same effect. More importantly, Lizardi's notion of cultural destructiveness relies on rather large and unsubstantiated assumptions about the reception of films and media in general. While a film like *The Texas Chainsaw Massacre* (2003) does reflect cultural attitudes and may in turn shape the atti-tudes of its audience in some way, studies like Lizardi's or mine are ill-equipped to draw conclusions on the latter. Still, it is evident that the filmic text features numerous gender stereotypes, some of which are reinforced in comparison to the 1974 film, while others are subverted in keeping with broader social and genre developments.

In summary, there are a number of key differences between the 1974 and 2003 films. Where the first film broke new ground with its relentless rejection of taste and sanity, the remake is overall a more coherent and conventional horror experience that barely stands out from contemporary examples of the genre. It tempers the apocalyptic nihilism of its predecessor, administers torture in a more balanced manner, and ends on a more optimistic note for its empowered protagonist. With a more pronounced logic of transgression and punishment, and a re-affirmation of family, the remake is arguably much closer to conservative family values. The 2003 film is about the Final Girl not just transcending the monstrous, but also the lifestyle of immoral youth to become a more upstanding citizen. The first film, informed by a sense of a declining post-1960s counterculture, could not conceive of any future in its random, uncaring universe. Therefore, even though the slaughter of youths takes place in a similar fashion, the two films are divided by different worldviews. They do share one central cultural fear, however, and that is a deep suspicion of an uneducated rural underclass perceived as savage and violent. As the 2003 film removes the rationalizations of economic decline and joblessness, it only increases the monstrous difference of its cannibal rednecks, and cements their evil as inborn and absolute, independent from their socio-economic surroundings.

8. Suburban Stalkers and Final Girls

Halloween (1978) is widely considered the starting point for the dominant horror film subgenre of the 1980s, the slasher film. Even though films like *Psycho* (1960) and *The Texas Chain Saw Massacre* (1974) are frequently cited as earlier influences, it is *Halloween's* combination of narrative elements (masked killer, teenage victims, suburban setting, and holiday theme) and a distinct visual style (featuring shots from the killer's point of view) that set the paradigm for a wave of sequels and similar films. In a genre infamous for reproduction, then, *Halloween* (1978) stands out as particularly reproducible.

While the film enjoyed considerable success, its depiction of a psycho killer stalking and murdering teenagers also invited criticism. The focus on female victims led to accusations of misogyny, and the apparent punishment for youthful transgressions was also taken as evidence for a conservative turn in horror. At the same time, examinations of the protagonist's arc (as a "Final Girl," cf. Clover) produced a more complex view of gender dynamics in *Halloween* (1978) and the genre at large. The 2007 remake hardly addresses these critical concerns, but instead expands its focus to explore the background of its monstrous killer, much to the detriment of the previous protagonist. This shift in attention, along with the introduction of new elements and motives, leads to significant thematic departures. While this contrast alone offers plenty of material for analysis, the two films also serve as a frame to a crucial period of horror film production. *Halloween* (1978) marks the launch of the full-fledged slasher film, and its 2007 remake comes in after the genre's demise and revival.

HALLOWEEN (1978)

Halloween (1978) firmly established John Carpenter, who had been moderately successful with the low budget science fiction film *Darkstar* (1974) and the horror-tinted Western remake *Assault on Precinct 13* (1976), as a horror director. The film was independently produced on a tight budget, and Carpenter not only directed, but also wrote the script, based on an idea by producer Irwin Yablans, and wrote and performed the soundtrack (Rockoff 50-53). The film turned out a remarkable success at the box office.[1] Compared to its peers, critical reception was quite positive, and even though much of the praise focused more on the technical aspects of the film, it is now universally recognized as a landmark in the horror film genre. *Halloween* (1978) not only went on to shape the slasher genre, its successors also pioneered the mass production of horror sequels, clocking in at seven sequels, followed by a remake and a sequel to that remake (as of this writing).[2] When it comes to the combination of popularity and lasting influence, it is "arguably, the most successful horror film in American history" (Phillips 125).

The film opens in 1963, where the camera takes the point of view of a stalker in a suburban home. Having observed a teenage girl and her boyfriend, the stalker sneaks inside, kills the girl with a knife and is then revealed as her six year old brother Michael. The action then moves to contemporary 1978. Declared a lost cause by his psychotherapist Loomis, Michael Myers has spent the past fifteen years locked up in a mental institution, until he escapes and travels back to his old hometown of Haddonfield, Illinois. There, Myers begins to stalk Laurie, a high school student, along with her friends Annie and Lynda, while Loomis, convinced of Myers's "pure evil," tracks his traces and desperately tries to alert the police of his presence. Laurie and her friends notice the mask-wearing Myers, but fail to realize the danger. On Halloween night, Laurie is babysitting while Myers goes through the teenagers' homes and murders first Annie, then Lynda and her boyfriend. When Laurie goes looking for Annie, she is also attacked by Myers. During the following chase through suburban homes, Laurie stabs Myers several times, only for him to rise and attack her again. Finally, Loomis arrives and shoots Myers, but the body disappears. The final scenes show locations around the suburbs while Myers's heavy breathing is heard, implying that he is still alive.

---

1   Muir lists the budget at a meager $300,000 and mentions that *Halloween* (1978) held the record for top grossing independent film until 1990 (*Horror 1970s* 25).

2   The lengthy and convoluted *Halloween* series also challenges film categories. Beyond the title, *Halloween III: Season of the Witch* (1982) has nothing to do with Michael Myers, making it a "nonsequel," to use the term Perkins adapts from Druxman (Perkins 15). *Halloween H20: 20 Years Later* (1998), the seventh film in the series, ignores the three previous sequels and effectively starts a new sequence from *Halloween II* (1981).

The core narrative of *Halloween* (1978) proved extremely well-suited to re-production, thanks to a simple, but effective and adaptable structure. Producers and studios appreciated the appeal to the valued teenage demographic, along with the fairly cheap production. With a small cast of young actors, a limited location and timeframe, and masks and stabbings requiring little in terms of special effects, horror films following the *Halloween* paradigm promised sizeable profit margins. Furthermore, invoking a holiday in the title adds recognition value, and in the case of Halloween in particular, channels the popularity of an already horror-themed holiday.

It is worth pointing out that the high reproducibility of *Halloween* (1978) is hardly rooted in any particular innovation in form or content. On the contrary, the film is perceived as highly derivative by numerous critics. For example, Dika views it as a "conscious remake of Psycho" (18), and Wood likewise asserts that *Halloween* (1978) offers nothing new, but forms a "resourceful amalgam of *Psycho, The Texas Chainsaw Massacre, The Exorcist* and *Black Christmas*" (193). It would appear only logical, then, that a film that already represents a distillation from a variety of key examples of the genre, constructed with a clear purpose, would form an effective blueprint for reproduction.[3] Intriguingly, *Halloween* (1978) openly invokes a slightly different cinematic legacy by having Laurie and her charges watch *The Thing from Another World* (1951) (which Carpenter would remake four years later, see chapter 3) and *Forbidden Planet* (1956) on television. The latter is categorized as a science fiction film, but features an invisible monster sprung from the Freudian id, which is a close enough approximation of the stalking Michael Myers.

While the long trail of sequels and remakes undeniably attests to the reproductive potential of *Halloween* (1978), Nowell contests the established narrative concerning its significance to the slasher genre. He points out that the slasher structure had already been evident four years earlier, in the Canadian film *Black Christmas* (1974), which would more accurately represent the genre's actual point of origin (105). Furthermore, Nowell insists that *Halloween* (1978) was not responsible for starting the teen slasher cycle of the early 1980s. It did moderately well, he argues, but failed to pick up MPAA distribution (104-05). Rejection from the major film studios meant a major commercial setback, and only the later success of *Friday the 13th* (1980) inspired a number of "cash-ins," meaning the bulk of the early 1980s slasher films (145). In short, *Halloween's* (1978) iconic status is vastly overrated. Nowell is of course correct in pointing out the network of influences that shaped *Halloween* (1978) and the genre, as well as the

---

3   Indeed, Nowell names "calculated hybridity," the recombination of previous hits to assure commercial success, as a general method of film production (25).

complexities of the film industry. Carpenter did not single-handedly reinvent the horror film genre with *Halloween* (1978), but originality is not required for the film to be significant, and even though it did not create the slasher tropes from scratch, it played a major part in refining and bringing them to critical attention.

Even though the slasher formula is generally considered as obvious and predictable, there are still many variant attempts at definition. For example, Jones identifies four key plot points: (1) "a past misdeed creates a psychopathic killer," who (2) returns to the "site of the misdeed" on a specific date in the present to (3) stalk and kill a group of teenagers, except for (4) one girl, who "survives to thwart the killer" (quoted in Ní Fhlainn 180). As another example, Nowell states that the teen slasher story structure requires "three iconographic elements: a distinct setting, a shadowy killer, and a group of youths" (20), and unfolds in three steps, "setup," "disruption," and "resolution" (21). Dika goes into more detail, and outlines the narrative structure of what she terms the stalker film in seventeen points (59). This last example already hints at some of the difficulties in finding a common slasher formula, namely that there is no definite critical consensus in delineating the edges of the slasher genre. While the various iterations of *Halloween* and *Friday the 13th* form an undisputed core canon, the generic affiliation of the *Texas Chainsaw* films is already problematic. Key studies of the genre operate with different definitions, and where Dika is very narrow in focus, limiting what she terms the "stalker film" to horror films featuring a first person camera (14), Clover is rather broad, liberally listing variant genre designations in her introduction to the "slasher (or splatter or shocker or stalker) film" (21).

Although its persistence points to a certain popularity with audiences, the slasher film enjoys a fairly negative reputation among critics, even compared to the already disreputable horror genre. Clover famously located it "at the bottom of the horror heap," beyond respectable audience and criticism (Clover 21). While other types of horror film have reached acceptance and lasting popularity among critics and academics, the proponents of the slasher have not been as successful in elevating the genre to respectability. In fact, some of the critics that had worked to defend horror film against accusations of being immoral or artistically worthless in the 1970s ended up reviling this new wave of horror in similar ways, albeit for slightly different reasons. Wood, for instance, dismissed them as "teenie-kill-pics" and as evidence of a worrisome turn in horror (195). Admittedly, the publication of Clover's study and others throughout the 1990s has at least established the slasher film as a valid subject for research, albeit not as a medium of artistic expression. As a technically accomplished forerunner of the type, *Halloween* (1978) is usually elevated above the bulk of the genre (cf. Dika 9), but such goodwill is rarely extended to its many successors.

Halloween (1978) presents a fairly clear-cut conflict between normality and monster, and the following analysis will focus on three focal points in this conflict. First, it will examine the location and background, suburbia and the social structure of which it is a part, followed by the portrayal of the monstrous intruder Michael Myers, and finally, the victims and the last survivor Laurie in particular.

A Suburban Landscape of Constant Danger

Halloween (1978) exemplifies the basic horror motif of a monster intruding and disturbing normality. In the suburbs of fictional Haddonfield, Illinois, the film constructs a completely generic white middle class world to effectively represent any American suburb. If the film did not name Haddonfield's home state, it could be located almost anywhere across the US, given its lack of local color. The fact that a Californian shooting location stands in for Illinois is standard practice for Hollywood, but it also underlines the exchangeability of the suburban setting. Haddonfield is thus not a particular place, but *the* American suburb, an archetypal site of normality to go with the archetypal evil of *the* boogeyman Michael Myers. Whereas the hillbilly or urbanoia horror film in the mold of *The Texas Chain Saw Massacre* (1974) has its ensemble of young middle-class victims travel into the realm of the monsters, a desolate rural wasteland, *Halloween* (1978) hits them right where they live. As Ní Fhlainn points out, the film draws a horror scenario for home owners, whose property is under assault from incomprehensible forces (182).

Haddonfield appears as an average, that is, perfectly normal American suburb: individual houses, situated on neatly trimmed lawns, and inhabited by nuclear families of parents and their children. Older teenagers like Laurie and Annie babysit younger children from the neighborhood in a support network that is built on communal trust. The only insinuation of violence is bullying at high school, and the only sign of decay is the Myers residence.[4] Abandoned since the 1963 murder, it appears as a foreign body in an otherwise flawless community. Efforts to reabsorb the house into normality are made, as Laurie's realtor father tries to sell it, but so far remain unsuccessful.

---

4 There is another hint towards the possibility of murder and domestic violence around the otherwise idyllic Haddonfield. When showing the grave of Judith Myers to Loomis, a groundskeeper says "Every town has something like this happen" and begins to recount the story of (presumably) a family murder in a neighboring town. That suggests the occurrence of more such murders and perhaps the existence of more psychotic killers.

This space of normality, however, proves woefully unprepared for the threat of just one individual whose resilience may appear supernatural, but whose means are utterly ordinary and material. Michael Myers moves freely in the streets and stays unnoticed and unchallenged. While many typical film monsters only come out at night and stick to the shadows, except for occasional glimpses to build tension, Myers makes his presence known to Laurie by appearing in broad daylight. Remarkably, he stays unnoticed by everyone except her. The suburban landscape is almost empty, offering an open hunting ground for Myers, and the community is fundamentally unsafe with no boundaries or guardians to stop him.[5] Thresholds between public and private spaces are penetrated with ease, as cars, doors, and windows are unlocked all around Haddonfield. Until the climax, Myers never has to use force to enter any room. Suburbia, and thus the normality of *Halloween* (1978), is dangerously oblivious to possible dangers. The single-family home, symbol of middle class independence, is not only unsafe against attack; it also turns into a trap for its inhabitants. Once Myers is present, the architecture stands in the way of a safe escape. Annie locks herself in the laundry room by accident, and Laurie finds herself locked out of the house during her escape from Myers.

The vulnerability of suburbia is realized fairly late by Sheriff Brackett. Once he accepts Loomis's view of Myers and his capabilities, he remarks that Haddonfield is "Families, children, all lined up in rows up and down these streets. You're telling me they're lined up for a slaughterhouse?" Suburbia is defined by families, and the manner in which they are arranged only serves to escalate the scale of potential atrocities. The formative idea of suburbia as a safe, pastoral idyll for nuclear families is violently upended by the arrival of just one extraordinary psychopath. As Gill suggests for the genre in general, slasher films "seem to mock white flight," the large-scale relocation of white middle-class families away from the inner cities, by depicting suburbia as fundamentally unsafe (16). Gill's reading is highly applicable to *Halloween* (1978), and indeed, the suburb and school of Haddonfield appear to be exclusively populated by white parents and children. The film thus serves not only as a paradigmatic example for slasher films, but also for what might be called suburban horror.

The architecture of suburbia is not the only opening for the monstrous to enter; its social structures are also insufficient. Throughout the film, parents are rarely seen. Laurie's father briefly appears at the start of the film, and Annie's

---

5   Considering Carpenter's well-known passion for the classic Hollywood Western, and the propensity of Western themes to creep into his work (Maddrey 131), the suburbs could be read as a frontier here, which would match their emptiness and seeming lawlessness, not to mention the need for a lone gunman (Loomis) to administer justice.

father plays a recurring role as the town Sheriff, but neither is present during any of Myers's attacks. Not only are the fathers absent during crisis, there are no mother figures present at all, and Laurie has to assume the parental role in protecting her wards during Myers's attack. Haddonfield's teenagers and children are conspicuously left on their own on Halloween (cf. Gill 17). The authorities are similarly absent or ineffective. Sheriff Brackett may be well-meaning, but turns out to be no help at all, as he underestimates Myers and is never around when needed. In a dangerously oblivious community, only psychiatrist Dr. Loomis, an outsider, is aware of the threat. As Loomis explains, he had to manipulate the legal system to keep Myers locked up, and even after Myers's escape, the police are reluctant to heed his warnings. It appears to be a systemic failure that allows Myers to escape and murder: legal and mental health institutions are too soft to keep him contained, and the police are incapable of retrieving him. Only Loomis, a determined individual who defies the rules and structures of society according to his own judgment, is able to save Laurie and stop Myers, if only for the moment. There is a case to be made for the character of Loomis as a rugged individualist, considering that he is a lone, gun-toting psychiatrist, but even if he does not exactly match the archetype, he certainly fits the mold of anti-authoritarian characters in the films of John Carpenter (cf. chapter 3).

In summary, none of the protections of an ostensibly safe society function adequately in *Halloween* (1978), as Muir notes, including the failure of parents, law, and science (by which he means psychiatry and medicine) (*Carpenter* 77). These shortcomings could be read as a critique of suburbia as caught in a false sense of security, thanks to negligent parents and authorities. The concentration of families in suburbs and established cultural habits like parents leaving their children with teenage babysitters could furthermore be argued as enabling Myers's killing spree. The stress on Myers's inexplicable and unpredictable, in short: monstrous evil serves to absolve these institutions to some extent, however, and Gill suggests a slightly more ambiguous stance for slasher films, in that they both mock and yearn for the middleclass family (17). In that case, *Halloween* (1978) could be read as both a critique of as well as a statement of concern for the archetypal, or perhaps idealized suburbia represented by Haddonfield.

That concern for the normality of suburban families can of course be read as historically specific. Dika links the stalker film, of which *Halloween* (1978) is a key example, with a move towards political conservatism in the late 1970s and early 1980s, which included a reconciliation with "marriage, family, and religion" (132). Since Haddonfield is defined as a site for families, at least, the film may be read as part of that movement. Wood takes a similar stance and is highly critical of reactionary tendencies in the film and genre (193-94). Phillips follows in the same vein, but also vastly expands the historical context. *Halloween* (1978), he claims, is informed by the turn towards a more conservative America, the backlash against the permissiveness of disco culture and cultural narcissism, as well as by nostalgia for the 1950s, Jimmy Carter's malaise, and the rise of the religious right (Phillips 130-32).

The Faceless Killer

Halloween's (1978) monster is easily summarized: Michael Myers is a silent masked psychopath who stalks, stabs and strangles teenagers on Halloween, in what is most likely a recreation of the murder he committed on the same day as a six-year-old. Going by this description alone, Michael Myers would hardly seem to compare to the more colorful and outlandish monsters of the horror genre, but he nevertheless achieved iconic status among the genre canon. Myers is far from an ordinary killer, since the film systematically strips him of his humanity and exalts him into a mythical figure. While still technically human and unremarkable at first glance, Myers is depicted as thoroughly monstrous.

First off, the audiovisual presentation of Myers leaves no doubt that he is a threat. For much of the film's first half, the audience does not get a good look at him, as he either appears in the foreground, with his head outside the frame, or far in the background. In accordance with genre traditions, his appearances are accompanied my music cues that signify danger. Myers's movements are slow and purposeful, even during chase scenes, and his body language is minimal. He never speaks and utters no sound when wounded; in fact, the only sound he makes is the heavy breathing that hangs over his point of view shots. Tellingly, Myers's defining feature is an accessory: a formless human mask, worn at all times, which serves to further dehumanize him. The resulting reduction of the character to a pale reflection of a human being is so thorough that the masked Myers is only listed as "The Shape" in the credits.[6] Myers, then, is presented not as a full human being, but as an empty and therefore monstrous husk. For this reason, his eventual unmasking has little effect, as the face underneath is as expressionless as the mask. The combination of mask, silence, and complete ruthlessness recalls *The Texas Chain Saw Massacre's* Leatherface, but where

---

6   Apart from "The Shape," the film's end credits list two actors for Michael Myers, at 6
     and at 23 years, but the latter is only used for the asylum escape and the short unmasking scene. (As an aside, the ages do not add up with the timeline of the film, but that
     seems to be an oversight.)

Leatherface is excessive and grotesque, Myers evokes monstrosity from a more subdued demeanor.

Arguably, the most iconic scenes of Michael Myers are those in which he is not visible at all, as the camera adopts his point of view. Carpenter's use of a subjective camera for Myers has been the subject of some controversy, as it allegedly makes the audience active participants in the depicted acts of sadistic violence. Dika, who sets point of view shots as the distinctive mark of what she terms the stalker film (14), takes a more differentiated view. These shots, she claims, allow viewers to share the killer's perspective, but without or at least lessened responsibility. In the case of *Halloween* (1978), the subjective camera creates distance and no empathy because Myers is not really defined as a character (Dika 36-37). In addition, Clover suggests that point of view shots can be "pro forma," and that they can destabilize as much as stabilize identification (45). Jancovich arrives at a similar conclusion, stressing that the killers of slasher films do not offer much to identify with, and that their point of view may be used to alienate audiences (*Horror* 106). In short, even moving the camera behind Myers's eyes only serves to underline his inhumanity.

On the diegetic level, Myers's monstrous status is further cemented by his psychiatrist Loomis, who serves as the film's only expert and authority on the matter. In frequent expository monologues, Loomis repeatedly points out just how dangerous Myers is. He relates the story of their first encounter, during which the six year old Myers displayed "No reason, no conscience, no understanding; even the most rudimentary sense of life or death, good or evil, right or wrong." Loomis claims that Myers has "the devil's eyes," calls him "purely and simply evil," and as the simplest example of dehumanization, refers to him as "it." As he tells Sheriff Brackett, "This isn't a man." Since the characters of a horror narrative give the audience a reference on how to read the monster (Carroll 18), Loomis's desperate warnings firmly establish Myers as an inhuman, monstrous Other. Notably, thriller and horror films featuring psychopathic killers had proliferated since *Psycho* (1960), but *Halloween's* (1978) embrace of "pure evil" as a defining trait for Myers represents a break in the subgenre (Muir, *Horror 1970s* 25).[7]

---

7 Remarkably, some characters take over the role of the boogeyman. Tommy, the boy babysat by Laurie, decides to scare Lindsey, the neighbors' kid, but is preempted by Myers. In another scene, Loomis poses as a monster to scare a group of children away from the Myers house, and appears to enjoy the experience. The fact that Loomis, who has firsthand experience with an actual human monster, takes pleasure in switching roles strongly suggests that the capability to cause terror is indeed more widespread.

Taking a step further, the depiction of Michael Myers also verges on the fantastic. Loomis not only exalts him into a figure of pure evil, but equates him with the mythical monster, the boogeyman, at the film's conclusion. Myers's actions also stretch the limits of what is humanly possible. For instance, he manages to lift Bob with one hand, and using a knife in his other hand, pierces his body with such force as to pin him to a wall. Myers's resilience to injury may likewise seem supernatural, as he is stabbed in the eye with a knitting needle, stabbed in the chest with a knife, shot six times, and falls out a second story window, only to disappear again. At times, Myers appears in the frame like a ghostly apparition (see fig. 9). Phillips sees more hints towards supernatural means in the convenient opening and closing of doors, and in the fun house-like display of bodies towards the climax (136). An imaginative viewer can find rational (or rather, material) explanations for these events, but as the film proceeds, these become strained, at least. As a narrative device, the uncertainty whether or not Myers possesses supernatural abilities generates tension, and the challenge to categories of knowledge again serves to emphasize his monstrosity.[8]

Like his physical limitations, Myers's motivation remains uncertain and ultimately unknowable. The opening scene, which shows six-year-old Michael Myers murdering his sister Judith after watching her intimate encounter with her boyfriend, may suggest incestuous desire as the motive for the deed. According to Wood, the murder of Judith Myers points towards family horror, implicating the "child-monster" as a "product of the nuclear family," along with the sexual repression of children and the incest taboo (193). From this vaguely psychoanalytic point of view, Myers's repressed urges regarding his sister are enacted as violence, in a variation of the "psychosexual fury" prevalent in the genre (Clover 27). The later murders may not quite fit into that pattern, but the general similarities in age and lifestyle between Myers's sister and his later victims might be sufficient to read them as a sort of compulsive repetition.

However, much to the frustration of Wood and other critics, the film appears to reject any such theories through the voice of Loomis. To Loomis, there are no complexities to explore, and the only explanation is that Myers is evil. Therefore, by identifying Myers with the boogeyman, an "embodiment of an eternal and unchanging evil," the causality of sexual repression and murder is undone (Wood 193). Wood criticizes Loomis's assessment of Myers as the "most extreme instance of Hollywood's perversion of psychoanalysis into an instrument of repression" (194). If Loomis is correct, then society is not responsible for Myers's monstrosity, and if the monster is not caused by (and rebelling against) so-

---

8 *Halloween 6: The Curse of Michael Myers* (1995) confirmed a supernatural origin for Myers, only for later sequels to retract that idea again.

ciety's surplus repression, then it only serves to uphold repression and the status quo. Wood adds that reading the film against Loomis (that is, dismissing his expert opinion as false) is an intriguing possibility, but ultimately concludes that such a reading is neither legitimate nor coherent (194). Williams, however, has no such reservations and accuses Loomis of using Myers as a scapegoat, in service of society that wishes to disavow "social crisis" (*Hearths* 216).

Even though Loomis's expository monologues play a large part in shaping possible readings of Myers's character and actions, and – as outlined above – frustrate some approaches, there are still a few more blank spaces left for interpretation, even without resorting to the development of counternarratives. The film offers no counterpoint to Loomis's judgment that Myers was already pure evil at age six, but it says nothing about how Myers reached that point. For a narrative invested in tension, that gap simply serves to heighten the mystique of the monster Michael Myers, but it also leaves a potential that the 2007 remake will go on to explore at tremendous length.

In *Halloween* (1978), Michael Myers functions as a monstrous intruder into the normality of suburbia, but although he has spent the previous fifteen years at the margins, in a mental institution, it is worth mentioning that he is still from Haddonfield, as the film's tagline, "The night HE came home," clearly points out. Despite Loomis's insistence, and Wood's critical disappointment, Myers is not from beyond, or hell, or outer space, or even the Texas backwoods; he is indeed from the heart of normality. Moreover, the survival of Myers not only opens the door for sequels, but it signals an end to normality and the impossibility of safety. Normality is not restored, but still under threat, as the heavy breathing over the various locations of the town suggests. By disappearing, Myers is potentially everywhere.

Teenage Targets and the Final Girl

A significant part of the critical discourse on *Halloween* (1978) is closely intertwined with discussions of the slasher genre in general and focuses on the roles of the mostly female victims and the final survivor. Given the paradigmatic role of *Halloween* (1978) and the close replication of many of its narrative tropes and filmic techniques in the plethora of generic successors, it should come as no surprise that film is taken as a representative sample by Dika, Clover and others. As the slasher genre and its later excesses are also the subject of distinct critical resentment, it may however be necessary to filter out generic points that are not applicable to *Halloween* (1978) itself, in order to arrive at a valid reading of the text.

As mentioned earlier, the slasher genre has frequently been decried as an especially low form of exploitation cinema,[9] indulging in the graphic murder of teenage girls in particular to a degree that is at least questionable. Indeed, Michael Myers's favored targets in *Halloween* (1978) are teenage girls: the first victim is his older sister Judith in 1963, and in the present, he murders Annie and Lynda, and repeatedly tries to kill Laurie. His other victims are a truck driver, killed off-screen, and Lynda's boyfriend Bob. The headcount alone does little for an analysis, though, and the characterization of the victims and the circumstances of the murders are crucial for any reading.

For a start, Laurie, Annie and Lynda act as the main representatives of a threatened normality, since their parents and indeed any adults are practically absent from the narrative. Specifically, they depict a slice of late 1970s suburban middle-class teenage life. All three attend high school, and Annie and Laurie babysit children of the neighborhood whose parents are out for the night. Even though their backgrounds seem similar, their priorities are somewhat different. Judging by their conversations, Annie and Lynda appear more interested in dating than school, whereas the more bookish and less social Laurie is treated as a bit of an outsider. That dynamic suggests that Annie and Lynda, with their confidence and lack of responsibility, are more representative of the average teenage girl, at least as constructed by the film. The difference between Laurie's and her friends' behavior is striking, and has widely been read as a factor in the respective characters' demise or survival, and as revealing a particular political or moral stance for the film.

In short, Annie and Lynda exhibit a variety of transgressive behaviors, at least in terms of a strict conservative morality (cf. Dika 44-45). Annie is verbally aggressive, disrespectful of her father, smokes what is most likely marihuana while driving, and shirks her babysitting duties in favor of meeting with her boyfriend for sex. Lynda and her boyfriend Bob take advantage of Annie's babysitting to have sex in another family's home and engage in underage drinking. All three are killed by Myers, while the survivor Laurie is a good student, responsible as a babysitter, sexually not active, and even though she partakes in Annie's joint, she is clearly not used to smoking. *Halloween* (1978) can thus be read as a morality tale: the naughty Annie and Lynda die, and the virtuous Laurie survives. Michael Myers acts as a punishing force which suppresses those teenagers that transgress against suburban morality and conformity. This logic of sin and punishment is by no means new for the horror genre, especially when unruly youths are concerned (cf. *The Texas Chain Saw Massacre*, ch. 4.3.1), but *Hal-*

---

9   Inaccurately, as Nowell argues, since slasher films mostly aimed for mainstream distributors and ratings, as opposed to independent "grindhouse" venues (Nowell 30-31).

loween (1978) again refines preexisting motives into a paradigm. According to Clover, the murder of Lynda and Bob starts the slasher genre tradition of sexual transgression leading to death (33), which amounts to a "generic imperative" that "crosses gender lines" (34).

This underlying logic has rather drastic implications, and Wood, for instance, considers *Halloween* (1978) the "decisive" film for a "reactionary direction change" in the horror genre (191). Since the victims are promiscuous and the survivor a virgin, the monster becomes "simply the instrument of puritan vengeance and repression rather than the embodiment of what Puritanism repressed" (194). Specifically, the monster acts as a "superego figure, avenging itself on liberated female sexuality or the sexual freedom of the young" (195). Williams makes essentially the same argument about the slasher films of the 1980s. He characterizes these films as politically conservative, as they try to "assert patriarchal power" and remove the monster's association with the return of the repressed (*Hearths* 211). Much like Wood, Williams concludes that "The monster is now the patriarchal father" (211), and that its survival "now symbolizes a dominant patriarchal hegemony ruthlessly attempting to deny viable counterhegemonic alternatives" (211-13).

Phillips reads *Halloween* (1978) in a similar vein. He argues that the film inverts the sense of invading chaos that typically characterizes the horror film, and instead positions Myers as an avenger imposing order in a chaotic world (126). Since all of the teenage victims are involved in sexual activities, the murders follow a punitive logic, and Myers stands in for a "disciplining parental figure" (137-38). Laurie, then, survives thanks to being prude and possessing maternal qualities (139-40). With all that in mind, Phillips speculates that the film's success is the result of a young audience seeking discipline or "to purge their guilt" (142). Of course, this theory assumes that teenage audiences identify with the victims and their actions on screen, perceive their behavior as morally transgressive, and are relieved by reading Myers's murders as a substitute punishment for their own deeds. Although Phillips does not consider *Halloween* (1978) a conservative film, he finds that it resonates with a contemporary "rise in conservative sentiment" (143).

By contrast, Jancovich mounts a defense of *Halloween* (1978). Drawing on Tudor, he argues that the film never presents any of the women as immoral or their activities as problematic or abnormal, and certainly not as inviting punishment (*Horror* 106-07). To Jancovich, the source of the film's horror is precisely that the "audience *does not* want to see even the most irritating of the teenage characters get killed" (107). Furthermore, he denies that Lynda and Annie are victimized because of their threat to a patriarchal order, since Laurie is (by her own admission) the one who is threatening to men (107). In more general terms, Jancovich identifies masculinity as the problem in this type of slasher film, which features no positive or effective male characters (107). In the case of *Halloween* (1978), Sheriff Brackett and Loomis are ineffectual, and Loomis is no better at stopping Myers than Laurie is (108). This lack of male heroes is attributed to a "wider loss of faith in the structures of American society," and the slasher genre accordingly presents normality as unstable, with "traditional forms of authority" as either the root cause of the threat or ineffectual at combating it (108). Even though Jancovich reads slasher films as critical of masculinity and male authority, he stresses that this stance does not make these films feminist (108).

Indeed, few critics would consider *Halloween* (1978) a feminist film. On the contrary, Dika finds that the film treats the victims as "devalued characters," and views Lynda and Annie in particular as "grotesque parodies" of females who deserve to die because of their transgressions, which include not only sex, but also their aggressive attitude (44-45). If these characters are indeed, as Dika puts it, "parodies of 'new women'" (46), the film would assume a reactionary, anti-feminist stance. Such readings are commonplace for the slasher and related subgenres of the 1970s and 80s, whose marked focus on female victims has been explained as pushback against 1960s and 70s feminism (Wood 196). However, Wood adds that women have always been prime targets in horror for a variety of reasons, from the assumption of weakness to the enactment of patriarchal "wife/whore" oppositions (196-97). Clover, too, notices a trend towards female victims in slasher films, and states that even films featuring an equal distribution of male and female victims will show the murders of women "at closer range, in more graphic detail, and at greater length" (35). She also concedes that this pattern forms a "cinematic standard" with a "venerable history" that is not created, but carried on by the slasher (35).

However, beyond the restaging of familiar and problematic genre tropes, *Halloween* (1978) also breaks new ground when it comes to its protagonist. The character of Laurie marks the full realization of what Clover calls the Final Girl, a new, invariably female type of horror protagonist that unites the functions of victim and hero (17). The Final Girls thus suffers numerous horrors, but is strong enough to either resist the killer until she is rescued, or to destroy him on her own (35). Clover sees that development rooted in the women's movement and the "image of an angry woman" it has given to the horror genre, a female archetype credible enough to act as "perpetrator" and protagonist (17). She traces the emergence of the Final Girl through *Psycho* (1960), *The Texas Chain Saw Massacre* (1974), and *Halloween* (1978), with the phase starting in 1974 responding to "the values of the late sixties and early seventies" (24-26). In contrast to *The Texas Chain Saw Massacre's* (1974) Sally, Laurie makes the crucial step from passive to active defense, from merely surviving to fighting back, and in the wake of *Halloween* (1978), Final Girls manage to defeat monsters on their own (37). The fact that Laurie still needs Loomis to save her in the end may not be significant here – according to Clover, "the quality of the Final Girl's fight" and the "qualities of character that enable her, of all characters, to survive" are more important than who stops the killer (39). The Final Girl is clearly the main character, "not sexually active," "watchful to the point of paranoia" (39), and "boyish" or "not fully feminine" (just as the killer is not fully masculine) (40).

Since critiques of the slasher film and its reception fail to take the Final Girl into account, Clover takes the character type as a departure point to rethink questions of gender and identification. Quoting theories that assume the identification of female viewers with male characters on screen, Clover suggests that the reverse is true for the Final Girl. As the slasher offers no male characters to identify with, and the killer doesn't invite empathy, the likely explanation for the popularity of the female victim-hero with predominantly male audiences is that male viewers identify with her, at least by the end of the film (43-45). While the emergence of the Final Girl would seem to point at changing conceptions of gender (16), and thus hold progressive potentials, Clover undercuts those with "figurative readings" that stress the Final Girl's function as a male surrogate. The Final Girl therefore reads as male, after all, not as a feminist development, and the male viewer's use of her to enact his own fantasies amounts to "an act of perhaps timeless dishonesty" (53).

Clover's concept of gender and sex, and especially her assertion that the sex of a horror character is derived from the gender of her function (16), are met with harsh criticism by Pinedo. Clover's adherence to sexual difference, she claims, denies female agency – if a female character has to be read as male when she is aggressive, there can be no female agency, and "Clover dismisses the progressive potential of this gender trouble" (83). Instead, Pinedo suggests that the Final Girl breaks down binary notions of gender and "violates the taboo against women wielding violence" (84). Consequently, the slasher functions as a fantasy of female rage and an opening for feminist discourse because women are not only victims, but allowed to retaliate, thereby offering pleasure to female audiences (86-87). Williams, by contrast, attacks Clover for *over*estimating the progressive potentials of the slasher film. He dismisses the significance of the Final Girl, as her victory is undercut by sequels or insanity, accuses Clover of ignoring textual complexity, and rejects her thesis on the masochistic tendencies behind horror –

even if there is a masochistic identification, it may still serve repression (*Hearths* 214, cf. "Trying").

Few elements of Clover's study have been spared by criticism. Nowell, for example, takes issue with what he views as faulty assumptions and inconsistent categorization of films. Clover's concept of the slasher film, a term she invented, is particularly problematic. Not only do her examples not match her definitions, she also created a critical category – the slasher – that "did not exist on celluloid in the years before her piece was published," but went on to influence scholarly perceptions (Nowell 17). Repeated by other writers, Clover's claims would pro-liferate and reinforce misconceptions about the genre, in particular, that it is mainly concerned with male psychopaths torturing women (Nowell 17-18). More pertinent to this chapter, Clover's reading of *Halloween* (1978) is also con-tested by other authors. Gill contradicts her on the "gender bending" of the Final Girl, denies that Laurie is androgynous, and finds that Final Girls bend age in-stead, having more maturity and responsibility than their peers (23). Likewise, Connelly argues that Laurie is not empowered in her final fight and fails to reach "Final-Girl status" (16), despite the fact that Clover coined the Final Girl as a concept in the first place, with Laurie as a key example. Still, for all its short-comings and limitations, Clover's study was highly influential, and her analysis of the Final Girl remains relevant to both *Halloween* (1978) and much (though not all) of the genre at large. As the most recent remakes featured in this study demonstrate, female victim-heroines are alive and well in the horror genre.

The discussion of female teenage victims and the Final Girl dominates much of the critical discourse on *Halloween* (1978), yet there are of course a few more readings worth mentioning. For Telotte, the film deals with a struggle over the perception of self and others and the consequences thereof ("Through" 140). Laurie has to transcend the "narcissistic vision" of the victims and the "voyeur's vision" of Myers (141-42) and undergo a "visual awakening" to survive (146). As another approach, Dika offers a symbolic reading, according to which "Lau-rie and Michael are meant to represent opposing aspects of a single self" (50). Accordingly, she sees Freudian symbolism in Laurie placing a key at Myers's door, thereby unlocking him and/or her own repressed sexuality. Dika concludes that Michael is "openly" Laurie's id because the metatext *Forbidden Planet*, seen on TV at the Doyle house, involves a monster manifested from the id (51). The battle with Myers finally replaces sex to mark Laurie's passage into adult-hood (51).

In summary, then, *Halloween* (1978) features a horror scenario that dispels the presumed safety of the suburbs, and channels adolescent anxieties by placing teenagers in danger, without help from parents or institutions. That the mon-

strous killer is driven by pure evil may have questionable ideological consequences, but proves effective enough for more than one horror film.

HALLOWEEN (2007)

Since *Halloween* (1978) shaped both the horror film genre as well as its mode of
reproduction, a remake seemed inevitable once the sequels started to peter out
(*Halloween Resurrection*, the eighth film in the series, was released in 2002).
While the horror film industry often hands sequels and remakes to new or less
reputable directors, *Halloween* (2007) was headed by a director who had already
made a name for himself in the horror genre. As his chosen name implies, Rob
Zombie (born Robert Bartleh Cummings) modeled his persona and his media career on his infatuation with horror. As a heavy metal musician, his band was
called *White Zombie* (after the 1932 horror film) and treated horror subjects,
among others; when that disbanded, he continued his musical career as Rob
Zombie while also turning to film. Zombie acted as writer and director on *Halloween* (2007), exerting a great deal of control over the film and working less as
a studio hired hand, but as an avowed fan. Needless to mention, that background
failed to impress mainstream film critics, who found little to like in the remake
and were less than enthused by the drastic increase in graphic violence.[10] As is
frequently the case with horror, such dismissal did little to discourage audiences,
and *Halloween* (2007) performed well at the box office. Adjusted for inflation,
however, the remake's earnings stay far behind the 1978 version.[11]

Halloween (2007) vastly expands on the 1978 film. Almost half of the film's
running time is spent on the back story of Michael Myers, from his life as a troubled kid and the murder of his family to the failed attempts at therapy and his escape and return to Haddonfield. Two scenes that take up less than seven minutes
in the 1978 film, the flashback to 1963 and Myers's escape from the mental institution, are extended to 53 minutes, while the film's total length comes to 111

---

10 The remake earned 24% positive reviews on *Rotten Tomatoes* ("HALLOWEEN
(2007)").

11 *Box Office Mojo* reports a domestic gross of $58 million ("Halloween (2007)," *Box
Office Mojo*). The site has no entry for the budget, but *IMDb* estimates $15 million
("Halloween (2007)," *IMDb*). For comparison, the 1978 film is listed with $47 million
on a $325,000 budget ("Halloween"), which in 2007 dollars roughly correspond to
$149 million and 950,000, respectively. These numbers should suffice to show that
the 1978 film did more with much less, at least in purely commercial terms.

minutes (discounting the end credits). Arguably, the added material on Myers's time in treatment also has a precedent in the TV version of *Halloween* (1978), first broadcast in 1981, which was expanded with a number of new scenes filmed during production of *Halloween II* (1981), including a conversation of Loomis with a six year old Michael Myers. Nevertheless, these brief scenes are hardly comparable in scope or content to the narrative laid out in Rob Zombie's version. More accurately, the 2007 film serves both as a prequel, introducing a completely new back story for the characters of Michael Myers and Loomis, and as a remake, staging a new version of the 1978 film's main narrative. Due to the considerable length of the prologue, the main narrative (Halloween in contemporary Haddonfield) is actually given less running time than in the 1978 film.

The remake begins with an ominous introductory quote by Loomis and then moves to the home of the Myers family in Haddonfield, presumably during the late 1980s or early 90s. Michael Myers is seen as a disturbed ten year old, who struggles with a broken home and bullying at school, and only feels affection towards his mother, who works as a stripper, and his baby sister. After a fight at school, psychiatrist Dr. Loomis is brought in as a counselor and diagnoses worrying tendencies towards animal cruelty. Despite Loomis's efforts, Michael murders a school bully and later, on Halloween night, goes on to kill his mother's boyfriend, his older sister and her boyfriend. After a trial, Michael is confined to a mental institution under Loomis's care, where he increasingly retreats over the next year. When Michael murders a nurse, all hopes for therapy are abandoned, and Michael's traumatized mother commits suicide.

The action resumes fifteen years later. Since no therapeutic progress has been made in the meantime, Loomis finally abandons Michael Myers and goes on to promote a book he wrote on the on the case. Myers himself manages to escape from his cell thanks to criminal staff and returns to Haddonfield, committing numerous murders in the process. Hiding in his old family home, Myers encounters Laurie and begins to stalk her and her friends Annie and Lynda. In the meantime, Loomis tracks Myers and attempts to get law enforcement on the case. On Halloween night, Lynda enters the Myers house to have sex with her boyfriend; both are subsequently killed by Myers. He then goes on a killing spree in the suburbs, murdering Laurie's parents, Annie's boyfriend (with Annie barely surviving the attack) and two police officers. Myers then captures Laurie and takes her to his family home, where he reveals that Laurie is in fact his little sister, given up for adoption after the suicide of their mother. Still terrified, Laurie stabs her captor and tries to escape, aided by Loomis who reluctantly shoots Myers. However, Myers survives, overpowers Loomis, and continues his attack, until Laurie manages to shoot him in the head. Laurie's hysterical screams fade into the end credits, which show snippets of home videos featuring the young Michael Myers.[12]

The competing goals of a remake (cf. Leitch 53) stand in stark contrast in the 2007 film. On the one hand, Rob Zombie pays homage to the 1978 film by closely replicating a few key scenes, such as the murder of Lynda, featuring Myers's improvised ghost costume (see fig. 10). Loomis's dialogue also repeats many of his lines from the first film, with "the devil's eyes" now serving as the title of his book. Furthermore, the soundtrack re-uses the unchanged *Halloween* theme by John Carpenter as well as the song "(Don't Fear) The Reaper" by Blue Öyster Cult, and televisions in the film show *The Thing from Another World* (1951) and *Forbidden Planet* (1956), which were also quoted in the first film.

On the other hand, these attempts at homage frequently turn into an upstaging of the previous film. The aforementioned sequence leading to the murder of Lynda, for instance, is fairly similar to the original scene: Lynda's boyfriend Bob goes downstairs to get beer, where he is stabbed and pinned to a wall by Myers, who then dresses up with a bed sheet and Bob's glasses. Lynda is at first tricked by the costume, prompting her to expose her breasts (with the comment "See anything you like?"), before Myers moves to strangle her. The remake recreates this sequence almost bit for bit, but adds coarser dialogue regarding Bob's sexual performance and full frontal nudity for Lynda. Afterwards, the film goes on to raise the bar further with the assault on Annie, which is a complete departure from the 1978 film. Instead of being killed on the way to her boyfriend, she is caught in the middle of the act, and the scene's dialogue tops Lynda's coy question with Annie's more direct "wanna fuck me?"

As another example, the remake's climax seems to be geared towards audiences familiar with the 1978 film. Loomis's intervention plays out much like in the Carpenter version, with Loomis appearing just in time to save Laurie. The two then exchange the dialogue that concluded the 1978 film ("Was that the boogeyman?" – "As a matter of fact, I do believe it was"), only for Myers to re-appear and initiate yet another chase and fight scene. The narrative twist of having the seemingly dead monster return for another surprise attack is so common in the horror genre to count as the most predictable of clichés. In *Halloween* (2007), it is employed as a response to the previous iteration of the same scene, in order to shake up audiences who expect the film to end once Loomis has uttered his famous last line.

---

12 The plot summary is based on the *Unrated Director's Cut* DVD, which is twelve minutes longer than the theatrical version. The longer version adds and extends a number of scenes, features more graphic violence, and changes a few plot points, most significantly the escape of Michael Myers.

Overall, the remake ups the ante on several aspects of its predecessor. It aims to provoke contemporary audience sensibilities and ratings standards by featuring far more and more explicit nudity, sex, violence, and strong language. In addition, it tries to surpass the first film by deepening the characterization of Michael Myers and enhancing character relationships. The personal developments of Loomis and Myers are more closely interlinked, and Laurie is now Myers's primary interest due to family relation, as opposed to a chance encounter. The expansions in the remake also condense elements introduced in the *Halloween* sequels into one film. The revelation that Laurie is Myers's sister is taken from the sequel *Halloween II* (1981), and as another nod to the sequels, the soundtrack includes "Mr. Sandman," which featured in *Halloween II* (1981) and *Halloween H20* (1998).[13]

For the following analysis, the most significant tendency in the remake is its drastic revision of the monster Michel Myers and the resulting effect on every other part of the narrative, especially the (previous) protagonist.

Filling in the Blank and Humanizing "It"

With the extension the film's scope, the focus shifts significantly towards its monster Michael Myers. The nominal protagonist Laurie is only introduced after 53 minutes have been spent on Myers's growth into the masked killer (for comparison, 1978's Laurie appears after seven minutes). The main effect of spending so much time on Myers is a humanization. The first film took great care to depict Myers as inhuman and inscrutable, referring to him as "it," "evil," and the "boogeyman." 1978's Myers never speaks, and his actions are strictly limited to stalking and killing. Now, the remake offers a more complex, yet still psychopathic character. The aim of the film is twofold, and contradictory: first, it tries to explain Myers, to make him human and understandable. Second, it tries to undo this work by establishing distance and reasserting the monstrous Myers familiar from the 1978 film. The presentation of Loomis's book *The Devil's Eyes*, which segues from the prequel portion of the film into the remake portion, gives a short summary of how Myers should be read at this point: as a "psychopath without any boundaries" and an "irredeemable evil." Nevertheless, Loomis's evaluation is undercut as the film proceeds, and with the image of a troubled ten-

---

13 The 2007 remake also establishes an awkward intertextual relation to the disowned sequels of the *Halloween* series, by casting Danielle Harris, who played the lead in the disowned *Halloween 4* and *5*. Harris now plays Laurie's friend Annie, and even though Verevis's "celebrity intertextuality" may apply in only a limited fashion, she is at least recognizable to the more dedicated fans of the *Halloween* series.

year-old (who loves his mother and baby sister) imprinted on the audience, the adult Myers can hardly achieve the impersonal monstrosity he embodied in the 1978 film.

The role of Myers's mother, like most of his back story newly created in the remake, offers a rationale for his descent into violence. The young Michael Myers is presented as stuck in a dysfunctional family, between an abusive substitute father and a flawed, yet loving mother. The first, his mother's boyfriend Ronnie, is unemployed, lusts after his Michael's older sister and constantly insults Michael, questioning his sexual identity as a "queer," "fag" and so forth. Michael's mother Deborah, by contrast, provides the family income by working as a stripper, encourages Michael, and attends his school when he is in trouble. Oddly enough, in the crude underclass context drawn by the film, she functions both as a Fallen Woman and as the Angel of the House. Despite her best efforts, Michael feels neglected, as shown by a juxtaposition of her working while Michael waits alone, with the rock ballad "Love Hurts" on the soundtrack. Taking the song lyrics into account, the scene amplifies Michael's emotional neediness into unrequited love, which in turn colors possible readings of his subsequent murders. Due to Michael's problematic attachment to his mother, the murder of his substitute father strongly suggests the Oedipus complex, as Michael attempts to remove his (substitute) father to take possession of his mother.

The Freudian overtones in the remake echo psychoanalytic readings of the 1978 film, which saw Michael Myers's motive for the initial murder in his repressed incestuous urges (cf. Wood 193). Michael's desire for his older sister Judith, previously a plausible yet not necessary or inevitable reading, is fairly unambiguously inscribed in the remake's text with Michael stroking Judith's naked body right before the killing. The aforementioned Oedipus-setup with his mother and stepfather then adds another level of repressed sexual tension to his upbringing. Where the 1978 film denied any complexity behind Myers's motivations, and in fact derived much of his monstrosity from reducing him to "pure evil," the remake constructs a somewhat conventional causality chain from well-worn clichés including school bullies, abusive stepparents, and stifled sexual desire. Even though it stops short of justifying Myers's actions, the film renders them explicable and thereby less monstrous.

However, as the remake proceeds, the causality of Myers's actions is quickly diluted by the sheer number of indiscriminate murders. Every stage of the narrative raises the number of victims, from five in the 1978 film to a total of nineteen in the 2007 version, including a school bully, several sanitarium staff, Laurie's foster parents, and two police officers.[14] Between all this carnage, it comes as a surprise that Myers has no intention of killing his long-lost sister Laurie, and instead wants to reconnect with her (by murdering everyone close to her, perhaps in a bout of jealousy). In another display of unexpected humanity, Myers cannot bring himself to kill Loomis, either, even though Loomis has shown no such restraint regarding Myers. This final turn of events proves Loomis's expert opinion wrong: Myers does have boundaries after all, and despite his casual slaughter of Haddonfield's residents, he is still capable of feeling affection. In a major departure from the 1978 film, the remake resumes its effort to humanize its monster. Even Loomis, who previously proclaimed him the "antichrist," apologizes for having failed Myers. Finally, the end credits function as a paratextual confirmation of that humanization, listing "Michael Myers," the person, as opposed to "The Shape" of the 1978 film.

By definition, monsters disrupt normality, but a key factor in reading that disruption is the origin of the monster and the relationship to normality it implies. On the one hand, if the monster is the direct product of its decidedly normal environment, it amounts to an internal threat, implicating normality itself in its creation. On the other hand, if the monster originates from outside of normality, it represents an external threat, and normality is absolved of any responsibility. 1978's Michael Myers may have been raised in Haddonfield, but his portrayal as the inhuman boogeyman, a being of pure evil, shifts him towards the second category. Neither his parents nor the community of Haddonfield are ever blamed for the existence of the monster Myers. *Halloween* (2007) seems aware of the distinction and tries to have it both ways. This aim becomes evident during Loomis's book presentation, in which he blames a "perfect storm" of nature and external circumstances for Myers's mental state. Therefore, the abusive stepfather and school bullying do not take the sole responsibility, but help bring out Michael Myers's psychopathic predisposition. This balanced approach softens any stance that may be read into the film, as society may be at fault, but only partly. At the same time, Myers cannot be understood as an absolute evil, because whatever innate evil he possesses forms only half of the equation (cf. Halfmann 392).

There is however a significant change in Michael Myers's origin that shifts his relationship to the normality of the narrative. As Ní Fhlainn points out, his family is clearly marked as "white trash" (191), as members of a poor, uncultured lower class that is completely distinct from the middle class victims Myers later stalks. Ní Fhlainn's claim that "the discrimination that figures the slasher is

---

14 The exact count deviates for the theatrical version of the film, which features an alternate escape scene for Myers, but at this point, the difference is negligible.

not one of skin color but of strict social hierarchy" (183) may be debatable for the 1978 film, as the Myers family of that film looks perfectly middle class, but it clearly applies to the remake. By changing Myers's class origins, the remake reinforces his status as an intruder into the middle class normality of Laurie's adoptive family. Furthermore, it would be easy to argue that the damaging upbringing of Myers that shapes him into a monstrous killer is due to his lower class origins, and that it is "white trash" brutality that finally spills over into the otherwise perfectly safe suburban idyll of contemporary Haddonfield.

In addition, the Myers family is not the only instance of "white trash" violence in the film. Myers's return to killing is somewhat forced on him, after fifteen years of passivity at his high security mental institution. Two corrupt guards, conforming to redneck stereotypes in appearance and language, not only provoke Myers, but use his cell to rape a female patient in his presence. Finally pushed too far, Myers's kills the two and uses the opportunity to break out. The scene marks an odd break in the narrative, as it positions the nominal monster in a heroic position: compared to a couple of redneck rapists, the film would seem to suggest, Myers is morally superior. At this point, Myers has been developed into a moderately complex, at times even sympathetic character, yet the "white trash" characters are simply irredeemable. Not only is Myers's abusive stepfather partly responsible for his monstrous turn, it takes another pair of crass and violent "rednecks" to provoke and enable his subsequent killing spree.

This theme marks a trend, not in the *Halloween* series, but in the work of its current writer and director. Upon its release, *Halloween* (2007) was already the third film by Rob Zombie in which "middle class victims are sadistically abused, tortured, sexually violated and humiliated at the hands of vicious, unsympathetic and so termed 'white trash villains'" (Ní Fhlainn 190). To some extent, these villains echo a monster type prevalent in the 1970s horror and exploitation cinema, especially in the films of Tobe Hooper and Wes Craven. A key example is the family of monstrous hillbillies in *The Texas Chain Saw Massacre* (1974), already mentioned in the previous chapter. Moreover, the transmedia persona of the director Rob Zombie is already fashioned as a sort of monster redneck. As a musician, Rob Zombie released an album of horror-themed songs titled *Hellbilly Deluxe* in 1998, with a sequel in 2010. The monstrous redneck, then, appears to be a favorite character type of Zombie's, which might explain the role this type of character plays in *Halloween* (2007). Regardless of the writer/director's tastes and intentions, rednecks are at the very least the supporting monsters of the film, which introduces an element of urbanoia, the combination of class anxiety and economic guilt (Clover 124-34); only in this case, it might be more appropriate to call it suburbanoia.

Suburban Normality and the Other Family

While the 1978 film only portrayed contemporary Haddonfield at length, the re-make's expanded focus adds a historical perspective for the narrative's site of normality. The dysfunctional Myers family home stands in sharp contrast to the idyllic suburban community featured in the 1978 film, yet it remains unclear to what extent it is representative of its time and place, and whether Haddonfield has been transformed from a "white trash" neighborhood into the safe middle class town it appears to be in the remake's second half. Contemporary Had-donfield no longer features strip clubs, and the decayed Myers home remains as a foreign body between more stereotypically wholesome family homes.

Overall, the sense of isolation and emptiness that characterized 1978's Had-donfield is decreased in the remake. The streets look less empty, and the removal of Myers's lengthy stalking sequences reduces the sense of architectural vulner-ability. Furthermore, while the authorities may not be effective, they are at least present. Early in the film, Michael Myers's school instantly acts on his violent behavior and involves Dr. Loomis, who correctly diagnoses dangerous tenden-cies in young Michael. Towards the end, two police officers show up at the Wal-lace home after Laurie's 911 call and manage to shoot and wound Myers. Both examples show that the system works to some extent, even though it still fails to stop Myers. That task is again left to determined individuals, namely Loomis and Laurie. Yet despite Michael Myers's unchecked rampage, *Halloween* (2007) is just slightly more trusting in institutions than its predecessor.

Among the various structures and institutions of normality, the remake is however most interested in the family unit. The families of Michel Myers and Laurie Strode, barely sketched in the 1978 film, are expanded into opposing models in the 2007 version. The "white trash" Myers family is a site of incessant abuse, whereas the Strodes are a stereotypically liberal, middle aged, middle class couple that genuinely cares for their (adoptive) daughter. The opposition can easily be read as an expression of class anxiety, with the Myers family serv-ing as an Other, or more precisely, an Other family to the Strodes. As a logical consequence of the remake's underlying sense of suburbanoia, the Myers pro-duce a monster in Michael, whereas the Strodes raise a (relatively) virtuous and responsible young woman. Arguably, the Strodes' sole flaw is that they are, like most representatives of normality in the film, incapable of mounting a defense against Myers. Yet even so, Cynthia Strode's final words only emphasize her dedication to family, as she implores Myers to "leave my baby alone."

Remarkably, family is even central to the motivations of the film's monster. As mentioned in the previous section, Myers aims for a family reunion with his sister, which implies that family ties are strong enough to transcend even years of isolation, emotional withdrawal and murder sprees. Despite the fervor with which *Halloween* (2007) disrupts all these human connections, it is surprisingly affirmative of family ties.

Cutting (Out) the Victims

As a result of the narrative's expansion, the girls who were at the center of the 1978 film are pushed to the sidelines. Since they are introduced around the midpoint of the film, Laurie, Lynda and Annie are inevitably allotted less time. Strangely enough, the vastly increased number of deaths and the demographic diversity of Michael Myers's victims mean that the dismissive term of "teenie-kill pic" (Wood 195) is hardly applicable to *Halloween* (2007) anymore, even though it still qualifies as a slasher film. In total, Myers kills more adults than teenagers, and when he does target teenagers, he goes for couples instead of lone girls. Judith Myers's and Annie's boyfriends are added to the list of victims, and contrary to the trend, Annie actually survives in this version (if only until the sequel). Out of nineteen dead, only five are teenagers, and only two are girls. Judging by these numbers alone, it would appear that the remake diverges from the much criticized age and gender dynamics of its predecessor and the slasher genre as a whole. At closer inspection, however, this turns out not to be the case.

Even though Myers murders numerous people who just happen to stand in his way, from sanitarium staff to police, these deaths are generally less elaborate than those of the teenagers he deliberately seeks out. Furthermore, the logic of transgression and punishment is still pronounced, and in some regards reinforced. As in the 1978 film, Judith and Lynda are killed right after secretly meeting with their boyfriends, and the remake further emphasizes the sexual nature of those encounters. In a significant deviation from the first film, Annie is no longer stalked while doing laundry, but attacked during sex, which means that all of Myers's assaults on teenagers now coincide with sexual activity. Laurie marks an exception, but then again, Myers has no intention of killing Laurie, at least not at the start. More than the first film, the remake thus matches Clover's observation that sexual transgression leads to death (or almost, for Annie) in the slasher film (34). As in the 1978 film, provocations of the monster and indulgence in alcohol are at least aggravating factors.

While sex is equally fatal for teenagers of both genders, there is still a noticeable difference in the depiction of male and female deaths. It is not so much that female deaths are shown in more detail and at greater length, as per the pattern common in the genre (cf. Clover 35); in fact, *Halloween* (2007) revels in the explicit depiction of every single act of violence. However, Judith, Lynda, and Annie are all attacked in various states of undress, and the camera lingers on their nude bodies to an extent that easily reads as fetishistic and objectifying. While the 1978 film already featured brief topless shots of the female victims, the remake again follows a more excessive visual regime. Therefore, even though Myers remains sexually stunted, the murders evoke sexual violence more strongly. Overall, sexual aggression is a more noticeable undercurrent throughout the 2007 film, from the charged language of school bullies and various redneck characters to the graphic rape scene inside the mental institution.

As in the 1978 film, Laurie performs a different role than her friends. She embodies most of the traits of the typical Final Girl as laid out by Clover (39-40): she is the main character (of the film's second half, at least), watchful, and sexually inactive. At the same time, these characteristics are less pronounced than in her 1978 counterpart, and Laurie is presented less as an outsider among her peers, but as an average girl. Her bookishness is reduced to wearing glasses; there is no mention of boys being scared of her, although she admits to her Annie that she does need a boyfriend. While Laurie is the least transgressive member of her circle of friends, she is not above making obscene gestures at her parents. It would be difficult to read her as "not fully feminine" (Clover 40). For the most part, Laurie seems to handle the terror of Myers with slightly less composure than her predecessor, even though she still manages to keep her babysitting charges safe. Once the threat is obvious, she is mostly reduced to screaming and running away, only fighting back when Myers willingly renders himself vulnerable.

Completing the trajectory of the Final Girl, Laurie assumes full agency at the very end. Even though Loomis repeatedly interferes on her behalf, it is still up to her to shoot the (unconscious) Myers in the head and end the threat. Unlike her 1978 counterpart, 2007's Laurie is the one to defeat the monster in a seemingly permanent manner, but that gain in agency is arguably outweighed by her absence during the first half of the film. More importantly, not only does the focus on Myers reduce the size of Laurie's role, his added complexity also diminishes the significance of her struggle. Up to this point, the film has made an unprecedented effort to portray Myers both as a monster and a sympathetic victim, and it has been made clear that Myers did not even seek to harm Laurie in the first place. Therefore, Laurie's violent response, previously a high point of Final Girl empowerment, becomes ambiguous. Opposing pure evil elevated 1978's Laurie, but opposing her misunderstood, albeit murderous sibling does not do the same for 2007's Laurie.

Ultimately, *Halloween* (2007) undertakes a massive change in the core narrative taken from its source. It toys with turning its monster into its protagonist by focusing much of its runtime on the development of Myers, adding depth to his character, and reducing the role of Laurie. This is not strictly an unprecedented development for horror films or franchises that go through many sequels and re-iterations.[15] By definition, the victims are subject to rapid attrition, and even successful Final Girls are eventually removed from the ongoing narrative. As the monster is the distinguishing mark of the horror genre, and a memorable monster is the foundation of a horror film franchise, it is kept around with ever more elaborate explanations. The prequel portion of *Halloween* (2007) and its character study of Michael Myers is therefore indicative of a long-running engagement with a horror franchise, aimed at filling in every last blank left by the previous works in the series, even as its remake portion aims to erase and reconceptualize the preceding texts.

It is evident that the remake has more interest in and perhaps even adoration for its monster. Formerly an inhuman force preying on the insecurities of suburbia and the permissiveness of its teenage inhabitants, Michael Myers is transformed into a more explicitly oedipal figure, monstrous as well as tragic, that is also a victim of its environment. This reassessment offers intriguing possibilities in light of Wood's critique of the 1978 film. After all, one of Wood's main complaints was the disavowal of family horror and the resort to inhuman evil as the explanation for Myers's deeds (193). The 2007 film corrects this perceived misstep by tracing Myers's monstrosity to an abusive family structure, at least in part. While Wood considered but ultimately rejected the idea of reading the film against Loomis, the remake effectively retracts Loomis's analysis, and has him apologize for his failure to Myers. By discrediting Loomis and unambiguously establishing young Michael Myers's incestuous desires, the 2007 film restores the "causality of sexual repression and murder" that Wood saw removed from the 1978 film (193).

Perhaps inadvertently, the revisions of *Halloween* (2007) appear to comply with the criticisms issued by Wood, Williams and others and enable more subversive readings than the 1978 film. The emergence of the monster Michael Myers can be read as the return of the repressed, or as a failure of social structures, including family, education, legal and medical systems. Despite these potentials, the remake is still a far cry from the radical stances of Wood and Williams. Myers is still presented as a unique specimen, systemic problems are never fully acknowledged, and much of the blame is shifted onto a distorted underclass milieu. Even as the 2007 film dismantles the concept of pure evil, it introduces

---

15 For example, *Texas Chainsaw 3D* (2013) does the same with Leatherface.

monstrous rednecks, who form as much of an evil outside force threatening suburban normality as any other horror monster. Taking the exploitative depiction of the teenage victims and the pronounced logic of transgression and punishment into account, it becomes obvious that the film is still indebted to many of the more controversial slasher film traditions, in some regards even more than its predecessor.

Halloween (1978) has frequently been read in the context of a late 1970s, early 1980s turn towards political conservatism in the genre as well as the US at large (Wood 191; Dika 132; Williams, *Hearths* 211; Phillips 143). The associated suburban anxieties of home invasion and adolescent insecurities are still in place in the 2007 remake, which suggests that the precarious safety of suburbia has retained its potential for horror over the past thirty years. The most significant new addition of the remake lies in the expanded back story of Michael Myers, and this might be an area in which the cultural discourses of the mid-2000s are a more noticeable influence. The depiction of ten-year-old Myers draws on contemporary media narratives of adolescent psychopaths, firmly established by recurrent and intensively covered school shootings (cf. Halfmann 392). Myers corresponds to almost every stereotype: a socially withdrawn young male from a broken home, a bullying victim turning to violent revenge; he even has a taste for horror films and loud rock music. In a familiar progression, the Myers family tragedy turns into a media circus capped off by Loomis's book tour.

If the remake's depiction of Myers is informed by the news media of the 2000s, the addition of monstrous rednecks appears largely disconnected from contemporary concerns. Instead, that element represents a throwback to earlier cinematic trends, to the 1970s hillbilly horror and rape-revenge movies that the director Rob Zombie seems fond of, judging by his work. It may be difficult to read *Halloween* (2007) as a fully accomplished updating of its source and a commentary on its own historical moment, and it might be tempting to speculate that Zombie, an avowed genre fan, is more interested in recreating and expanding on bits of his favorite films from past decades than in dealing with the present. Such criticism, though, would be on shaky ground at best, considering the nature of remaking and the fact that John Carpenter's *Halloween* (1978) was likewise received as a fan's exercise in style (cf. Wood 193).

Fig. 8. Family dinner at the cannibals' in The Texas Chain Saw Massacre *(1974)*

Fig. 9. The apparition of Michael Myers in Halloween *(1978)*

Fig. 10. Myers's disguise in Halloween *(1978), restaged in* Halloween *(2007)*

Conclusion

The discussion of the sample horror remake complexes has shown that the structure of normality and monstrous disruption remains highly adaptable due to its simplicity, which allows it to work in any context, and the inherent narrative potency of transgression. Even though the selection of sample films does not evenly cover the past 50 years, it is obvious that there is always something to be feared. Indeed, the critical perception that the current moment is particularly subject to crisis and more filled with anxiety is often overstated, at least when it comes to a genre in which fear is a constitutive feature (as the name "horror" implies). Cultural fears of the Other, of individual outsiders, of repressive groups, or of bodily or mental failure may transform, but hardly vanish, and recur in variations of familiar patterns.

The analysis leaned on a number of compound terms to better approach the intersection of concepts involved in the reproduction of horror. The *horror remake complex* aimed to elevate neglected remakes, delineating sets of related films as functional units and objects of study. *Cultural fears* pointed out that these films reflect and feed a broader cultural condition, an always lingering, historically contingent sense of insecurity that stems from social changes as much as from the basic challenges and flaws of the human condition. The *monster discourse* sought to grasp that film monsters are subject to ongoing development. The point was to substantiate the claim that horror and remake are such a prevalent combination because their respective functions support each other. To that end, I investigated how monsters absorb and personify cultural fears and how they are refigured in the remaking process. The results have been highly variable.

The first horror remake complex on the list already challenged several of my basic definitions. While most remake cycles enshrine the initial film as *the* original, *The Thing from Another World* (1951) is arguably displaced from its own remake cycle. Even though *The Thing* (1982) pays homage to its filmic predecessor, it mostly works in the mode of readaptation, restoring the novella as the primary source of the narrative. The 2011 film, then, works both as a prequel to and remake of *The Thing* (1982), which cuts out the 1951 film entirely and again shifts the center of the narrative, only this time to the 1982 film. The relevant historical contexts and cultural fears shift along with the focus of the individual films, and where the 1951 film calls for watchfulness and unity in the face of the Cold War, its 1982 successor depicts a complete dissolution of social structures and relations, which is repeated in milder form in the 2011 version. The monster discourse of the Thing likewise changes in leaps and bounds, but settles around this notion of distrust in fellow humans, amplified by a shapeshifting threat.

By comparison, the textual relations of the *Body Snatchers* cycle are more clearly oriented towards the canonized first film, which quickly supplanted its literary source. Viewed as a horror remake complex, this sequence of films offers a wealth of material, not only because of the remarkable number of remakes, but also because of the ambitions towards social commentary that permeate each version. The subtle takeover of human communities by identical pod duplicates showcases a fundamental conflict between individual and group, which easily adapts to a variety of contexts. The 1956 version resonates with fears of communist subversion and/or anticommunist fervor, as well as concerns about encroaching social conformity. The latter are further emphasized and developed into a critique of consumer culture and pop-psychiatry in the 1978 film, again refigured into a critique of the nuclear family and military discipline in 1993, and finally reshaped into an assessment of post-9/11 despair in 2007. The pod monster discourse invariably casts a callous conformity as monstrous, whereas it positions the downsides of human experience, whether anxiety, conflict, or other issues, as the inevitable cost of being human.

The scenario of *The Crazies* (1973) has some superficial similarities to that of *Body Snatchers*, in that normal small-town Americans are subtly transformed into monstrous threats, but the film functions more narrowly as an allegory of the Vietnam War. By relocating disastrous containment strategies to rural Pennsylvania, it drives home their brutal inefficiency, along with the absurdity of political and military decision making. Only the barest core of this approach is transported to the 2010 remake, which resonates with the fear that the US government might turn the methods employed in its War on Terror on its own population. At the same time, a renewed focus on shock effects and a constriction of narrative perspective leave little room for the extensive institutional critique that fueled the first film. Still, both versions of *The Crazies* share a distrust of basically all institutions above the local level, as well as fears of a dormant violent potential of rural Americans.

A similar trajectory can be observed between the two versions of *Dawn of the Dead*. Where the 1978 film uses the besieged shopping mall as a backdrop for a blatant satire of late-1970s consumer culture, the 2004 remake largely discards this aspect in favor of raising the pace and tension of its survival narrative. In the process, the function of the zombies takes a radical turn, from a human mirror that highlights the flaws of individuals, institutions and social conventions, to an inhuman horde that represents an implacable Other to its mostly decent human characters. As with *The Crazies*, the shift from message-heavy to effect-driven horror may be explained with changing cultural attitudes (perhaps external terrors seemed more relevant in 2004 than questioning consumerism) as well as the fact that low-budget independent productions are subject to different objectives and pressures than those with bigger budgets. Despite these differences, both films build on shared cultural fears of a collapse of civilization, against which the luxuries of consumer culture provide no safety whatsoever.

Perhaps even more than the previous example, *The Texas Chain Saw Massacre* (1974) possesses a radical edge that the slicker remake struggles to capture. As the result of a notoriously unrestrained small-time production, the 1974 film transgresses contemporary conventions of morality as much as those of genre and narrative in its rejection of sense and sanity. Its encounter with a barbaric leftover that still haunts the margins of modern America is also informed by the experience of late-1960s counterculture and its decline, as well as broader cultural fears of the countryside and lower classes. The 2003 remake retains this last element, but reorders the rest into a more conventional horror narrative. Far from the random nihilistic universe of the first film, the remake sees sin punished, virtue rewarded, and family affirmed, while also giving far more agency to its protagonist. Thus, despite raising the bar in terms of brutal violence and reiterating the fear of human monsters at the margins of society and geography, the remake ends up with an overall less pessimistic outlook.

While *Halloween* (1978) also focuses on a psychotic human monster, it moves its intrusion into the center of normality. The driving cultural fears behind the murder sprees of Michael Myers concern the vulnerability of suburbia and defenselessness of (barely coherent) families, contingent on the recklessness of youth and the denial that evil actually exists. With this resurgence of regressive fears, the film arguably occupies the threshold between the permissive 1970s and the morally reactionary 1980s. By contrast, *Halloween* (2007) complicates the straightforward setup of its source, since it not only restages the previous narrative, but massively expands on it. Shifting the narrative focus from the victims (and the previous protagonist) to the monster, the remake undermines the 1978 film's notion of pure evil. Even though that seems to imply a more nuanced conception of monstrosity, the remake mostly draws on current pop-psychological media clichés on adolescent spree killers and introduces a monstrous underclass. At its core, however, the *Halloween* complex reiterates the fear that the family home is not safe.

Comparing the remakes and their strategies of revision and reconstruction, some common threads emerge. Starting with the depiction of monsters, there is a general trend towards increasingly dangerous, inhuman, or incomprehensible monsters. The pods turn more callous and alien, the Thing's body starts to defy categorization, and both crazies and zombies become more aggressive and credible threats. All of these monsters are depicted as more distinctly *Other* to human normality in their respective films. A tendency towards dehumanization is particularly noticeable in *Dawn of the Dead* (2004) and *The Crazies* (2010), both of which dismiss their predecessors' common strategy of equating monsters and humans. In contrast, it is difficult to judge whether the redneck cannibals of *The Texas Chainsaw Massacre* (2003) are more or less monstrous than their 1974 counterparts. The only clear exception to the trend is *Halloween* (2007), which takes a major effort to humanize and redeem its monstrous killer.

While most of the featured remakes reshape their monsters to be more menacing Others, their use of markers of difference to that end is less uniform. The claim that monsters are assembled from discursive fragments taken from other social or cultural contexts has found ample evidence, but their particular links to "marginalized social groups" (Cohen 11) have been more difficult to substantiate. The *Body Snatchers* films tend to associate the monsters with dominant movements enforcing conformity, not any excluded minorities, and a similar argument may be made for the mass of consumer zombies in *Dawn of the Dead* (1978). A better example are class- and region-based fears in *The Crazies* (1973), both versions of *The Texas Chain Saw Massacre* (1974, 2003), and *Halloween* (2007). All of these films draw on stereotypes of a brutish rural underclass to construct their monsters, partly in the mold of Clover's "urbanoia" (124). In many other cases, however, the sample films and their remakes invoke a generalized fear of outsiders or deviants that is largely devoid of specific markers, employing the mechanics of othering more than their traditional targets. A possible explanation may be that the incessant refigurations and mutations of the horror genre have long severed the monstrous fragments from their origins, and reduced them to the elementary impact of fear that is, after all, the genre's main focus.

Another key factor for the reading of horror narratives is their outcome, specifically the question whether the monster is defeated and order restored. All of the featured remakes make at least minor adjustments to the conclusions of their narratives, but radical reversals – a defeated monster ending up triumphant in the remake or vice versa – are much less common. Leatherface remains in control of his patch of Texas in *The Texas Chainsaw Massacre* (2003), and the zombies again conquer the mall in *Dawn of the Dead* (2004). *The Crazies* (2010) wildly exceeds its predecessor's conclusion with a nuclear explosion, but the cycle of outbreak and containment is set to resume just as well. *The Thing* (1982) replaces the clear defeat of the monster with near-total ambiguity, and while the 2011 film preserves this outcome, it also adds a less ambiguous partial win for its human protagonist. And where *Halloween* (1978) made the survival of its monster and the ongoing disruption of order explicit, its remake strongly suggests the contrary. This would appear to be a significant reversal, but it is questionable how meaningful such outcomes are for established horror franchises, in which there is always a way for the monster to return for another sequel (and indeed, the apparent death of Michael Myers is undone for *Halloween II* (2009)). Therefore, the only cases of complete reversal are found in the *Body Snatchers* sequence, with the 1978 film's total pod victory as the crass opposite of 2007's utter defeat of the aliens and return to the geopolitical status quo.

Judging purely by the fate of the monsters, it is hard to identify a general tendency among the various remakes. Monsters do not appear to be any more or less successful overall, and taking the notion of restored or disrupted order into account, it becomes apparent that few of the films trust in a return to the status quo to begin with. Two of the exceptions are from the 1950s, *The Thing from Another World* (1951) and *Invasion of the Body Snatchers* (1956), which would seem to support Tudor's claim that the genre transitions from secure to paranoid horror around the 1960s (*Monsters* 102-04). Yet even these films exhibit a distrust of institutions, and the same applies to *The Invasion* (2007). Even though the latter film unambiguously eliminates its monsters and restores the previous order, it characterizes that state as deeply flawed. Therefore, it is difficult to read that outcome as truly supportive of a sociopolitical status quo. At least when it comes to the cross-comparison of remakes, then, the survival of monsters alone fails to deliver crucial insight, but fortunately, the other half of the horror equation offers yet more material.

Just like monsters are updated between iterations, their targets need to keep up with the times as well. For the monster's assault to reach the desired effect of horror, normality needs to be at least somewhat relatable. The remaking process thus involves a conscious updating of characters (or victims) and setting, as well as unconscious reflections of changed cultural conditions and attitudes. With my sample films ranging from the 1950s to the present day, one of the most glaring areas of change is the representation of genders and the associated roles. While gender stereotypes abound in any given film, there is also a clear progression towards more prominent and independent female characters.[1] Most importantly, the most recent versions of the *Body Snatchers* story (1993, 2007) and *The Thing* (2011) switch from male to female protagonists, with the latter two fully replacing the narrative roles of their male predecessors. *The Texas Chainsaw Massacre* (2003) strengthens its female protagonist, turning her into a proactive leading character instead of a survivor through happenstance. Less remarkable changes are found in *Dawn of the Dead* (2004), which replaces an outspoken, but passive female lead with several more active characters, and *The Crazies* (2010), which slightly improves on a weak love interest. Both films are still driven by their male characters, however. Next to the all-male *The Thing* (1982), *Halloween* (2007) is perhaps the only step back, due to the fact that it relegates the previous protagonist to the second half of the film and raises the exploitative depiction of female bodies. It is worth noting that any assessment of character agency is made in the context of the horror genre, which generally leaves little room for heroic protagonists, or even fully developed characters. Victimization is to be expected, but it matters whether male and female characters are terrorized and murdered in distinctly different manners, and who gets to survive for what reason. Expanding the mold of the slasher film's final girls, the remakes show both minor and major steps towards a more varied portrayal of genders, while still preserving genre stereotypes like screaming female victims, often relegated to minor characters.

This often slow and stuttering progression is arguably diluted by what may be read as an increase in conservative family values. Recent remakes show a notable upswing in support for family ties of all kinds, with romantic partnerships, kinship and nuclear families, or the desire towards any of these, being portrayed more prominently and favorably. *The Invasion* (2007) centers on a mother whose main concern is her child's safety, the protagonist of *The Texas Chainsaw Massacre* (2003) wants to abandon her hippie lifestyle to start a family, *Halloween* (2007) introduces backdrops of dysfunctional as well as idyllic family life, *Dawn of the Dead* (2004) plays up the importance of various human bonds in a crisis, and even the drastic resolution of *The Crazies* (2010) leaves the core of a nuclear family intact. Admittedly, this development may not indicate a global trend as much as it points out the distinctions between a particular set of 1970s horror films, which resonate with a low point of trust in relationships and family structures during their historical moment, and their 2000s remakes. Similar reservations may apply for the subtly increased presence of Christian motifs or imagery,

---

1 By contrast, racial diversity in casting rises slightly in a few cases (e.g. *The Thing* (1982), *Body Snatchers* (1993)), but remains far less noticeable.

from the ambiguous portrayal in *Dawn of the Dead* (2004) and the messianic figure of Oliver in *The Invasion* (2007), to the images of crucifixion in *The Texas Chainsaw Massacre* (2003) and the expulsion from Paradise evoked in the final shots of *The Crazies* (2010).

Still, these trends conspicuously align with the further dehumanization of monsters to match the criteria Wood observed in the "reactionary wing" of horror film during the 1980s (192-93). It would seem that the current remakes largely continue on the ideological path described by Wood, but as the detailed analysis has shown, the stances of the individual films are usually more complex than Wood's political dichotomy suggests. The magnitude of the ideological shift in the genre may also be skewed by the selection of examples. The counter-culturally attuned independent horror film of the 1970s has drawn a lot of critical attention, but it still represents just one small (if influential) segment of the prolific genre of horror. Due to the limited scope of my study, I have given comparatively less attention to other waves of horror production and reproduction, which may be subject to less pronounced or even opposite ideological shifts.

Changing cultural attitudes have an undeniable impact on remakes, but the refiguration of narratives and themes is also affected by changing production circumstances. All of the remakes covered in this study were produced on larger budgets than their predecessors (accounting for inflation), which exerts different pressures on their production.[2] A higher financial investment raises the need for a larger box office (and secondary market) intake to recoup costs. Therefore, it discourages taking risks that might impact a film's marketability, and encourages staying closer to current, presumably safer genre standards.[3] Common critical approaches view this correlation as a threat for the artistic value of a film, which is expected to flow from individual vision as opposed to pragmatic studio or distributor interests. Consequently, the loss of a personal (auteur) perspective is a frequent criticism of remakes, and as mentioned earlier, the curtailed allegories of *The Crazies* and *Dawn of the Dead* may serve as examples of that tendency.

---

2   Since film remaking is tied to the ownership or acquisition of the rights to the literary and/or filmic source, it is almost by definition a production practice limited to the established film industry. Between distribution and sequelization deals, the move of film properties from independent filmmakers to larger studios appears practically inevitable, with all that entails for subsequent productions.

3   This line of argument might seem to contradict one of the main reasons for film remaking: that a remake of a previously successful film is already a relatively safe bet. The proven material of the original film is just one half of the equation, though, and it is still necessary to adapt it to current viewer sensibilities.

Nevertheless, the analysis has shown that these remakes are still attuned to their moment in cultural history (not to mention genre history), and even though they may be less obviously topical, they also adapt contemporary fears to function. In addition, some of the sample remakes work as counterexamples. *The Invasion* (2007) is an expensive, impersonal studio remake that desperately strives for relevance and offers social commentary that is sharply focused on its historical moment. Evidently, the tremendous budget did not impede these ambitions, even though the result was not met with critical approval. As another example, *Halloween* (2007) was written and directed by a horror auteur of sorts with a great deal of personal control over the production, and while Rob Zombie's handwriting is all over the remake, the reception was also rather mixed. Judging by the examples in this study, then, the influence of commercial concerns on remaking is undeniable, but its results are far from uniform, and while individual flourishes tend to vanish, the adjustment to genre standards tends to improve on at least some of the more technical aspects of filmmaking craft.

At this point, it is worth repeating that few horror films are made purely to deliver an artistic or political statement, and that neither is required for the film to function. *The Texas Chain Saw Massacre* (1974), for example, is now appreciated for its bold transgressiveness and the countercultural attitudes that seeped in through its creators. Yet, these same creators had only turned to horror in the first place since it offered the best chance to make a profit (Macor 20). The same applies to George Romero and his groundbreaking *Night of the Living Dead* (1968). As Gagne reports, "the decision to do a horror film was made purely for commercial reasons" since "a low-budget horror film is simply more marketable than a low-budget art film" (23). The celebrated *Dawn of the Dead* (1978), then, only came into being because Romero had failed with his other filmic ventures (cf. Gagne 23; 83). Simply put, Tobe Hooper, George Romero and their respective associates started making horror films because they understood them to be an easy sell, and the same still applies to filmmakers and remakers today. The assumption that horror films are easy moneymakers with a built-in audience makes them attractive for beginning filmmakers and those with limited means, and this idea of safety due to simplicity of purpose goes a long way towards explaining their appeal for remaking as well.

With this study, I set out to question the genre canon by probing its boundaries, and specifically, the remakes dismissed as lesser derivatives. By pointing out continuities, I tried to shift attention beyond an understanding of individual films as unique and exceptional works and towards the recognition of the ongoing processes of reproduction that shape them. For this purpose, the audacity that renders remakes an affront to many critics and fans is their greatest asset. Remakes not only revere, but dare to question their sources and initiate a reevaluation of previous films. Even when they come up short, and they usually do, their challenge revitalizes interest in the originals and invites new readings. In a sense, remakes even help to support a sense of nostalgia, as they frequently make their predecessors look better by comparison and inadvertently cause newfound appreciation of what may have been deeply flawed films. Remakes thus have the potential to both challenge and confirm the genre canon. This pattern was evident in the critical discourse surrounding most of my sample films, and I am confident that it will be repeated once the commercially successful horror films of the past decade, like *Saw* (2004) and *Paranormal Activity* (2007), will be remade. I am just as confident in putting it as a question of *when*, not *if* these films are revisited. Regardless of the exhaustion of critics, the reproduction of horror shows no signs of subsiding. Given the constant evolution of cultural fears, the demand for horror to deliver matching monsters is likely to keep up, assuring that the monster always returns.

Of course, the constant permutation of monsters offers more opportunities for research beyond the scope of this study. Starting with the selection of films, there remain many promising subgenres and periods of production that I have barely touched upon. The 1970s and 2000s have been well represented, but every other decade still offers a wealth of intriguing texts that have been revisited in one form or another. There is also vast potential to study the reproduction of horror outside the narrow definition of the film remake. Any of the monster discourses identified in the sample films also interacts with the respective genre (or subgenre) discourses formed by imitators, competitors and their own sequels. This is particularly relevant for *Dawn of the Dead* (1978) and the zombie genre, as well as *The Texas Chain Saw Massacre* (1974) and its various pre- and sequels, along with the host of backwoods horror it inspired. The case is even stronger for *Halloween* (1978), its seemingly endless procession of sequels, and the slasher genre it helped to define. Moreover, for this type of prolific horror franchise, the web of remakes, sequels, prequels and spinoffs becomes so convoluted that the distinctions between these types of intertextual relations become blurred. The strict distinction between remake and other derivative forms may seem rather arbitrary, as these texts emerge from a similar production process and pursue many of the same conflicting goals. That does not mean that we need to give up on these distinctions and pull back to genre as a larger concept; it does, however, point out the potential in a study of the textual transformations and discursive developments within a horror film franchise, or even larger transmedia franchises, to gain a fuller appreciation of the entwined workings of remaking and horror.

Works Cited

PRIMARY SOURCES

Body Snatchers. Dir. Abel Ferrara. Perf. Terry Kinney, Meg Tilly, Gabrielle Anwar. Warner, 1993.

The Crazies. Dir. George A. Romero. Perf. Lane Carroll, Will MacMillan, Harold Wayne Jones. Cambist, 1973.

The Crazies. Dir. Breck Eisner. Perf. Timothy Olyphant, Radha Mitchell, Joe Anderson. Overture, 2010.

Dawn of the Dead. Dir. George A. Romero. Perf. David Emge, Ken Foree, Scott H. Reiniger. United Film Distribution, 1978.

Dawn of the Dead. Dir. Zack Snyder. Perf. Sarah Polley, Ving Rhames, Jake Weber. Universal, 2004.

Halloween. Dir. John Carpenter. Perf. Donald Pleasance, Jamie Lee Curtis, Nancy Kyes. Compass/Warner, 1978.

Halloween. Dir. Rob Zombie. Perf. Malcolm McDowell, Scout Taylor-Compton, Tyler Mane. Weinstein/MGM/Paramount, 2007.

The Invasion. Dir. Oliver Hirschbiegel. Perf. Nicole Kidman, Daniel Craig, Jeremy Northam. Warner, 2007.

Invasion of the Body Snatchers. Dir. Don Siegel. Perf. Kevin McCarthy, Dana Wynter, Larry Gates. Allied Artists, 1956.

Invasion of the Body Snatchers. Dir. Philip Kaufman. Perf. Donald Sutherland, Brooke Adams, Jeff Goldblum. United Artists, 1978.

Psycho. Dir. Alfred Hitchcock. Perf. Anthony Hopkins, Vera Miles, John Gavin. Paramount, 1960.

The Silence of the Lambs. Dir. Jonathan Demme. Perf. Jodie Foster, Anthony Hopkins, Scott Glenn. Orion, 1991.

The Texas Chain Saw Massacre. Dir. Tobe Hooper. Perf. Marilyn Burns, Allen Danziger, Paul A. Partain. Bryanston, 1974.

The Texas Chainsaw Massacre. Dir. Marcus Nispel. Perf. Jessica Biel, Jonathan Tucker, Erica Leerhsen. New Line, 2003.

The Thing. Dir. John Carpenter. Perf. Kurt Russell, Wilford Brimley, T.K. Carter. Universal, 1982.

The Thing. Dir. Matthijs van Heijningen. Perf. Mary Elizabeth Winstead, Joel Edgerton, Ulrich Thomsen. Universal, 2011.

The Thing from Another World. Dir. Christian Nyby. Perf. Margaret Sheridan, Kenneth Tobey, Robert Cornthwaite. RKO, 1951.

SECONDARY SOURCES

Allen, Graham. *Intertextuality.* London: Routledge, 2000 (The New Critical Idiom).

Anderson, John. "Homicidally Unhinged, But for a Cause." *New York Times* 21 Feb. 2010 late ed. AR21.

Arend, Wolfgang. *Auf der Jagd nach Hexen und Zuschauern. Mediensoziologische Bausteine zu einer Theorie des Remakes am Beispiel von Hexenfilmen.* Mainz: Bender, 2002.

Beard, Steve. "No Particular Place." *Sight and Sound* 3.4 (Apr. 1993) 30-31.

Becker, Matt. "A Point of Little Hope: Hippie Horror Films and the Politics of Ambivalence." *Velvet Light Trap* 57 (Spring 2006). 42-59.

"Birth, Death and Shopping. The Rise and Fall of the Shopping Mall." *The Economist* 22 Dec. 2007: 102-04.

Bishop, Kyle. *American Zombie Gothic. The Rise and Fall (and Rise) of the Walking Dead in Popular Culture.* Jefferson: McFarland, 2010.

---. "Dead Man Still Walking. Explaining the Zombie Renaissance." *Journal of Popular Film and Television* 37.1 (2009): 16-25.

Biskind, Peter. *Seeing Is Believing. How Hollywood Taught Us to Stop Worrying and Love the Fifties.* New York: Pantheon, 1983.

Bloody Disgusting. <http://bloody-disgusting.com/> (18 Sep. 2014).

"Body Snatchers (1993)." *IMDb* <http://www.imdb.com/title/tt0106452/reference> (6 May 2014).

"BODY SNATCHERS (1993)." *Rotten Tomatoes.* <http://www.rottentomatoes.com/m/body_snatchers/> (6 May 2014).

Bogdanovich, Peter. "B-Movies." *Invasion of the Body Snatchers.* Ed. Al LaValley. New Brunswick: Rutgers UP, 1989. 173-76.

Borrowman, Shane: "Remaking Romero." *Fear, Cultural Anxiety and Transformation. Horror, Science Fiction and Fantasy Films Remade.* Ed. Scott A. Lukas and John Marmysz. Lanham: Lexington, 2009. 61-82.

Braucourt, Guy. "Interview with Don Siegel." *Focus on the Science Fiction Film.* Ed. William Johnson. Englewood Cliffs: Prentice Hall, 1972.

Braudy, Leo. "Afterword: Rethinking Remakes." *Play It Again, Sam. Retakes on Remakes.* Ed. Andrew Horton and Stuart Y. McDougal. Berkeley: U of California P, 1998. 327-34.

Brenez, Nicole. *Abel Ferrara.* Urbana: U of Illinois P, 2007.

Brophy, Philip. "Horrality – The Textuality of Contemporary Horror Films." *The Horror Reader.* Ed. Ken Gelder. 2006. 276-84.

Campbell, Joseph W. (as Don A. Stuart). *Who Goes There?* [1938] <www.goldenageofscifi.info/pdf/Who_Goes_There.pdf> (24 Sep. 2014).

Canavan, Gerry. "'We Are the Walking Dead': Race, Time, and Survival in Zombie Narrative." *Extrapolation* 51.3 (2010). 431-53.

Carroll, Noël. *The Philosophy of Horror. Or: Paradoxes of the Heart.* New York: Routledge, 1990.

Catsoulis, Jeanette. "Scientific Trek Turns Into a Game of Spot the Alien." *New York Times.* 13 Oct. 2013. <http://movies.nytimes.com/2011/10/14/movies/the-thing-with-mary-elizabeth-winstead-review.html?smid=twnytimes movies&seid=auto&_r=0> (6 Mar. 2013).

Clover, Carol. *Men, Women, and Chain Saws. Gender in the Modern Horror Film.* Princeton: Princeton UP, 1992.

Cohen, Jeffrey Jerome. "Monster Culture: Seven Theses." *Monster Theory. Reading Culture.* Ed. Jeffrey Jerome Cohen. Minneapolis: University of Minnesota Press, 1996. 3-25.

Connelly, Kelly. "From Final Girl to Final Woman. Defeating the Male Monster in *Halloween* and *Halloween H20.*" *Journal of Popular Film and Television* 35.1 (April 2007): 12-20.

Crane, Jonathan Lake. *Terror and Everyday Life. Singular Moments in the History of the Horror Film.* Thousand Oaks: Sage, 1994.

"The Crazies." *Box Office Mojo.* <http://www.boxofficemojo.com/movies/?id=crazies.htm> (30 Mar. 2011).

"The Crazies (1973)". *IMDb.* <http://www.imdb.com/title/tt0069895/> (30 Mar. 2011).

"THE CRAZIES (2010)." *Rotten Tomatoes.* <http://www.rottentomatoes.com/m/1205380-crazies/> (30 Mar. 2011).

Cumbow, Robert C. *Order in the Universe: The Films of John Carpenter.* 2nd ed. Lanham: Scarecrow, 2000.

"DAWN OF THE DEAD (2004)." *Rotten Tomatoes.* <http://www.rottentomatoes.com/m/dawn_of_the_dead/> (14 Sep. 2013).

Derry, Charles. *Dark Dreams 2.0. A Psychological History of the Modern Horror Film from the 1950s to the 21st Century.* Jefferson: McFarland, 2009.

Dika, Vera. *Games of Terror. Halloween, Friday the 13th, and the Films of the Stalker Cycle.* Rutherford: Farleigh Dickinson UP, 1990.

Druxman, Michael B. *Make It Again, Sam. A Survey of Movie Remakes.* South Brunswick: Barnes, 1975.

Eberwein, Robert. "Remakes and Cultural Studies." *Play It Again, Sam. Retakes on Remakes.* Ed. Andrew Horton and Stuart Y. McDougal. Berkeley: U of California P, 1998. 15-33.

Fanfiction.net. <https://www.fanfiction.net/> (18 Sep. 2014).

Fiske, John. *Reading the Popular.* Boston: Unwin Hyman, 1989.

---. *Understanding Popular Culture.* London: Routledge, 2004 [1988].

Forrest, Jennifer, and Leonard R. Koos. "Reviewing Remakes: An Introduction." *Dead Ringers: The Remake in Theory and Practice.* Ed. Jennifer Forrest and Leonard R. Koos. Albany: State U of New York P, 2002. 1-36.

Foucault, Michel. *Abnormal. Lectures at the Collège de France 1974-1975.* Trans. Graham Burchell. London: Verso, 2003.

Franklin, H. Bruce. "The Vietnam War as American Science Fiction and Fantasy." *The Fantastic Other. An Interface of Perspectives.* Ed. Brett Cooke, George E. Slusser and Jaume Marti-Olivella. Amsterdam: Rodopi, 1998 (Critical Studies vol. 11). 165-85.

"Frequently Asked Questions About the National Film Registry." *National Film Preservation Board.* 20 Aug. 2014. <http://www.loc.gov/film/faq.html> (15 Dec. 2014).

Gebhard, Gunther, Oliver Geisler, and Steffen Schröter. "Einleitung." *Von Monstern und Menschen. Begegnungen der anderen Art in kulturwissenschaftlicher Perspektive.* Ed. Gunther Gebhard, Oliver Geisler, and Steffen Schröter. Bielefeld: Transcript, 2009. 9-30.

Gelder, Ken. "Introduction: The Field of Horror." *The Horror Reader.* Ed. Ken Gelder. London: Routledge, 2000. 1-7.

Genette, Gérard. *Palimpsests: Literature in the Second Degree.* Lincoln: University of Nebraska Press, 1997 [Paris, 1982].

Gill, Pat. "The Monstrous Years: Teens, Slasher Films, and the Family." *Journal of Film and Video* 54.4 (Winter 2002): 16-30.

Glasberg, Elena. "'Viral Things': Extended Review." *Women's Studies Quarterly* 40.1-2 (Spring/Summer 2012): 201-10.

Grant, Barry Keith. *Invasion of the Body Snatchers*. Houndmills: Palgrave Macmillan, 2010.

Gregory, Charles T. "The Pod Society Versus the Rugged Individualists." *Journal of Popular Film* 1.1 (Winter 1972): 3-14.

Grindstaff, Laura. "Pretty Woman With a Gun: La Femme Nikita and the Textual Politics of 'The Remake.'" *Dead Ringers: The Remake in Theory and Practice*. Ed. Jennifer Forrest and Leonard R. Koos. Albany: State U of New York P, 2002. 273-308.

Guins, Raiford, and Omayra Zaragoza Cruz. "Revisionings: Repetition as Creative Nostalgia in the Films of John Carpenter." *The Cinema of John Carpenter: The Technique of Terror*. Ed. Ian Conrich and David Woods. London: Wallflower, 2004. 155-66.

Hagner, Michael. "Monstrositäten haben eine Geschichte." *Der Falsche Körper. Beiträge zu einer Geschichte der Monstrositäten*. Ed. Michael Hagner. Göttingen: Wallstein, 1995. 7-20.

Halfmann, Miriam. "The Night(s) HE Came Home! Rob Zombies *Halloween* (2007) als Remake und Reopening der Horror-Saga im neuen Millennium." *Dawn of an Evil Millennium. Horror/Kultur im neuen Jahrtausend*. Ed. Jörg Van Bebber. Darmstadt: Büchner, 2011. 389-94.

"Halloween." *Box Office Mojo*. <http://www.boxofficemojo.com/movies/?id=halloween.htm> (17 June 2011).

"Halloween (2007)." *Box Office Mojo*. <http://www.boxofficemojo.com/movies/?id=halloween07.htm> (17 June 2011).

"Halloween (2007)." *IMDb*. <http://www.imdb.com/title/tt0373883/reference> (17 June 2011).

"HALLOWEEN (2007)." *Rotten Tomatoes*. <http://www.rottentomatoes.com/m/1179254-halloween/> (17 June 2011).

Hanich, Julian. *Cinematic Emotion in Horror Films and Thrillers. The Aesthetic Paradox of Pleasurable Fear*. New York: Routledge, 2010 (Routledge Advances in Film Studies vol. 5).

Hantke, Steffen. "Shudder As We Think: Reflections on Horror and/or Criticism." *Horror*. Ed. Steffen Hantke. Vashon Island: Paradoxa, 2002. 1-9.

---. "They Don't Make 'Em Like They Used To. On the Rhetoric of Crisis and the Current State of American Horror Cinema." *American Horror Film. The Genre at the Turn of the Millennium*. Ed. Steffen Hantke. Jackson, University Press of Mississsippi, 2010. vii-xxxii.

Harper, Stephen. "Zombies, Malls, and the Consumerism Debate: George Romero's Dawn of the Dead." *Americana: The Journal of American Popular*

Culture (1900-present) 1.2 (Fall 2002). <http://www.americanpopularculture .com/journal/articles/fall_2002/harper.htm> (15 Apr. 2013).

Hills, Matt. *The Pleasures of Horror*. London: Continuum, 2005.

Hoberman, James. "Paranoia and the Pods." *Sight and Sound* 45.2 (May 1994). 29-31.

Holston, Kim R., and Tom Winchester. *Science Fiction, Fantasy and Horror Film Sequels, Series and Remakes. An Illustrated Filmography*. Jefferson: McFarland, 1997.

Horton, Andrew, and Stuart Y. McDougal. "Introduction." *Play It Again, Sam. Retakes on Remakes*. Ed. Andrew Horton and Stuart Y. McDougal. Berkeley: U of California P, 1998. 1-11.

"Horror Remake." *Box Office Mojo*. <http://www.boxofficemojo.com/genres/ chart/?id=horrorremake.htm> (10 Oct 2011).

Huet, Marie Hélène. *Monstrous Imagination*. Cambridge: Harvard UP, 1993.

Huygens, Ils. "Invasions of Fear: The Body Snatchers Theme." *Fear, Cultural Anxiety and Transformation. Horror, Science Fiction and Fantasy Films Remade*. Ed. Scott A. Lukas and John Marmysz. Lanham: Lexington, 2009. 45-59.

"The Invasion." *Box Office Mojo*. <http://www.boxofficemojo.com/movies/?id= invasion.htm> (5 May 2014).

"The Invasion (2007)." *IMDb*. <http://www.imdb.com/title/tt0427392/ reference> (5 May 2014).

"THE INVASION (2007)." *Rotten Tomatoes*. <http://www.rottentomatoes.com /m/invasion/> (16 Dec. 2014).

"Invasion of the Body Snatchers." *Box Office Mojo*. <http://www.boxofficemojo .com/movies/?page=main&id=invasionofthebodysnatchers.htm> (5 May 2014).

Jancovich, Mark. "General Introduction." *Horror: The Film Reader*. Ed. Mark Jancovich. London: Routledge, 2002.

---. "Genre and the Audience. Genre Classifications and Cultural Distinctions in the Mediation of *The Silence of the Lambs*." *Horror: The Film Reader*. Ed. Mark Jancovich. London: Routledge, 2002. 151-61.

---. *Horror*. London: Batsford, 1992.

---. *Rational Fears. American Horror in the 1950s*. Manchester: Manchester UP, 1996.

Jaworzyn, Stefan. *The Texas Chain Saw Massacre Companion*. London: Titan, 2003.

Jenkins, Henry. *Convergence Culture. Where Old and New Media Collide*. New York: New York UP, 2006.

---. *Textual Poachers. Television Fans and Participatory Culture.* New York: Routledge, 1992.

---. *The Wow Climax. Tracing the Emotional Impact of Popular Culture.* New York: New York UP, 2007.

Jones, Darryl. *Horror. A Thematic History in Fiction and Film.* London: Arnold, 2002.

Kaminsky, Stuart. "Interview with Siegel." *Invasion of the Body Snatchers.* Ed. Al LaValley. New Brunswick: Rutgers UP, 1989. 153-57.

Katovich, Michael A., and Patrick T. Kinkade: "The Stories Told in Science Fiction and Social Science: Reading 'The Thing' and Other Remakes from Two Eras." *The Sociological Quarterly* 34.4 (Nov. 1993): 619-37.

Kaufman, Philip. "Audio Commentary." *Invasion of the Body Snatchers.* Dir. Philip Kaufman. 1978. MGM, 2003. DVD.

Kawin, Bruce. "The Mummy's Pool." *Planks of Reason: Essays on the Horror Film.* Ed. Barry Keith Grant. Metuchen: Scarecrow, 1984. 3-20.

Kiefer, Bernd and Markus Stiglegger. "Die bizarre Schönheit der Verdammten. Abel Ferrara und die Suche nach Erlösung." *Die bizarre Schönheit der Verdammten: Die Filme von Abel Ferrara.* Ed. Bernd Kiefer and Markus Stiglegger. Marburg: Schüren, 2000.

King, Stephen. *Danse Macabre.* New York: Everest 1981.

Knöppler, Christian. "Intertextualität und das Filmremake." *Polyphonie, Intertextualität, Intermedialität: ein interdisziplinäres Forschungsfeld.* Ed. Marion Grein, Miguel Souza and Svenja Völkel. Aachen: Shaker, 2010. 113-46.

---. "The Mark(er) of Evil: Die Markierung von Monstrosität." *Was Machen Marker? Logik, Materialität und Politik von Differenzierungsprozessen.* Ed. Eva Bonn, Christian Knöppler, and Miguel Souza. Bielefeld: Transcript, 2013. 189-212.

Kristeva, Julia: "Word, Dialogue and Novel." *The Kristeva Reader.* Ed. Toril Moi. New York: Columbia UP, 1986. 34-61.

Kühle, Sandra. *Remakes. Amerikanische Versionen Europäischer Filme.* Remscheid: Gardez, 2006.

LaValley, Al. "*Invasion of the Body Snatchers:* Politics, Psychology, Sociology." *Invasion of the Body Snatchers.* Ed. Al LaValley. New Brunswick: Rutgers UP, 1989. 3-17.

LeGacy, Arthur. "*The Invasion of the Body Snatchers:* A Metaphor for the Fifties." *Literature Film Quarterly* 6.3 (1978): 285-92.

Lehmann, Johannes. "Der Verbrecher als Monster? Oder: warum Menschen Monster brauchen, Monster aber nicht." *Monster. Zur ästhetischen Verfas-*

sung eines Grenzbewohners. Ed. Roland Borgards, Christine Holm, and Günter Oesterle. Würzburg: Königshausen und Neumann, 2009. 191-217.

Leitch, Thomas. "Twice-Told Tales: Disavowal and the Rhetoric of the Remake." *Dead Ringers: The Remake in Theory and Practice*. Ed. Jennifer Forrest and Leonard R. Koos. Albany: State U of New York P, 2002. 37-62.

Lemke, Thomas. *Biopolitics. An Advanced Introduction*. Trans. Erin Frederick Trump. New York: New York UP, 2011.

Lizardi, Ryan. "'Re-Imagining' Hegemony and Misogyny in the Contemporary Slasher Remake." *Journal of Popular Film and Television* 38.3 (2010): 113-21.

Loock, Kathleen. "The Return of the Pod People: Remaking Cultural Anxieties in Invasion of the Body Snatchers." *Film Remakes, Adaptations and Fan Productions. Remake – Remodel*. Ed. Kathleen Loock and Constantine Verevis. Basingstoke: Palgrave Macmillan, 2012. 122-44.

Loudermilk, A. "Eating 'Dawn' in the Dark. Zombie Desire and Commodified Identity in George A. Romero's 'Dawn of the Dead.'" *Journal of Consumer Culture* 3.1 (2003) 83-107.

Lukas, Scott A.: "Horror Video Game Remakes and the Question of Medium: Remaking Doom, Silent Hill, and Resident Evil." *Fear, Cultural Anxiety and Transformation: Horror, Science Fiction and Fantasy Films Remade*. Ed. Scott A. Lukas and John Marmysz. Lanham: Lexington, 2009. 221-42.

Macor, Alison. *Chainsaws, Slackers, and Spy Kids: Thirty Years of Filmmaking in Austin, Texas*. Austin: U of Texas P, 2010.

Maddrey, Joseph. *Nightmares in Red, White and Blue: The Evolution of the American Horror Film*. Jefferson: McFarland, 2004.

Maes, Hans. "A Celestial Taxonomy of Remakes?" *Cinemascope* 2 (May – August 2005) <http://www.madadayo.it/Cinemascope_archive/cinema-scope.net/Numero%20due/articolo05.html> (14 Apr. 2010).

Mann, Katrina. "'You're Next!': Postwar Hegemony Besieged in Invasion of the Body Snatchers." *Cinema Journal* 44. 1 (Fall 2004) 49-68.

McCarthy, Joseph. "The History of George Catlett Marshall, 1951." *Internet Modern History Sourcebook*. <http://www.fordham.edu/halsall/mod/1951mccarthy-marshall.html> (2 July 2013).

Michel, Frann: "Life and Death and Something in Between: Reviewing Recent Horror Cinema." *Psychoanalysis, Culture & Society* 12. 4 (Dec. 2007): 390-97.

Morrison, Michael A. "A Few Remarks about a Couple of Things: Hawks and Carpenter Reconfigure Campbell." *Trajectories of the Fantastic. Selected Essays from the Fourteenth International Conference on the Fantastic in the*

Arts. Ed. Michael A. Morrison. Westport: Greenwood, 1997 (Contributions to the Study of Science Fiction and Fantasy 70).

Muir, John Kenneth. *The Films of John Carpenter*. Jefferson: McFarland, 2000.

---. *Horror Films of the 1970s*. Jefferson: McFarland, 2002.

---. *Horror Films of the 1980s*. Jefferson: McFarland, 2007.

---. *Horror Films of the 1990s*. Jefferson: McFarland, 2011.

"National Film Registry Titles 1989-2013." *National Film Preservation Board*. 26 Sep. 2014. <http://www.loc.gov/film/registry_titles.php> (15 Dec. 2014).

Neale, Steve. *Genre and Hollywood*. London: Routledge, 2000.

---. "'You've Got To Be Fucking Kidding!' Knowledge, Belief and Judgement in Science Fiction." *Alien Zone: Cultural Theory and Contemporary Science Fiction Cinema*. Ed. Annette Kuhn. London: Verso, 1990. 160-68.

Nelson, Erika. "Invasion of the Body Snatchers: Gender and Sexuality in Four Film Adaptations." *Extrapolation: A Journal of Science Fiction and Fantasy* 52.1 (Spring 2011): 51-74.

Neumann, Frank. "Leichen im Keller, Untote auf der Straße. Das Echo sozialer Traumata im Zombiefilm." *Untot. Zombie Film Theorie*. Ed. Michael Fürst, Florian Krautkrämer, and Serjoscha Wiemer. München: Belleville, 2011. 65-84.

Nowell, Richard. *Blood Money. A History of the First Teen Slasher Film Cycle*. New York: Continuum, 2011.

"Our Mission." *Participant Media*. <http://www.participantmedia.com/company/about_us.php> (30 Mar. 2011).

Paffenroth, Kim. *Gospel of the Living Dead. George Romero's Visions of Hell on Earth*. Waco: Baylor UP, 2006.

Patterson, Natasha. "Cannibalizing Gender and Genre: A Feminist Re-Vision of George Romero's Zombie Films." *Zombie Culture. Autopsies of the Living Dead*. Ed. Shawn McIntosh and Marc Leverette. Lanham: Scarecrow, 2008. 103-18.

Perkins, Claire. "Remaking and the Film Trilogy: Whit Stillman's Authorial Triptych." *Velvet Light Trap* 61 (Spring 2008). 14-25.

Phillips, Kendall. *Projected Fears. Horror Films and American Culture*. Westport: Praeger, 2005.

Pinedo, Isabel Cristina. *Recreational Terror. Women and the Pleasures of Horror Film Viewing*. Albany: State U of New York P, 1997.

Pym, John. "Invasion of the Body Snatchers." *Sight and Sound* 29.1 (Spring 1979): 128-29.

Quaresima, Leonardo. "Loving Texts Two at a Time: The Film Remake." *Cinémas: Journal of Film Studies* 12.3 (2002): 73-84.

Rigby, Jonathan. *American Gothic. Sixty Years of Horror Cinema*. Richmond: Reynold & Hearn, 2007.

Robinson, Juneko J. "Immanent Attack: An Existential Take on the Invasion of the Body Snatchers Films." *Fear, Cultural Anxiety and Transformation. Horror, Science Fiction and Fantasy Films Remade*. Ed. Scott A. Lukas and John Marmysz. Lanham: Lexington, 2009. 23-43.

Rockoff, Adam. *Going to Pieces. The Rise and Fall of the Slasher Film, 1978-1986*. Jefferson: McFarland, 2002.

Rodriguez, Rene. "Review: 'The Thing' (R)." *Miami.com*. 13 Oct. 2011. <http://www.miami.com/039the-thing039-r-article> (6 Mar. 2013).

Röttgers, Kurt. "Monster gibt es nicht – oder doch?" *Monster*. Ed. Kurt Röttgers. Essen: Blaue Eule, 2010 (Philosophisch-literarische Reflexionen vol. 12). 7-16.

Russell, David J. "Monster Roundup. Reintegrating the Horror Genre." *Refiguring American Film Genres. History and Theory*. Ed. Nick Browne. Berkeley: U of California P, 1998. 233-53.

Russell, Jamie. *Book of the Dead. The Complete History of Zombie Cinema*. Guildford: FAB, 2005.

Sahota, Shalimar. "What Went Wrong: The Invasion." *Boxofficeprophets*. 3 Mar. 2011. <http://www.boxofficeprophets.com/column/index.cfm?column ID=13741&cmin=10&columnpage=1> (6 May 2014).

Samuels, Stuart. "The Age of Conspiracy and Conformity: Invasion of the Body Snatchers." *American History – American Film*. Ed. John O'Connor and Martin Jackson. New York: Ungar, 1980. 203-17.

Sanjek, David. "Fans' Notes: The Horror Film Fanzine." *The Horror Reader*. Ed. Ken Gelder. London: Routledge, 2000.

Sayre, Nora. "Watch the Skies." *Invasion of the Body Snatchers*. Ed. Al LaValley. New Brunswick and London: Rutgers UP, 1989. 184.

Schaudig, Michael. "Recycling für den Publikumsgeschmack? Das Remake: Bemerkungen zu einem Filmhistorischen Phänomen." *Positionen Deutscher Filmgeschichte. 100 Jahre Kinematographie: Strukturen, Diskurse, Kontexte*. Ed. Michael Schaudig. München: Diskurs Film, 1996. 277-308.

Seed, David. *American Science Fiction and the Cold War. Literature and Film*. Edinburgh: Edinburgh UP, 1999.

Sharett, Christopher. "The Horror Film in Neoconservative Culture." *The Dread of Difference. Gender and the Horror Film*. Ed. Barry Keith Grant. Austin: U of Texas P, 1996. 253-76.

---. "The Idea of Apocalypse in *The Texas Chainsaw Massacre*." *Planks of Reason. Essays on the Horror Film*. Ed. Barry Keith Grant. Metuchen: Scarecrow, 1984. 255-76.

Shaviro, Steven. *The Cinematic Body*. Minneapolis: U of Minnesota P, 1993 (Theory out of Bounds, vol. 2).

Skal, David. *The Monster Show. A Cultural History of Horror*. New York: Norton, 1993.

Smith, Steve. "A Siege Mentality? Form and Ideology in Carpenter's Early Siege Films." *The Cinema of John Carpenter: The Technique of Terror*. Ed. Ian Conrich and David Woods. London: Wallflower, 2004. 35-48.

Snakes on a Blog. <http://www.snakesonablog.com/> (13 Dec. 2009).

Snider, Eric D. "Review: The Thing (2011)." *Film.com*. Oct 14, 2011. <http://www.film.com/movies/review-the-thing> (6 Mar. 2013).

Southern, Nathan. "Marcus Nispel." *International New York Times*. <http://www.nytimes.com/movies/person/359417/Marcus-Nispel/biography> (16 Dec. 2014).

Stevens, Brad. *Abel Ferrara: The Moral Vision*. Godalming: FAB, 2004.

Stichweh, Rudolf. "Der Körper des Fremden." *Der Falsche Körper. Beiträge zu einer Geschichte der Monstrositäten*. Ed. Michael Hagner. Göttingen: Wallstein, 1995. 174-86.

Telotte, J.P. "Human Artifice and the Science Fiction Film." *Film Quarterly* 36.3 (Spring 1983): 44-51.

---. "Through a Pumpkin's Eye: The Reflexive Nature of Horror." *Literature/Film Quarterly* 10.3 (1982): 139-49.

"THE TEXAS CHAINSAW MASSACRE (2003)." *Rotten Tomatoes*. <http://www.rottentomatoes.com/m/texas_chainsaw_massacre/> (10 Oct 2011).

"The Thing (1982)." *IMDb*. <http://www.imdb.com/title/tt0084787/reference> (5 Mar. 2013).

"The Thing from Another World (1951)." *IMDb*. <http://www.imdb.com /title/tt0044121/reference> (5 Mar. 2013).

Tudor, Andrew. "From Paranoia to Postmodernism? The Horror Movie in Late Modern Society." *Genre and Contemporary Hollywood*. Ed. Steve Neale. London: BFI, 2002. 105-16.

---. *Monsters and Mad Scientists. A Cultural History of the Horror Movie*. Oxford: Blackwell. 1989.

---. "Why Horror? The Peculiar Pleasures of a Popular Genre." *Horror. The Film Reader*. Ed. Mark Jancovich. London: Routledge, 2002. 47-55.

Twitchell, James. *Dreadful Pleasures. An Anatomy of Modern Horror*. Oxford: Oxford UP, 1985.

Underhill, Stephen. "J. Edgar Hoover, 'Speech before the House Committee on Un-American Activities' (26 March 1947)." *Voices of Democracy* 3 (2008): 139-61.

Verevis, Constantine. *Film Remakes*. Edinburgh: Edinburgh UP, 2006.

---. "Redefining the Sequel. The Case of the (Living) Dead." *Second Takes. Critical Approaches to the Film Sequel*. Ed. Carolyn Jess-Cooke and Constantine Verevis. Albany: State U of New York P, 2010. 11-29.

Warren, Bill. *Keep Watching the Skies! American Science Fiction Movies of the 50s*. Vol. 1. Jefferson: McFarland, 1982.

Watts, Peter. "Things." *Clarkesworld* 40 (Jan. 2010). <http://clarkesworld magazine.com/watts_01_10/> (6 Mar. 2013).

Waxman, Sharon. "After Hype Online, 'Snakes on a Plane' Is Letdown at Box Office." *The New York Times*. 21 Aug. 2006. <http://www.nytimes.com /2006/08/21/movies/21box.html?_r=1&ref=arts> (20 May 2009).

Wetmore, Kevin. *Post-9/11 Horror in American Cinema*. New York: Continuum 2012.

White, Dave. "I Spit on Your Horror Movie Remakes, Sequels: A Horror Fan Laments the State of One of His Favorite Genres." *MSNBC.com*. 25 Oct. 2005. <http://www.msnbc.msn.com/id/9805698/> (22 Mar. 2010).

White, Eric: "The Erotics of Becoming: *Xenogenesis* and *The Thing*." *Science Fiction Studies*, 20.3 (Nov. 1993). 394-408.

Williams, Tony. *Hearths of Darkness. The Family in the American Horror Film*. Madison: Farleigh Dickinson UP, 1996.

---. *Knight of the Living Dead: The Cinema of George A. Romero*. London: Wallflower, 2003.

---. "Trying to Survive on the Darker Side: 1980s Family Horror." *The Dread of Difference: Gender and the Horror Film*. Ed. Barry Keith Grant. Austin: U of Texas P, 1996. 164-80.

Wood, Robin. *Hollywood from Vietnam to Reagan*. New York: Columbia UP, 1986.

Woods, David. "Us and Them: Authority and Identity in Carpenter's Films." *The Cinema of John Carpenter: The Technique of Terror*. Ed. Ian Conrich and David Woods. London: Wallflower, 2004. 21-34.